Introductory Marketing

Stephen Page

Stanley Thornes (Publishers) Ltd

First published in 1995 by:
Stanley Thornes (Publishers) Ltd
Ellenborough House
Wellington Street
CHELTENHAM
Glos. GL50 1YW

A catalogue record for this book is available from the British Library.

ISBN 0 7487 1783 8

Typeset by P&R Typesetters Ltd, Salisbury
Printed and bound in Great Britain by Redwood Books, Trowbridge, Wiltshire

Contents

Dedication

To my father, who did not live to see this book completed.

Introduction

Every day of our lives calls for decisions. Sixth form or College? GCE A Level or GNVQ? This marketing textbook, or another one?

Many of our decisions are about consumption. As consumers, we get swept along in a stream of marketing messages. They touch and shape almost every aspect of our lives. So it is vital to understand marketing, whether from the point of view of those who do it, or of those to whom it is done.

Many marketing messages are based on the attraction of work-avoidance. For example, in taking the back-breaking labour out of housework.

Fortunately, learning does not happen like that. It occurs most effectively when people are interested, and making discoveries for themselves.

That is why I have written this book in a style which I hope will keep you turning the pages. It includes plenty of activities to set you off on your own investigations. Current examples are used to illustrate the theory. There are sample assignments to prepare you for assessment.

This book is based upon many years of teaching Marketing and Advertising to students. I have also drawn upon my experience in helping small businesses to draw up business and marketing plans. My aim throughout has been to provide you with a clear, readable, user-friendly book to act as companion to your Marketing course.

In doing that I have been helped by many people, including staff at the publishers, Stanley Thornes, colleagues at Matthew Boulton College in Birmingham, and especially by my wife, whose encouragement has been invaluable.

This book is better for their contributions, but any mistakes are wholly my own responsibility.

Thank you for reading this. I hope that you will decide that this book is right for you, and that you will find it of real value in your studies.

Stephen Page

Acknowledgements

The author and publishers are grateful to the following for permission to reproduce previously published material:

CACI Ltd (pp. 48, 49, 50)
Foresight (0171 405 4455) (p. 86)
Newspaper Publishing plc (p. 95)
NEC (UK) Ltd (p. 99)
Butterworth-Heinemann Ltd (p. 152)
Sara Lee/Household & Personal Care and NDI Display Ltd (p. 183)
Advertising Standards Authority (p. 204)

Every attempt has been made to contact copyright holders, and we apologise if any have been overlooked.

CHAPTER 1

Making sense of marketing

Done by spivs?

Why learn about marketing?

Marketing is sexy; the word is on everyone's lips. Big brands turn over millions of pounds each year, so inter-company rivalries make good copy for the media. Politicians make no moves until they have consulted their 'spin doctors' for advice on public reaction. Top marketing professionals can command fat salaries.

Then there is the glamour of new product launches, advertising campaigns, and research conferences at international venues. Compared with many other business disciplines, marketing seems to offer scope for imagination and creativity. So, is it surprising that people are intrigued by the subject? In 1992, 27,000 students in 50 countries around the world were studying for professional qualifications offered by the Chartered Institute of Marketing in London.

Sex is used openly as a selling tool. The clothes company Joe Bloggs had young couples in steamy clinches appear in adverts with the strapline 'Everyone snogs in Joe Bloggs'. In the Levi's launderette commercial, the male model stripped down to his boxer shorts.

Anyone contemplating a career in marketing needs to be able to see behind the glamorous facade, to the demanding, frustrating and sometimes repetitive activity which is just as much a part of working in marketing as in any other discipline. It is important to be aware too of the public's love-hate relationship with marketing. Woe betide the product, sales promotion or advertising claim that does not live up to expectations.

Public perceptions of marketing

Activity

Before you go any further, try to find out what other people (not students or professionals in the subject) think about marketing. Ask them what the word 'marketing' means to the them and how they feel about the activities they associate with marketing.

It may be helpful to work within a small group for this activity. Report back and discuss your findings together in the group.

DISCUSSION

It would be surprising if, during your investigation, you did not encounter criticisms of, for example, junk mail, the improper use of market research as a guise for a sales pitch, or the argument that marketing tries to sell people things they do not really want.

Even within the business there is controversy. Anthony Pye Jeary, the marketing brain behind some of Andrew Lloyd Weber's musicals, feels that the word itself creates a problem:

> *'It doesn't mean anything. It's embarrassing – it has a reputation for being done by spivs'*

(*Independent*, 4 August 1993).

Such comments have closely allied the concept of marketing with manipulation. The argument runs like this. First organisations find out public likes and dislikes. Then they use that information to devise cunning promotional gimmicks. Poor old Joe and Josephine Public cannot resist.

But is this not rather a limited view? To begin with some of the criticisms are of tactics. Although they may be misused at times, that does not invalidate their use for legitimate purposes. Have you never tried to find out about a person's likes and dislikes before trying to arrange a date? Have you never tried to sell a bicycle through a local paper? Were your uses legitimate?

Marketing should be persuasive. But for people to be persuaded along a course of action, it is likely that there was a tendency for them to behave in a particular way in the first place. Also people who are persuaded to buy things they do not want or which are no good will not be caught out a second time.

Markets and marketing: some definitions

Exactly what is meant by a market and by the term marketing?

Activity ——————————————————————

How many uses can you identify for the word 'market'? Jot down different examples in your note-book, and then compare them with the following comments.

DISCUSSION

You will probably have noted four slightly different meanings for the word 'market' in current use:
* a place (such as the spot where stallholders sell their wares),
* a system of exchange between buyers and sellers (as in 'the stock market'),
* total demand for particular products (as in 'the housing market is in decline'), and
* the consumers for a particular product or service (as in the phrase 'the market for package holidays is primarily concerned with value for money').

You will find all four uses of the word in this book.

The word 'marketing' is often used so loosely to cover a multitude of activities that it is easy to overlook the fact that is has a clear and precise definition. It is this:

'Marketing is the identification, stimulation, and satisfaction of customer requirements, at a profit.'

You may want to copy the definition into your note-book, and commit it to memory.

So, *marketing* requires an organisation to consider whether the product is what the consumers want in the first place, while *advertising* (with which marketing is often confused), is concerned with dreaming up a persuasive message to communicate to the target audience.

At the heart of this definition is the concept of consumer requirements. Why did you buy this book? Because you want to keep the author and publisher in business? Or because you hope it will help you to pass your exams? Consumers will only buy what they think they want or need, so it is important for a seller to identify those requirements (by research), stimulate them (by promotion) and satisfy them (by ensuring quality).

However, achieving all that will still not guarantee that the activity is profitable. There are substantial numbers of organisations which have traded from time to time without being profitable, for example, during a recession. There are also types of organisation for which the phrase might not seem appropriate, for example, a fire brigade, or a doctor's practice. Yet even these organisations will be expected to work within financial constraints, making effective use of the public money they are given.

Such organisations are likely to satisfy the basic requirements of the marketing mix, to provide:

* the right product
* at the right price
* in the right place
* promoted to the right people
* within agreed financial constraints (e.g. at a profit).

(The marketing mix is covered in detail in Chapter 5.)

Marketing in action

The easiest way to understand the application of marketing in modern businesses is to look at some examples.

Activity

Do you eat at McDonalds, the fast food restaurant? How well do you think that McDonalds has identified, stimulated and satisfied the needs of its customers? (Remember there are many people who are not McDonalds' customers because it does not meet their needs.)

Start by making a list of what you think are McDonalds' customers' needs. Then make a second list of the ways in which they are satisfied. Afterwards, think about the way the company stimulates those needs or makes consumers aware that the fast-food chain can satisfy them.

DISCUSSION

If you do eat regularly at McDonalds, then you will know that this is a company with a clearly understood market for its products, and one which built a remarkably clear brand image in the UK during the 1980s.

Consider the situation before McDonalds erupted into the UK fast-food market. Most such outlets were small traders – fish and chip shops, oriental carry-outs, and corner cafes. Of course, many of these places remain in business, but their collective market share has fallen. Large chains, such as Wimpey or Golden Egg in the sixties, anticipated the McDonalds' policy of standardised menus and uniform house style, but provided an 'at table' service. Where counter service was offered, it was normally of the cafeteria type, with a single queue, slowly snaking past a wide range of food and drink, only one or two items of which interested each consumer. Before McDonalds, the 'drive-thru' was virtually unknown in the UK.

Based on its experience in the USA, McDonalds believed that the UK was ready for a chain of fast-food outlets which would provide:

* both eat-in and take-away facilities,
* a range of products of known quality at inexpensive prices,
* speedy service – cutting queuing or time spent waiting for table service,
* a clean bright environment,
* an image which appeals particularly to young people.

The development of these restaurants also accompanied a predicted growth in the total market for catering services, as real disposable incomes grew, and people were less willing to spend time cooking, or waiting for their meals. The results speak for themselves: by the early 1990s, McDonalds was serving more than one million meals each day in the UK.

This outline picture of the McDonalds' phenomenon emphasises the key elements of successful marketing:

* knowing exactly *to whom* you are trying to sell,
* knowing what those people want,
* providing products that meet their requirements,
* promoting the products and services to the market, and
* doing it at a profit (or within other constraints).

This seems like such commonsense that you would think all businesses worked on this basis, but a few moments reflection should convince you that this is certainly not so. How often have you seen a new shop open up in your district, only to close down, with hopes dashed, a few months later? No doubt the proprietor had the inclination and the capital to start the business – all that was missing was the market!

In such a case, the proprietor's mistake is to assume that he or she is in business to make or provide things. However, as the US writer on management, Peter Drucker, had asserted as long ago as 1959, businesses exist not to make things, but to create customers. This point was developed a few years later by another American, Theodore Levitt, who argued that an obsession with products, rather than customers, explained the demise of US railroad firms. Their mistake, he said, was to assume that they were in the railroad – rather than the transportation – business. In other words, if they had looked for means other than railroads with which to satisfy people's transport needs, they might still have been in business, albeit not as railroad companies.

Business orientations

The reason that the US companies failed was that they clung to a product orientation, or focus. However, other orientations are possible for businesses, and these can be expressed diagrammatically (see Figure 1.1).

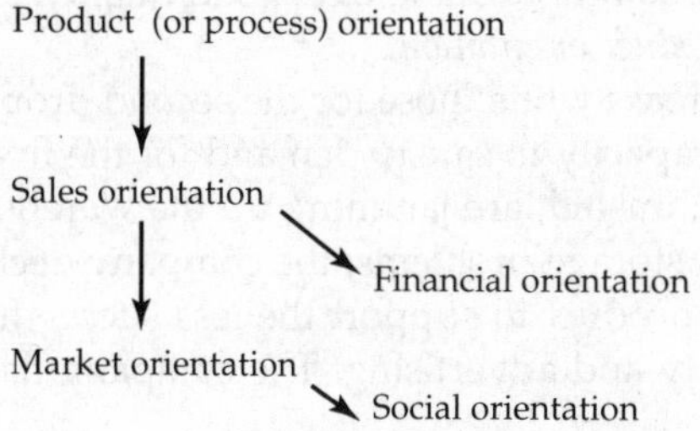

Product (or process) orientation

Sales orientation

Financial orientation

Market orientation

Social orientation

Figure 1. 1 – Possible business orientations

Figure 1. 1 implies that organisations will pass through these orientations sequentially, and indeed some do. However, many businesses remain stuck at one particular stage, while others may short-circuit some stages altogether.

Each of these orientations may be described as follows:

* **product orientation** is characterised by:
  - a preoccupation with the organisation's existing products,
  - production being the lead function within the organisation,
  - being appropriate only for a seller's market, where all output is immediately consumed,
  - any unsold output being blamed upon unappreciative customers or ineffectual salespeople;
* **process orientation** is equivalent to product orientation in the service sector;
* **sales orientation** is characterised by:
  - great emphasis being attached to promotion and personal selling to sustain production,
  - sales being the lead function in such organisations,
  - being appropriate only when substantial untapped demand exists (e.g. people would buy, but are unaware of the product's availability),
  - a pre-occupation with sales volume, rather than profitability,
  - the dominance of short-term planning;
* **financial orientation** develops from sales orientation and is characterised by:
  - an emphasis on profitability, not just turnover,
  - finance being the lead function in such organisations,
  - Ford during its 'We don't make cars, we make money' phase,
  - the tendency for long-term product development being jeopardised for short-term profit gains;
* **market orientation** is characterised by:
  - the organisation's thinking being dominated by consumers (not products),
  - profit targets geared to market forecasts being used for operational control,
  - the predominance of long-term planning;
* **social orientation**, an extension of market orientation, is characterised by:
  - non-economic objectives (e.g. care for the environment or non-exploitation of Third World suppliers).

Changing orientation over time

Let us look at how this theory might apply to an imaginary manufacturing company. Assume it has two main products, both of which are selling well without any significant promotional activity. Management at the works is free to concentrate almost entirely on maintaining trouble-free, good quality production. The business at this stage has a *product orientation*.

Then, orders for one product increase while those for the second drop off. There is no longer sufficient production capacity to satisfy demand for the first product, while boxes of the second product, unsold, are jamming up the warehouse. In an attempt to solve their capacity and storage problems, the company decides to use revenue from the more successful product to support the less successful one, through increased salesforce activity and advertising. The company has now moved to a *sales orientation*.

Only when the business realises its short-sightedness in switching its resources from its most successful product to its least successful one, and begins to examine the market for the second product, with a view to redeveloping or replacing it, can the company claim to have reached a *market orientation*.

However, just as this stage has been reached, the company becomes aware of growing public disquiet about polluting by-products in the production process of its goods. In deciding to switch to alternative, albeit more expensive materials, which are not harmful, even though this has not been demanded by customers, the company has also achieved a *social orientation*.

Activity

Apply the categories outlined above to some organisations that you know. For example, you might choose your school or college, your employer, or a business of which you are a customer. Compare your impressions with those of others.

Marketing in the public sector

You may have been tempted to conclude that much of what has been said so far was only appropriate to companies in the private sector. This is not the case. Organisations in the public sector – that is central and local government and the remaining publicly-owned utilities such as the Post Office – have turned to marketing with enthusiasm in recent years.

This very much reflects the influence during the 1980s of a right-wing think-tank called the Adam Smith Institute. It presented the Conservative government elected in 1979 with a radical set of proposals to reverse a long-term trend towards greater public control of economic activity. These proposals had three elements:

* 'privatisation' – the selling off of state-owned enterprises into the private sector, as has happened with gas, water and electricity supplies;
* the creation of an internal market where privatisation is not considered suitable, as has happened in the health service, and in many local authority activities; and
* producing consumers' charters for services likely to remain (at least temporarily) in the public sector.

Many of these developments were the subject of controversy, with opponents claiming that in some cases public monopolies have simply become private ones, or that service standards have declined.

Activity

The privatisation of British Rail provoked bitter criticism at the time. Bring the story up to date. How have rail services changed as a result? Has the introduction of free market practices to what had been a state-run monopoly benefited the travelling public?

Market forces in the public sector

Local authority leisure services are a good example of this change to free-market practices. The original principles upon which swimming pools and other public leisure facilities were provided by local authorities was as an act of public policy, shaped by the desire to improve public health. Even as late as the Wolfendon Report of 1960, and the subsequent establishment of the Sports Council, improved public health was seen to be the main justification for investment in facilities. In other words, the new public sports centres which emerged from the late 1960s onwards were not provided primarily because of demand from the marketplace, and they were certainly not expected to pay their way from receipts at the ticket office.

Some of this philosophy remains true today. Charging policies are still determined by local authority committee, and often reflect the political objectives set by the council rather than the prevailing market conditions. However, many changes have occurred in the last two decades, which betray the influence of free-market ideas. Most obviously, there has been the introduction of competitive tendering, under which local authorities become the clients, determining their general leisure and recreation strategy. They in turn appoint contractors to operate the authority's swimming baths, sports halls, squash courts and so on. Such contractors are selected by competitive tender. Secondly, there has been a growth in the 'customer-care' approach to local authority services under which greater care is taken to ensure that users and taxpayers are happy with the range and quality of an authority's recreation services.

Even the profit motive has entered the local authority landscape. Although the authority as the client – that is to say the purchasing agent on the public's behalf – may decide to provide leisure facilities at less than their cost, the contractor who operates the facilities on behalf of the authority, will endeavour to do so profitably. In some cases these contractors are genuine private companies, such as Ladbrookes, but more often the contractor is a self-contained department of the authority itself. In either case the bulk of an operator's income may well come in the form of a subsidy from a local authority, and only partially from money taken at the door.

Activity

Read the following case study about the swimming pool in a fictitious town. Can you identify any of the four orientations so far discussed – product, sales, marketing or social?

Case study

In at the deep end

When the public baths were opened in Muddleborough in 1890, they were a great success, and for many years were the pride of Muddleborough. Periodically the borough engineer installed new pumps and filters to ensure that the latest facilities were provided for local people to use. For decorum, men and women swam in separate pools, strict conventions about bathing attire were observed, and most of the things that people enjoyed doing were prohibited by bye-laws.

Then in the 1970s attendances started to wane. Various minor improvements were made but the situation did not improve. So the Parks and Leisure Committee decided to take an advert in the *Muddleborough Courier* every week, giving opening times and prices of admission.

There was still no improvement. Then one day, the Parks and Leisure Committee appointed a new manager for the baths. 'Why don't you ask the public what they would like?' she asked. 'Because we know what the public like,' explained the Committee. So she took them to see the baths run by her old authority. She showed them a flume slide and a long queue of people waiting to use it. She showed them a wave machine that made the baths more like the seaside. She showed them inflatables covered with laughing children. And she showed them the potted plants and easy chairs which were used for all the private family party bookings on Saturday nights. The committee liked it. 'We'll do this, too, if it makes our baths more popular!' the members said.

The implications of a market orientation

For an organisation to achieve a market-oriented philosophy significant changes in the way in which it has traditionally operated may be required. Organisations which are market-oriented possess some or all of the following characteristics:

* they are **consumer-driven**
* they undertake **long-term strategic planning**
* they are **research-driven**
* they use **market management techniques**
* they use **product management techniques**
* they use **distribution management techniques**
* they maximise **salesforce effectiveness**
* they understand **critical success factors**.

Consumer-driven organisations

Market-oriented businesses will be pre-occupied with consumer needs. This will manifest itself in formalised consumer care policies and the monitoring of satisfaction-levels. Such organisations understand consumers' requirements and set about meeting them. One frequent manifestation of this is a keen emphasis on quality, to make sure that every product reaching the customer is in perfect working order. When complaints are made, they are regarded as a resource, and procedures exist for investigating and rectifying the problem – both for the complainant and for future purchasers. (The concept of customer care is dealt with in Chapter 5.)

Product-oriented organisations are more likely to tolerate a few defects – 'Nobody's perfect, are they?' – and to regard complaints as a nuisance – 'Yeah, well, it's a computer error. It'll be put right on your next account.'

Long-term strategic planning

Businesses without a market orientation are more likely to live from crisis to crisis. 'We mean to produce a plan, but there's just been no time during the last few years.' Only a little better are those which have a plan somewhere, produced to secure a bank loan two years ago and completely ignored since then. Such organisations are liable to drift, be surprised by changes in their markets, and to be slow to respond to threats from their competitors.

Long-term planning does not guarantee success. It does, however, increase its likelihood, because the organisation will have:
* analysed its existing position,
* examined its options for the future, and
* decided how it expects to get there.
(For more about marketing planning, see Chapter 12.)

Research-driven organisations

Planning which is not based upon sound information will be worthless. So organisations which plan must also be ones which research. The necessary categories are:
* economic data (e.g. the Retail Price Index)
* market research (e.g. Nielsen retail audits)
* behavioural and attitudinal studies (e.g. opinion polls)
* competitor research (e.g. Business Ratio reports)
* promotional activity research (e.g. advertising effectiveness research)
* distribution and sales data (e.g. internal records)
* product development research (e.g. snore-stopping pillows).
(For more about marketing research, see Chapter 2.)

Market management techniques

A market orientation will clearly require an organisation to stay in close touch with those who purchase or use its products, at least to maintain, if not enlarge, existing market share. As such, it requires that organisations understand their markets through research, including the identification of new markets, and those which are in decline. Organisations can also influence their markets by using advertising, sales promotion and other promotional tactics already mentioned. (These are dealt with in more detail in Chapter 9.)

Product management techniques

An organisation's existing brands need to be managed to maintain quality, and be modified if necessary (e.g. as a result of technological innovation). A process called 'benchmarking' can be used, whereby an organisation will compare its activities against those of its market leader to see how it might improve. A market leader can benchmark against its challengers, or against similar organisations in other markets (e.g. overseas).

At times, it may be necessary to rationalise products, for example, in a contracting market. The modification of existing products, the development of new ones, and the taking of important pricing decisions also come under product management. (There is more about this in Chapters 5, 6, and 7.)

Distribution management techniques

It is not enough to have winning products – people must be able to buy them. So good distribution is critical. The management of the process requires selection of appropriate distribution channels – via intermediaries, or direct to the consumer – and operational control of transportation methods, storage and warehousing. (You can read more about this in Chapter 8.)

Salesforce effectiveness

Although you might expect salesforce activity to be more important to businesses with a sales orientation, an effective salesforce is equally important to market-oriented businesses.

The organisation's activity should be geared towards:

* striving for improved salesforce effectiveness;
* ensuring sales activity is concentrated on key brands and consumers (presumably the most profitable ones);
* developing support for salespeople (e.g. training, relevant data, merchandising)
* gearing sales activity to promotional plans.

(See Chapter 8 for more detail.)

Critical success factors

When a business fails, it may be forced to close down altogether, sell out to a competitor, or simply withdraw from a problem market, as Prudential Assurance were forced to do when their venture into estate agency coincided with a collapse in the property market.

Lack of understanding of critical success factors, and of the importance of the various links in the value chain, will contribute to business failures. But as you might expect, there is no one single explanation for why businesses fail. The omission of any one of the eight characteristics of a marketing orientation may play a part. The main causes of failure can be summarised as:

* lack of a market orientation
* failure to control cashflow
* over-trading
* high gearing.

Lack of a market orientation ought now to be clear to you. It can be illustrated by example. Take that of the many small radio and TV sales and repair shops that existed in the 1950s and 1960s. The increase in chain retailers, like Comet and Curry's, together with a willingness by consumers to replace, rather than repair, old sets has condemned many of these businesses to oblivion.

The other causes might appear not to have much to do with marketing but they do. An organisation that is potentially very profitable can still go out of business if it cannot control its cashflow (i.e. if there is more money being paid out than is being paid in). There are many cases of such failure. One was Carlyle Engineering, a bus body builder that closed with full order books. It simply could not obtain payment from its customers fast enough to settle its own suppliers' bills.

Over-trading is another cause of cashflow problems. It occurs when an organisation wins more business than it can afford to finance. This nearly happened to a leading supplier of up-market wedding gowns, which suddenly won a big order from a national bridal chainstore. The company went beyond the limit of its bank overdraft in order to supply the new customer, and was very nearly closed down by the bank. Fortunately, the bank extended the overdraft limit, and the problem passed – for the moment.

High-gearing occurs when companies borrow heavily to finance expansion. While rates on the borrowed money can be met from turnover, all is well. However, during recession, turnover falls and interest payments may become too burdensome. This is the fate that befell the successful advertising company Saatchi & Saatchi, which borrowed heavily to buy other businesses – mostly outside advertising. When the company could no longer afford loan repayments, the bankers could only be bought off by being given a share in the ownership of the business empire.

Activity

Why is it important for marketing people to understand these potential causes of failure? Jot down your answers in your note-book.

DISCUSSION

There is no point in devising plans for new or existing products or markets if the organisation cannot raise the finance for, or sustain itself in, those markets. So understanding how a new venture will be financed, and how much that will cost, is of crucial importance. In this, the co-operation of other departments within the organisations is crucial. This point is dealt with again later in this chapter.

Activity

Read the article from *Marketing Week* (Figure 1. 2 overleaf). It gives an example of a market sector which has revitalised itself as a result of becoming market-oriented. Then answer the following questions.

1 What crisis did Butlins and Pontins face in the 1990s?
2 How did they deal with it?
3 Which techniques did they use in becoming market-oriented?
4 What has been the significance of:
   a Club 18–30
   b Time share holidays, and
   c Centre Parcs?

Holiday camps find a comfortable pitch

No more hi-de-hi days and holidays – these days the accent is on high standards.

Seven million holidaymakers can't be entirely wrong, especially when half of them go back to the same place year after year. That's how many Britons indulge annually in the holiday camp experience.

"Stalag Butlin's" they called them in the Seventies, which was more accurate than most people knew. Many of the UK's holiday camps began life as cheaply converted armed forces training camps, picked up for next to nothing after the war.

But during the past decade, the image of the holiday camp, as exemplified by Rank-owned Butlin's and Scottish & Newcastle subsidiary Pontin's, has undergone something of a sea change. In the past five years, £190m has been invested in Rank's ten Butlin's Holiday Worlds and Hotels. And last week it emerged that Holiday Club Pontin's, as it has been renamed, is talking to advertising agencies about redoubling its efforts to woo back consumers from the lower end of the foreign package market.

The holiday camp market, like so many others in the Eighties, has successfully spawned a premium sector of which Center Parcs, also owned by S&N, is the best known. The basic concept of an all-in-one site has been refined and transferred to a sylvan rather than seaside setting.

Some argue that corporate ownership of holiday camps has left an antiseptic, anonymous atmosphere. Others argue the big chains have underestimated the sophistication of the punters, or that the big chains have become too sophisticated, too expensive and have left their "real" market behind.

Butlin's and Pontin's do not agree. Always the industry heavyweights, both were a product of the fixed holiday allocation and grew rich on low-cost summer breaks for the working-class family. They argue the principle remains fundamentally unchanged and is as saleable to the same socio-economic group today as it was in the Fifties and Sixties.

That was the heyday of the holiday camp. But the dramatic 15-year growth of foreign package holidays beginning in the Seventies also contained the seeds of its own decline. This was of little comfort to Butlin's where the situation deteriorated until 1984. Yet by 1991, the number of visitors had more than doubled.

The key to this turnaround in fortunes was adaptation to market changes. This meant accepting the decline in the traditional summer holiday and concentrating instead on finding growth in short breaks, day trips and extending the season through the winter. A third of Butlin's visitors now stay for less than seven nights.

Managing director of Butlin's Jim Whittell describes the attraction of the holiday camp over the Mediterranean as "everything being predictable".

"People can get the food, drink and papers that they want," which, according to his definition of the clientele, would be The Sun or Daily Mirror. "And there is no hassle getting there. It is a first-class, entertainment-led holiday."

Whittell denies any charge that increased sophistication has left the punters behind. "Our market profile has not changed for 25 years," he says. "If anything, it has declined. Originally we were targeting the C1s. Now we are predominantly low C1, C2 and D."

All this dispels the popular notion that the investment was designed to take Butlin's up-market in any way apart from the standards on offer. The yuppie market is left to Yuppie Butlin's, otherwise known as S&N's second holiday wing, Center Parcs. Both Butlin's and Center Parcs are intensely irritated by the nickname.

This is quite understandable since the two have virtually nothing in common. Center Parcs, a country club in the middle of a forest", with villas at a discreet distance from each other, is the antithesis of the Butlin's experience, offering peace and relaxation in place of excitement and entertainment. Eighty per cent of the clientele is ABC1 - the definition in this case being Volvo drivers from leafy suburbs - and the tariff reflects this. A three bed villa costs upwards of £650 for a week during high season.

With occupancies averaging 98 per cent, Center Parcs has become the blueprint of where British tourism wants to be. S&N is not daunted by the cost - about £80m for each Parc - and more are planned. Two other companies are on its tail for sites.

There is no similar competition to build Butlin's lookalikes. Its viability stems from ownership of the sites and the inherited infrastructure and goodwill. Whittell admits "it would not be viable" to build a Butlin's from scratch today.

Source: Marketing Week

Figure 1. 2 – High standards rather than hi-de-hi

Organising the marketing function

All organisations are different; so too are their structures. In small companies, responsibilities may be fluid in order to achieve flexibility from a small workforce. At the other end of the scale, larger organisations may have rigid self-contained departmental structures and inflexible job roles. What follows is a description of a typical larger organisation and Figure 1.3 shows a typical corporate organisational structure.

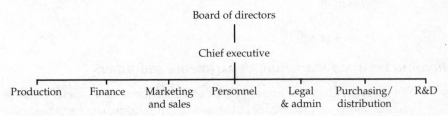

Board of directors

Chief executive

Production   Finance   Marketing   Personnel   Legal   Purchasing/   R&D
and sales   & admin   distribution

Figure 1.3 – Typical corporate organisational structure

Most organisations will have a marketing department, if only because it is fashionable to have one. Often the marketing role will be amalgamated with sales. In these cases, it is worth checking which comes first. If sales precedes marketing in the department title, it is a fairly safe bet that sales is more important. This indicates that a market orientation has probably not been achieved.

What are the roles of the non-marketing functions?

* **Production** is responsible for production planning, methods and control, establishing and monitoring quality systems, and cost control.
* **Finance** is responsible for raising capital, forecasting, budgetary control, accounting, internal audit and providing financial advice.
* **Personnel** is responsible for manpower planning, recruitment, training, remuneration, welfare, employee-relations, discipline and grievance procedures, termination of employment, health and safety policy.
* **Legal and administration** provides legal advice, support and internal communication systems.
* **Purchasing and distribution** is responsible for the ordering of raw materials, components and equipment, internal stores, warehousing, dispatch and transporting of finished goods.
* **Research and development (R&D)** is responsible for developing new ideas, and/or adapting them to existing products.

What is the role of the marketing and sales department?

Marketing and sales is responsible for:
* drawing up a strategic marketing plan,
* managing the organisation's brands,
* determining pricing strategy,

* forecasting sales and profit,
* commissioning market research,
* providing co-ordinated promotional activities, namely advertising, direct marketing, public relations, sponsorship, merchandising, and sales promotions,
* designing packaging to legal, image and market requirements,
* managing and co-ordinating the salesforce,
* order-taking,
* encouraging the development of a market orientation throughout the organisation.

Relationship between marketing departments and others

Not surprisingly, co-operation between departments is a crucial factor in business success. However, traditional business organisations have emphasised the separateness of functions and sections. Recent advances in the status of marketing can make the problem more difficult, especially if colleagues in other departments see marketing personnel as simply manifestations of a current fad, or worse, as overbearingly self-important.

Marketing as a function clearly needs to stay in touch with other departments because, as we saw earlier, marketing is not just a set of operational activities, it is also a philosophy concerned with meeting consumer requirements. For this reason it is important to inculcate a consumer-centredness philosophy throughout the organisation. For example, in a car plant, the old idea of the 'Monday morning' car is inimical. Production workers need to understand that their contribution is just as important to the consumer's satisfaction – and the business' success – as that of someone in sales. So careless working routines which are justified by the workforce on the grounds that anything wrong will be put right at dealer-inspection stage are just as much a headache for the marketing director as for the production director.

The extent of marketing's functional links with other parts of the organisation can be set out as follows:

* the production/marketing interaction results in agreement about the items to be produced, to what specifications, in what quantities and by what date;
* the finance/marketing interaction results in agreement on the investment required to maintain and develop the organisation's products and markets; the monitoring of financial targets; the establishment of user-friendly procedures for collecting payment;
* the personnel/marketing interaction results in agreement over the corporate image to be communicated in recruitment advertising; the messages to be communicated to the organisation's internal audience (i.e. its employees);
* the legal and administrative/marketing interaction results in advice on the legal basis for the organisation's activities (e.g. on a company's articles of association, legislation (UK and EU) and case law regarding, say, product liability);
* the purchasing and distribution/marketing interaction results in agreement on supplier specifications, the establishment of effective distribution networks and suitable management systems;

* the research and development/marketing interaction results in agreement on market-related criteria for research activity, and the nomination of competitor products for analysis.

Sadly, the comfortable interaction of roles described above does not always occur. Frequently, there is argument about who should determine prices – production or marketing. Similarly, sales people will promise quite unrealistic delivery dates, and then blame production if their customers complains. Research boffins may resent the way that their bright ideas are forever being rejected as impracticable by marketing.

Activity

B-Elec, a well-known giant electronics company has for some time been working in secret on a new electrical product, known as the Orb. This is sphere-shaped, and when held, induces a sensation of intense well-being. So far as the company knows, use of the orb is not addictive. However, development and material costs are likely to be extremely high, and to date it has only been possible to develop a mains-powered model, but battery or solar equivalents may follow.

As an individual activity, assume that you are B-Elec's marketing director, and have to prepare a briefing for the other department heads. How will you invite their co-operation in this project? In what way will each department need to be involved?

As a group activity, divide up the departmental roles between small groups, and prepare for the meeting. Think about each department's likely interests and worries about the project. After five minutes of discussion within your small groups, role-play the meeting.

Assignment 1

'Joolz – already on the rocks?"

Scenario
Assume that your group has decided to form a student company to take part in the annual Young Enterprise Competition. (Your tutor will have details of this.)

The group has also decided that the business it intends to set up will be called Joolz Y. E. Ltd., and will assemble and sell costume jewellery – mainly necklaces, bracelets and ear-rings.

The clinching argument for this business was that one student was keen on making her own costume jewellery, and claimed to have suitable trade contacts who would supply the company with beads and clasps. A number of eye-catching designs had been made up, and these were clearly a crucial factor. However, no statistical information about the size of the potential market or of trends within it were used to make the decision.

The decision has not been universally welcomed by everyone in the group – some male students expressed the view that assembling costume jewellery was unmanly and they would have preferred to do something else, albeit unspecified.

At the first general meeting of the company, you were elected marketing director. You now have to prepare for your first board meeting.

YOUR TASKS

1   Write notes for a short presentation you will make about the dangers of starting a busines without first assessing the strength of the market. Given that you will be unlikely to dissuade your colleagues from their decision, explain how they could quickly bring market-related factors to bear on their planning.

2   You have been asked to draft your own job description and present it to the board for approval. Assume that the other functions will be those set out in the structure diagram given in Figure 1. 3. Write down the job description you would suggest for the marketing director.

CHAPTER 2

Understanding marketing research

Suggers, fruggers and data muggers

The place of research in marketing

In Chapter 1 you learned about the development of the marketing concept, and how it is applied to business organisations. You will now appreciate that if organisations are to identify, stimulate and satisfy consumers profitably, then they must know what the consumer wants and whether the organisation is delivering that. Research is the means by which this information is obtained.

Unfortunately, research activity is sometimes used improperly as a front. It may be an attempt to disguise a salespitch, or fund-raising activity. A seemingly innocent fieldworker could be trying to obtain confidential information to use against an individual, or for the purposes of industrial espionage. These are the so-called suggers, fruggers, and data muggers. Needless to say, legitimate research excludes all such underhand practices, and controls exist to deal with the problem. These are discussed in more detail in Chapter 10.

Why bother with research?

There are six key benefits to organisations in undertaking research in marketing. These are as follows:
* research provides a basis for sound, market-led decision-making by providing information to reduce uncertainty;
* research enables organisations to match their products or services to the requirements of consumers;
* research indicates opportunities for product and market development;
* research provides objective explanations for success and failure in marketing;
* research enables product ideas to be tested without the expense of launching to the market (e.g. new pack designs);
* research enables advertising ideas to be tested during a campaign's development or prior to launch to ensure its effectiveness, and after launch to evaluate the success of the media used.

What does marketing research include?

Marketing research is an umbrella term. It covers all those research activities which provide information to guide and direct marketing functions within organisations. It should not therefore be confused with *market research* which provides information about actual and potential customers. Market research is only one component of the wider research that organisations undertake. The full list of research functions for marketing includes:

* product and development research,
* sales data collection,
* distribution research,
* advertising effectiveness and media usage research,
* trading environment analysis,
* market research.

Product and development research

Product and development research is that activity concerned with ensuring that an organisation's products currently satisfy consumer and legal requirements (and will do so in the future); will be able to compete with those of rivals; have a competitive cost-base and price; and will incorporate any technical improvements which lead to cost-reduction, enhanced performance, or both.

Sales data collection

Sales data is collected internally to enable the organisation to monitor trends in sales volume. This will take the form of statistical summaries, and of intelligence reports collected by field sales personnel. These would include customers' comments about rivals, new products, reasons for ordering and reasons for discontinuing orders. Such comments are often invaluable. Ironically, many organisations ignore this valuable source of intelligence, only taking notice of the message when it has been gathered through an expensive market research exercise.

Distribution research

Distribution research is undertaken to ensure that the organisations' products are available to purchasers at the right time and place. The performance of different types of sales outlets and methods needs to be monitored. So too does the amount of time for which products are in the system, as well as the extent to which they are lost or stolen in transit.

Advertising effectiveness and media usage research

Advertising effectiveness research attempts to resolve the dilemma once articulated by Lord Leverhulme, the soap-suds magnate. The head of Lever Brothers once remarked that he knew that half his company's advertising budget was wasted – he just wished he knew which half! These days, studies are undertaken to test consumers' reactions to advertising and of their attitude to the media in which the advertisements appear, in order to avoid wasteful spending.

Trading environment analysis

Trading environment analysis requires a company to look beyond its immediate markets to its wider trading environment.

One helpful acronym in analysing the trading environment is PEST. The initial letters stand for the Political, Economic, Social and Technological environment.

The *political* environment includes possible changes to laws and regulations governing the markets in which an organisation is operating. Possible changes in government policy, such as those affecting taxes and interest rates, are also of crucial importance, and need to be monitored. Activities by lobby groups, such as those which campaign against the use of animal fur in clothing, or for bans on the sale of harmful products such as firearms, must also be monitored.

The *economic* environment refers to trends in the world economy, and those in particular national markets. An organisation must be particularly alert to those which most affect its own business. For a company trading wholly in the UK, the range of economic indicators which it tracks might include:

* Gross Domestic Product (GDP): this assesses the size of the national economy and is very useful, showing whether an economy is growing or not.
* The Retail Price Index (RPI): this measures inflationary pressure.
* Average earnings (self-explanatory).
* Total consumer expenditure which can be calculated as follows:
  (Disposable income + Borrowing) − (Net savings + Debt repayment).
* Consumer confidence: differences between real disposable incomes and actual spending are often explained by consumer confidence. When the economy seems healthy, people's confidence often rises, and they borrow more money. When unemployment climbs, people take fewer risks, and may even concentrate on repaying debt (e.g. mortgages).
* Business confidence: measured quarterly by the Confederation of British Industry (CBI), usually on the basis of advance orders.
* Value of the pound (sterling) against major overseas currencies (e.g. US Dollar, German Deutschmark, Japanese Yen): influencing the relative cost of a company's imported supplies, and export sales.

The next element in PEST is the *social* environment. This refers to trends in the structure of society and in behaviour, and is the focus of much of what is called market research, to be dealt with in detail in the rest of this chapter.

The final element, the *technological* environment is that concerned with the use of raw materials, production processes and finished products, and particularly with innovation. For example, in the soft drinks industry, the development of a plastic material (called PET in short form) has reduced the use of glass bottles dramatically.

Activity

Take one form of research, trading environment analysis, and try applying PEST to a company or business sector with which you are familiar. Copy the table below into your note-book to provide a framework for your answers. The example printed here shows how it might be applied to the bus industry.

Political	Economic	Social	Technological
Privatisation of London buses	Recovery from recession – increased employment	Increasing car ownership	Development of environmental fuels
Pressure to ban cars from city centres	Competition from EU companies	Movement of population to outer suburbs	
	Declining consumer spend on public transport		

Market research

The final item in the list of marketing research activities is research into the markets themselves; this forms the major focus for this chapter. It provides information to enable the following questions to be answered:

* Market size
  - how many consumers does it contain?
  - how many purchases do they make?
  - how much do they spend?
* Market characteristics
  - who are the competitor organisations?
  - how efficient are they?
  - how profitable?
  - which are the rival brands?
  - what is their share of the market?
  - how easy is it for new products or services to enter the market?
  - what are the present trends in the market?
* Consumer characteristics
  - what are the characteristics of present consumers (individuals or business markets)?
  - how are they motivated to buy?
  - how sensitive are they to prices?
  - what are their buying cycles?
  - what image do they have of existing brands in the market?

Research or guesstimate?

Research is an expensive activity. Employing a market research agency on a small-scale project could cost an average of £15,000 (1993 prices). Even off-the-shelf data has a price. So it is important for organisations to be clear about the cost-effectiveness of research proposals they put forward. Not all the information necessary can ever be made available for decision-making purposes. The key questions for any business to ask are:

* What are the costs of the research likely to be?
* How far will data reduce the uncertainty regarding the outcome of the decision?
* What will the consequences be of making an incorrect decision?
* Are the expected benefits likely to outweigh the expected costs?

Types of research

There are two fundamental types of research activity:

* *Desk research* involves the use of existing data, which can be either internal or external to an organisation.
* *Field research* involves the collection of raw data by the research team, either by observation of actual behaviour, or by questioning respondents about their behaviour, attitudes or intentions.

Types of data

The two basic forms of research activity are matched by two basic types of data:

* *Primary data* is information generated by original research, for a purpose specified by the organisation requiring it; its advantage is its relevance to the user, but it is also likely to be expensive in time and money terms to collect.

* *Secondary data* is information from an existing source, probably published or held on a computer database. It is unlikely to have been gathered specifically to meet a particular organisation's requirements and is not always up-to-date. However, it is less expensive and time-consuming to obtain.

Data sources

Internal sources

Most organisations maintain records which provide some data which is likely to be of use. For example, this might take the form of a customer database, containing details of purchases made, contact name, telephone number and any complaints or compliments earned. In the days before computers, this data was often held on paper in a variety of unconnected locations. However, it is usually now a simple matter to collate information gathered by a variety of departments for different purposes. Many organisations now look for opportunities to gather information from their customers for internal use. One example is the guarantee registration card that purchasers of new appliances are asked to return. In addition to the customer's name and address, it is possible to find out how old the customer is, of what sex, whether the appliance was bought as a gift, which brands have been owned previously, and so on.

Activity

If you are currently in work, list in your note-book the internal sources of market research data existing within your own organisation. For those of you studying full-time, find out what information your college holds about its students, and what use is made of it.

DISCUSSION

You are likely to have been swamped with internal data once you started to dig. If your search was in college, you presumably discovered that, apart from students' names, addresses, and details of the courses they took, the college also logged the number of enquiries received, applications, offers of places, acceptances, commencements and successful completions. No doubt students' destinations, place of schooling, and levels of pre-qualification are also logged. Many of the colleges will also have records of the local organisations who use them for staff training.

Were you also able to obtain an impression about the usefulness of the system? Most internal systems began with a desire to record information, not necessarily to apply it to marketing purposes. You may have felt that administrative purposes were still the main justification for the existence of the data.

Published sources

More data is available in the public domain. The major categories of published sources are listed below.

Government statistics

Governments collect a great deal of information for their own use. As a by-product, much is made available to the public at a nominal price. The attraction of these sources lies not just in their cheapness, but in their availability and their comprehensive scope. Examples, all published by Her Majesty's Stationery Office (HMSO), include:

* economic trends – monthly reports on the main trends in the UK economy over the last five years;
* financial statistics – monthly reports on the health of the main sectors of the UK economy – industry, government, utilities, financial markets, leading companies and consumer spend;
* national income and expenditure – annual reports on national income, expenditure, and industrial output (called the 'Blue Book');
* regional trends – regional differences in economic, social and demographic trends;
* social trends – trends in household income/expenditure, demographics, housing and society.

Trade directories

Directories are used by researchers all the time. They are often listings of companies operating in a particular market, and provide data about scope, size, finances and management of a business. The *Yellow Pages* is one example of a directory. Other examples are:

* *Kelly's* – national and regional editions (business classification is by product/service),
* *Kompass* (in two volumes),
* *Key British Enterprises* and *National Business Directory*, published by Dun & Bradstreet,
* The *Municipal Yearbook*.

Standard works are held in public libraries, Chambers of Commerce, and in trade associations' libraries, so you should be able to gain access to these sources without charge.

Off-the-shelf research

A considerable number of market research companies now produce multi-client or commercial research, much more cheaply than client-specific (bespoke) research would cost. This is either available on a one-off basis or, more usually, by subscription with regular updates.

These published sources include:

* Keynote market reports – annual reports covering 200 plus key sectors of the UK economy;
* Mintel reports – covering whole markets, retail intelligence, leisure, personal finance, and new product launch reviews and case histories; published at intervals ranging from daily to occasional;
* Economist Market Reports – many of these are international;

* competitor analyses – for example, Business Ratio Reports (an annual analysis of 12,000 leading UK companies in 150 business sectors, assessing their profitability, liquidity, stock turnover, capital utilisation, productivity, credit period and export ratios);
* media usage reports – for example, BARB (Broadcast TV Audience Research), and OSCAR reports (on outdoor advertising);
* retail audits (e.g. Nielsen) – studies of sales of product types according to retail outlet; shows where competitor products are displayed and sold;
* consumer panels (e.g. AGB Super Panel, Television Consumer Audit) are on-going studies in which the same consumers regularly report their purchases of household goods, providing data about purchasing and storage before consumption (the so-called 'pantry audits');
* Target Group Index (TGI).

The *TGI* is a national survey of consumers' product and media usage patterns, produced by the British Market Research Bureau (BMRB). Its reports directly relate the purchase of products with the media habits of consumers, so that the manufacturers of products can find out which TV programmes or magazines their consumers seem to enjoy. This widely-used service is available on subscription to advertisers, agencies and to advertising media, although particular reports can also be purchased as and when required.

TGI users can find out about the social status of consumers, their levels of household income, household size, lifestyles, and appreciation indices for 80 top television programmes. Sales of more than 2500 fast moving consumer brands are tracked, together with 150 brands in consumer durables and the service sector. Purchasers are categorised as heavy, medium, light and non-users; and sales within these categories are analysed at both product group and individual brand level. For brands with more than one million purchasers, demographic and media use information is available.

Information is also provided about media usage, including 220 newspapers and magazines, the extent to which television is viewed, commercial radio listened to, and of exposure to outdoor media and cinema advertising. The data in TGI reports is particularly helpful when used in conjunction with other media audience research.

One of the strengths of the TGI survey is the large number of respondents throughout the UK who complete a questionnaire each month about their product and media usage. Their 24,000 responses provide the TGI with its raw data. Once processed and analysed, the results are made available to users in a variety of ways:

* through an on-line database, accessible only to subscribers;
* via computer bureaux, provided they hold the relevant volume; or
* in hard-copy, of which there are 34 separate volumes, covering demographics, food, household goods, pharmaceuticals, toiletries and cosmetics, drink, confectionery, tobacco, motoring, clothing and shopping, leisure, holidays and travel, financial services, and consumer durables.

In recent years, a further eight-volume set of reports, *AB TGI*, has been issued on high-status social groups A & B. It includes more detail about these high-disposable income groups than the mainstream reports.

The value of the TGI to companies is that it tells them who the consumers are, their loyalty (or otherwise) to brands, and which media they use. Organisations can also find out about their competitors' customers; the reverse obviously applies. In addition, the TGI enables an organisation's own data to be checked against, and synthesised with, national research data, thus increasing its accuracy and value.

Activity

In your note-book, list the sources you have access to in your college and local library. Use the list provided here as a check-list, but try to locate new sources too. When you list them, explain in a few sentences what they contain and how they might be used.

Commissioned research

Companies can either employ their own staff to undertake 'bespoke' research, or hire agencies to undertake it for them. Whether done on a DIY basis, or placed with an agency, commissioned research provides specific data which is not available in the public domain. This is particularly important where an organisation is planning innovations to its products.

Using market research agencies

The use of the specialist skills to be found in agencies provides organisations with a number of advantages. These are:
* experience in designing and implementing research programmes;
* familiarity with data resource systems;
* easier access to competitors than would be the case for an organisation's own staff;
* an unbiased and impartial view of the research outcome.

Set against these advantages are the potential drawbacks of greater cost, possible loss of confidentiality (e.g. by the use of third parties), and inappropriate results arising from poor briefing or misunderstanding on the part of the agency. It has to be pointed out that not even the most reputable research agency is immune from making mistakes.

To give you an idea of the range of work that such an agency can undertake, Figure 2.1 summarises the services that Research Associates (RA) offers to prospective clients.

Omnibus surveys

This type of survey is a variant to full-blown commissioned market research, in that it allows a number of different organisations to ask their own unique questions within one composite questionnaire. The process is known as 'taking seats on the omnibus'. In such cases, the responses will be released only to the organisation which 'bought the seat'.

A fee is charged for the service, usually determined by the sample size required, and the number and complexity of the questions to be posed. In 1993, one agency offered its weekly omnibus of 2000 UK adults at a rate card cost of £4000.

Case study

* **Marketing strategy in existing markets** – RA offers a full marketing planning service, analysing an organisation's markets and competitors, and assessing a business on 26 marketing issues. It will then generate a range of options and opportunities and produce an action plan.
* **Finding new markets at home or overseas** – for organisations contemplating entry into a new market, RA offers a thorough study, ranging from a description of that market's major characteristics (including the competition) to a recommendation about whether to enter the market, and how (e.g. through the use of agents or by acquiring an existing company in that market).
* **An image study** – this service enables RA clients to understand more fully how and why their own customers buy, what they think of the client's products, and those of its rivals. Again, the client's business is rated on 26 marketing issues, and specific actions are suggested to improve image, sales and profits.
* **Diversification and/or acquisition** – businesses which contemplate a move into wholly new products and markets, need reliable independent advice on the risks they run and the potential rewards. RA claims to provide this, by identifying markets, and suitable companies for possible acquisition, which satisfy clients' criteria for new development.
* **Consumer attitudes** – the last category of service provided by RA provides detailed information about the consumers who occupy clients' markets, what motivates buying decisions, how they rate clients' products and how they respond to sales promotions, advertising and price variation.

Figure 2.1 – Services provided by Research Associates (RA)

Methods of collecting primary data

There are three methods of collecting primary data: experimentation, observation, and survey.

Experimentation

Assume that a soft drinks manufacturer is contemplating a change to the recipe for one of its products. How would consumers react? One way to find out is by carrying out experiments in which the consumers sample the modified drink. There are two ways in which this can be done: by field experiments or by laboratory experiments.

Field experiments
Field experiments are made in 'real-market' situations. In such circumstances the modified product would be supplied to a small test market without announcing any change. The modification might be to the drink's recipe, pack, price or advertising. Sales to shops, cafes and pubs would be carefully monitored to detect any upward or downward trend.

Laboratory experiments

With *laboratory experiments* consumers are placed in highly-controlled and highly-artificial situations, although not actually in laboratories. So, the soft-drinks company might invite people to take part in tasting sessions in which they talk about their reactions. The method is widely used for new food and drink brands.

In any experimentation there are many factors susceptible to change. These are called *variables*. Those which are under the control of the experimenter are known as the *independent variables*. On the other hand, those beyond the control of the experimenter are called *exogenous variables*, while the observed result is known as the *dependent variable*. So any change, say, to the colouring of the soft drink would be a change in the independent variables. Changes in the weather, or competitors' reactions, however, being beyond the experimenter's control, are changes to exogenous variables. The problem is then to decide whether the dependent variable – sales of the drink – has been influenced by the independent or exogenous variables.

Observation

If the behaviour which an organisation wants to assess is already occurring, it may not be necessary to carry out an experiment, but simply to observe what is already going on. However, it may be necessary to contrive some artificiality in order that people may be observed without being aware of the fact.

Observation is excellent for recording behaviour, but it does not necessarily explain it. Questionnaires can help in this case. However, as a guide to behaviour observation is usually more reliable than using questionnaires because people may not be wholly honest in talking about their behaviour. For example, few people would admit to not wearing a seat belt on a car journey, but casual observation will show that there are still people who do not do so.

Survey

In circumstances in which it is not possible to observe people's behaviour, or where information about motivation and intention is required, the usual method for obtaining the desired data is the survey.

There are three basic survey methods:
*   personal interview
*   postal survey
*   telephone interview.

The advantages and disadvantages of each method are summarised in Table 2.1

A number of these points are common to each method. Generally, the method(s) chosen will be determined by:
*   the size of the research budget available,
*   the amount of information required,
*   the likely sensitivity of the respondents to making disclosure,
*   the size and distribution of the planned sample,
*   the motivation of respondents to take part,
*   whether the research is being undertaken by an organisation's own staff or by an agency.

For example, an organisation that wants quick results may opt for a phone poll. One that wants to obtain delicate data may prefer the personal approach, to reassure respondents about the integrity of the research. When a lot of questions need to be asked, the postal method may be chosen.

Table 2.1 – Survey methods: advantages and disadvantages

Method	Advantages	Disadvantages
Personal interview	Best response rates – demands little from respondents. Some information may be obtained by observation. Respondents' answers may be more accurate – less time to dissemble.	Expensive – particularly for nationwide surveys. Respondents' answers are influenced by the interviewer's presence. Difficulties in targeting an agreed sample.
Postal survey	Precise targeting is possible in sending out questionnaires. Relatively inexpensive. Enables detailed questioning of respondents. Answers not influenced by interviewer presence.	Response rate low and slow. Mailing list may be out-of-date. Questions cannot be explained if not understood. Stimulators required to prompt responses (e.g. free gifts, follow-up letters). Danger of unrepresentative responses.
Telephone interview	Low costs of reaching a wide audience quickly. Useful for carrying out initial research (e.g. to gain information about purchasing systems of industrial customers). Also enjoys advantages of personal interviews.	High levels of resistance in UK to 'intrusive' method. Not all the population have a phone at home. Other people are ex-directory. Intimate questions may seem threatening.

Activity

Assume that your college has decided to carry out the following market research projects. Which method above would you recommend in each case?

Project One: Noting the growth of tourism to its position as the world's largest industry, a decision has been made to approach the operators of local leisure and tourist facilities to try to quantify their possible demands for training over the next three years. Suggest a research method.

Project Two: In recent years, students completing NVQ Level III courses in Printing have expressed an interest in progressing beyond this level – until now not possible at this college. The supervisor of printing training courses is contemplating offering training and assessment at Level IV in the near future, and wants to assess likely demand. Suggest a research method.

Project Three: Recent concern about the spread of AIDS has led to the installation of contraceptive vending machines in male student toilets. Now a company vending female contraceptives has asked to be allowed to install such machines. However, there are concerns about the reaction of some students. The college wants to avoid a public relations blunder by assessing opinion beforehand. Suggest a research method.

DISCUSSION

Clearly, there is no single right answer; each challenge requires judgement to determine a suitable method. A postal questionnaire would probably be the most likely solution for Project One. However, if a close relationship exists with a small number of centres in the college's locality, personal interviews might be arranged at the respondents' premises. Telephone surveying would be difficult as it might be considered intrusive. However, for contacts with former part-time students in Project Two, this method could be expected to give a quick indication of likely interest. The sensitivity of the subject for Project Three suggests that a written response would be most suitable.

Organising a market research programme

Figure 2.2 represents a stage-by-stage plan for structuring a research programme:

1   Define the objectives for the research.
2   Carry out initial desk research in the chosen area to review the availability and usefulness of data from existing sources.
3   Plan the investigation:
    a   select the sources of data
    b   design primary research methods – survey/experiment
    c   Prepare data-gathering forms
    d   choose your sample.
4   Pre-test the method (i.e. undertake pilot) and refine if necessary.
5   Collect data.
6   Tabulate and analyse the data.
7   Present the findings in a written report.
8   Follow this up to validate the findings.

Figure 2.2 – The structure of a market research programme

Activity

Assume that you work in the marketing department of a confectionery manufacturer. Your R&D people have been working for some time on a low-calorie chocolate bar which tastes similar to existing products. Now they have produced a bar which meets taste requirements, but will cost about twice as much to produce as conventional products.

Draw up the outline for a market research programme which you would use to test the market potential for this idea.

Quantitative or qualitative data?

It is often assumed that survey data is all of a kind. This is not so; there is an important distinction to be drawn. One kind is called *quantitative data* – that is, information that can be counted and expressed in percentage terms (e.g. 55 per cent of all customers are women, 28 per cent are between the ages of 16 and 24 years, etc.). This is the type of data most often generated by surveys, and can easily be presented using sophisticated computer graphics. In practice, however, organisations also need to ask probing questions about people's motivations and attitudes. Above all, organisations need to know not just what people do, but why. Data about these underlying feelings, thoughts and motives is called *qualitative data*. Clearly, it requires a different approach and, by its very nature, cannot be presented statistically because it is impressionistic. This may make it sound very vague and wishy-washy. Yet some commentators believe that, when cash for research is limited, this method should be used. They argue that well-organised group interviews, while being relatively cheap to set up, can be very illuminating in helping to understand consumer attitudes and behaviour. However, if these sessions are to produce valid data, the interviewers will need to have good social skills and keep the purpose of the research clearly in mind.

The principal characteristics of the two data types are summarised in Table 2.2.

Table 2.2 – Quantitative and qualitative data

	Quantitative data	Qualitative data
Value to an organisation	'Hard facts' about what people do, think and want.	Insights into why people think and behave as they do.
Question-form most suitable for collection of this data	Close-ended questions, with choice of answers.	Open-ended questions with respondents given scope to say whatever they wish.
Suitable survey methods	Face-to-face, post and telephone.	All those listed left plus group discussion.
Likely report presentation formats	Tables, graphs, pie-diagrams, pictograms.	Evaluative reports.

Choosing a sample

In undertaking market research three questions need to asked:
* Which people are to be surveyed?
* How many people should be surveyed?
* How should they be chosen?

The sample unit – type and size

Those people in the population to be surveyed constitute the *sample unit*, or sample frame. Mostly it is not difficult to decide who these people are. However, sometimes there are problems. For example, a survey about purchases of men's pyjamas might mistakenly target male respondents, when more than half such purchases are made by women. It can also be difficult to identify just who makes up the sample unit, and where they are.

Suppose you wanted to survey people taking three or more holidays a year. Time and effort would be needed to construct the sample frame even before the survey could begin. The accuracy of the composition of the frame is particularly important when random sampling techniques are used, as will be made clear below.

Once a decision about the sample unit or frame has been made, it is then necessary to consider how large the sample should be. For most purposes it is neither economic nor feasible to contact the total market, and thus a representative number will be chosen. Where the sample unit is known to be composed of people with similar attitudes and behaviour, the number of subjects can be smaller. In addition, a larger sample size will require the data to be collected over a longer period of time, as responses at the end of the research period may differ from those at the beginning.

Random or non-random sampling?

The next decision will concern the nature the sample – a random, or a non-random one. The term *random sample*, which sounds rather as though it is ill-organised, simply means that the respondents are chosen in such a way that any member of the population has an equal chance of being selected. A *non-random sample* is one in which the respondents will almost certainly be selected on the basis of pre-determined characteristics.

The difference between the two options is that when random sampling techniques are used, it is possible to apply statistical techniques to assess the likelihood that sampling errors have occurred and thus affected the results. With non-random samples the use of statistical analysis to assess the effect of possible sampling error is not legitimate; however, it does occur.

Random and non-random samples can be further classified (see Figure 2.3).

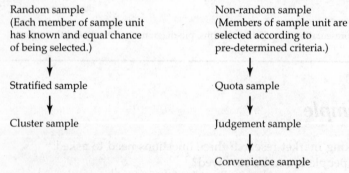

Figure 2.3 – Types of sample

Random samples require subjects to be selected according to some predetermined system for allocating the chances of participation. A common way is to number all the members of the sample frame then, if one-tenth of the frame is to be interviewed, to start at an arbitrary point within the first ten numbered names on the list and then approach every tenth person. The problem with this method is that it is time-consuming, and some of those selected at random will not agree to take part.

Stratified random sampling uses a similar approach, but this time the respondents are chosen randomly, but within pre-determined categories, such as socio-economic groups. *Cluster* random samples are again chosen at random, but rather than from within the entire population of the country, from within geographical concentrations. This method is used because it is cheaper and quicker.

However, it is the non-random sampling methods that are used most frequently for research, because these get results most cheaply and quickly. Of these *quota* samples are widely used. Here, the fieldworkers are asked to contact respondents in pre-determined categories (e.g. occupational groups) in the same proportion as the make-up of the sample frame. So, if OAPs make up 10 per cent of the population of the sample frame, researchers would be expected to interview a similar percentage of elderly people. *Judgement* sampling is less rigorous, and allows the fieldworker to make judgements about the representativeness of the subjects. *Convenience* sampling, being quick and cheap – respondents are chosen for convenience – is likely to be least representative. These latter methods increase the likelihood of interview bias in the results of the surveys.

Drawing up a questionnaire

In designing a questionnaire, there are broadly two types of question that can be asked:
* **Open-ended questions** allow respondents to exercise maximum discretion in answering. No alternatives are prescribed, and they are particularly suitable for gathering qualitative data. The main problem is in categorising the wide range of answers likely to result.
* **Closed-ended questions** prescribe a range of alternative answers between which respondents must select. They are particularly suitable for gathering quantitative data.

Examples of each type are given in Figure 2.4 (overleaf).

The seven principles

Following these seven principles will help you to design reliable survey forms:
* Questionnaires are research tools, and not an end in themselves. So start by thinking about what information is required, not by saying 'What questions should we ask?'
* Consider the circumstances in which the questions will be replied to; this will determine the length and number of questions that can be asked (e.g. postal questionnaires can be considerably longer than those answered in the street).
* Consider how the results are to be analysed and interpreted. The more open-ended the questions, the more difficult it will be to analyse and interpret the results.
* Avoid leading questions, which either make assumptions (e.g. How old were you when you first smoked a cigarette?) or telegraph a desired answer to the respondents (e.g. Don't you agree that hanging is too good for these perverts?).
* Only ask for one piece of information at a time, avoiding confusing questions. For example, the question 'Do you drink alcohol in pubs and clubs or at home?' fails to distinguish between consumption in public houses and clubs.
* Be precise in requests for information; vague questions will produce meaningless answers. For example, 'Do you drink a lot?' does not allow for the fact that 'a lot' will be interpreted differently from person to person.
* Keep sensitive or penetrating questions for the end of a questionnaire; start with safe topics until you have earned the confidence of the respondents.

Closed-ended questions

Dichotomous [1]
Respondents are offered only two choices.

Multiple choice [2]
Respondents have a wider choice, and may, if appropriate, answer more than once.

Graded/scaled [3,4]
Respondents can show their strength of feeling by choosing from a range of graded options (no middle option, thus forcing people to take one view or the other), or by putting list items in rank order [see question 4]

```
MAPLIN'S HOLIDAY CAMPS
Customer Questionnaire

1.  Have you ever stayed at a
    Maplin's camp before?

    Yes [ ]        No [ ]

2.  Did you see an advertisement
    for Maplin's camps in any of
    these places:
                TV Times          [ ]
                Radio Times       [ ]
                News of the World [ ]
                Sunday People     [ ]
                Chat              [ ]
                Daily Mirror      [ ]
                Tatler            [ ]
                Holiday Guide     [ ]

3.  "Maplin's Holiday Camps offer
    outstanding value for money"
        Do you :
                Strongly agree    [ ]
                Agree             [ ]
                Slightly agree    [ ]
                Slightly disagree [ ]
                Disagree          [ ]
                Strongly disagree [ ]


4.  Arrange these features of a
    Maplin's camp in their order
    of importance to you 1 = most
    important, 10 = least
    important
    ... Free rides for children
    ... Free evening entertainment
        for adults
    ... Guard dogs and security fence
    ... Cheerful camp host
    ... Radio Maplin's
    ... Free bus from railway station
    ... Friendly yellowcoats
    ... McMaplin's Burgerbar
    ... Novelty competitions
    ... Easy-payment scheme
```

Figure 2.4 - continued overleaf

Figure 2.4 - continued

Open-ended questions

Unstructured [5]
There is an almost infinite number of possible responses.

5. What is your opinion of Maplin's Holiday Chalets?
   _____
   _____

Word association [6]
Profound beliefs and reflex attitudes can be revealed by such questions.

6. What is the first thing you think of when you hear these words?

   Holiday   _____
   Campers   _____
   Hi-de-hi! _____

Sentence/story completion [7]
Questions like this attempt to assess the conscious and sub-conscious motives of respondents. Story completion is more demanding, and used less often than sentence completion.

7. On the first full day of their holiday at Maplin's, Angela and Geoff Smith woke with a feeling of eager excitement.The sun shone over the Hawaiian ballroom and in through their window."What shall we do today?" asked Greg. NOW COMPLETE THE STORY.
   _____
   _____

Picture completion [8]
A similar approach, but this time stimulating a response by the use of cartoons. Respondents write a reply in the empty bubble.

8.

Figure 2.4 - Specimen questionnaire

Activity

Read the questionnaire on page 34. Are there any mistakes which ought to be put right before trying it out on the public?

Banking services for young people
Please help us to improve how we serve you by filling in this 32-page booklet.

1 Have you ever been:
   * overdrawn?   (   )
   * refused credit because of bad debts?   (   )
   * in trouble with the courts over money?   (   )

2 Do you visit your branch of the bank:
   * regularly?   (   )
   * irregularly?   (   )
   * hardly ever?   (   )

3 Have you ever had to wait for an unreasonable length of time to use a bank counter or automatic cash dispenser?

   Yes   (   )   No   (   )

4 When did you decide to start acting responsibly with your money by opening a bank account?

   _____

   _____

5 I bank here because:
   * everybody is so friendly and helpful   (   )
   * the quality of service is brilliant   (   )
   * the bank has a first-class reputation   (   )
   * I wanted the free personal organiser   (   )
   * other (please specify)   (   )

PTO

DISCUSSION

You should have picked up the following errors to be corrected:

Question 1 – too intrusive a beginning. Sensitive or intimate questions should be asked towards the end of a survey, after a relationship of trust has been established with the respondent.

Question 2 – what is 'regularly'? Once a year may be regular, but not necessarily frequent. The question should have asked precisely about the intervals between visits.

Question 3 – this asks two things at once. When analysing the answers it will be impossible to tell if respondents are aggrieved at waiting too long for one or both types of service at branches.

Question 4 – this is guilty of the assumption that everyone is irresponsible with cash before they open an account.

Question 5 – this is incredibly conceited. Every answer option reflects well upon the bank, but they are not necessarily the reasons why people have accounts there. A fuller range of answers, including those not favourable to the bank, will be likely to provide more accurate information.

PTO – with another 31 pages to go, the compilers will be lucky to receive many responses!

Analysing and reporting research findings

The process of analysing the information obtained during research will be strongly influenced by the research methodology. If secondary sources of data have been used, the data has already been analysed and interpreted by someone else. In this case, the problem is to decide whether the presentation is helpful, or the interpretation placed on the data is correct. If however, you have been undertaking primary research using questionnaires, you will be required to tabulate the scores for closed-ended questions, and work out percentage responses. Open-ended questions, and observational and experimental research, pose problems about the data. Namely, deciding to which evidence the greatest significance should be attached.

Frequently, a researcher will be required to synthesise data; that is, to combine the results of two aspects of the research which appear to be related. In the example below, in a survey of soft drink consumption in the UK, there appears to be a connection between mean daily temperatures in summer (Table 2.3), and sales volume (Table 2.4). After the exceptionally warm years of 1989 and 1990, with high temperatures in the key months of July and August, sales volume slipped back in 1991.

Table 2.3 – Temperatures in England and Wales, 1989–91
(Source: *Retail Business*, October 1993, Economist Intelligence Unit)

Average	1951–80	1988	1989	1990	1991
Year	9.8	10.2	10.9	11.1	10.0
July	16.0	15.1	18.3	17.0	17.4
August	15.9	15.7	17.0	18.4	17.4

(°C mean daily air temperature at sea level)

Source: Meteorological Office

Table 2.4 – Consumption of Soft Drinks, 1988–92
(Source: *Retail Business*, October 1993, Economist Intelligence Unit)

	1988	1989	1990	1991	1992
Volume	7.0	8.0	8.4	7.9	8.0
% change	6	15	4	−6	1

(bn litres; percentage)

Source: Britvic

However, the interpretation that the sole factor behind the increased sales is mean daily temperature is dispelled when additional data is considered. Tables 2.5 and 2.6 show that there is a long-term trend towards soft drinks consumption, mainly at the expense of tea and coffee.

Table 2.5 – Consumption of soft drinks as proportion of all drinks consumption
(Source: *Retail Business*, October 1993, Economist Intelligence Unit)

1988	1989	1990	1991	1992
14.3	15.9	16.1	16.1	16.8

(% share of all drinks volume by all ages from 10 years)

Source: Annual Report of the Tea Council, from National Drinks Survey

Table 2.6 – Proportion of people drinking soft drinks and other drinks daily, 1988–92

(Source: *Retail Business*, October 1993, Economist Intelligence Unit)

	1988	1989	1990	1991	1992	Change* 1988/92
Soft drinks	49.0	51.6	51.8	51.7	53.7	4.7
Tea	81.4	80.7	80.1	80.0	78.7	−2.7
Coffee	58.3	57.9	57.6	56.6	56.9	−1.4
Alcohol	29.5	28.9	29.8	29.5	29.7	0.2

*Change in terms of percentage points
(Percentage from all ages from 10 years)   Source: Annual Report of the Tea Council, from National Drinks Survey

Activity

Carefully study the three tables below (Tables 2.7, 2.8 and 2.9) obtained from desk research relating to the consumption of carbonated soft drinks.

Assume that you are a market researcher for a major soft drinks company. Explain what you believe to be the significance of the figures to your market research manager.

Table 2.7 – Carbonated soft drink servings as a proportion of all beverage servings drunk, by age group, 1989
(Source: *Retail Business*, October 1993, Economist Intelligence Unit)

			Age group		
2–9	10–15	16–24	25–44	45–64	65+
17	26	15	8	5	3

(Percentage)

Source: National Drinks Survey, quoted by MMC

Table 2.8 – Consumption of carbonated soft drinks by age group, 1992–93 (from October 1992 to March 1993)
(Source: *Retail Business*, October 1993, Economist Intelligence Unit)

			Age group		
2–4	5–9	10–12	13–15	16–20	21–24
4	10	7	8	12	9

			Age group		
25–34	35–44	45–54	55–64	65–69	70+
17	12	8	6	3	4

(Percentage drinking yesterday)

Source: National Drinks Survey

Table 2.9 – Household consumption of unconcentrated soft drinks by household composition, 1991
(Source: *Retail Business*, October 1993, Economist Intelligence Unit)

Household type	Consumption per head	Expenditure per head	Share of consumption
	(index: all households = 100)		(%)
Old age pensioners	49	46	4
All single people	78	85	6
Other households without children	93	94	36
Households with 1 or 2 children	111	111	46
Households with 3 or more children	102	93	12

Source: *Retail Business* from NFS

Potential problems with research

Despite the best efforts of all those concerned with research things can, and do, go wrong. Why is this? There could be several reasons:

* Haste – in attempting to do too much in too little time, short cuts may be taken, and out-of-date or inappropriate secondary sources consulted.
* Inappropriate methodology – errors in project design, sampling techniques, lack of understanding by subjects and interview bias can all distort research findings.
* Lack of cash – financial constraints may limit the amount of research activity, leading to erroneous conclusions.
* Inexperience in interpreting research data – managers may see in the research merely what they wish to see, particularly where results are not clear-cut.

Examples of inaccurate research abound. Eddie Shah's *Daily Post* was launched in 1988 on the back of market research which showed that almost one in three tabloid newspaper readers were prepared to switch to a less sex-oriented, more 'respectable' tabloid than the *Sun*, *Mirror* or *Star*. In practice, the paper lasted only 18 days. There is often a difference between what people say and how they actually behave, as Eddie Shah discovered.

Likewise, the Japanese electronics giant Sony researched attitudes to the Walkman portable stereo before its launch. Results were unfavourable; people claimed they would not be seen in public wearing headphones. But Sony had a hunch that it was on to a winner and launched the product anyway. The rest is history.

Assignment 2

Bubbles

You are a marketing assistant for a small company making 'fizzy drinks'. The company's main products are rather weakly-branded mixer drinks (e.g. tonic water), to be added to alcoholic beverages. They are aimed primarily at women, and the products sell mainly in the North East of England and in the Scottish Borders. In recent years, an attempt has been made to target a younger market with cola and other similar drinks.

Last week, Mrs Dalgleish, the sales and marketing director called you into her office. 'I want you to undertake some desk research into the importance of the 16–24 year old segment of the soft drinks market. We believe that this could be the most important age group for the consumption of carbonated products. I want you to go away and prove me right', she said.

The first source you consulted was the invaluable office copy of the *Lifestyle Pocket Book*, produced by the Advertising Association. From there you obtained the population figures by age for the UK from the 1991 census:

Age group	Population ('000s)
0–4	3882
5–9	3670
10–14	3498
15–19	3727
20–24	4483

From these you calculated the size of the 15–24 age group in the population for the years 1991, 1996, and 2001.

You then turned up some commercial market research. From the National Drinks Survey, you discovered the percentage of all beverages drunk, by age in 1989, which were accounted for by carbonated soft drinks. The results were:

Age group	Carbonated soft drinks as a percentage of all beverage servings
2–9	17
10–15	26
16–24	15
25–44	8
45–64	5
65+	3

a   Does this confirm or contradict Mrs Dalgleish's assumption?

However, the National Drinks Survey also provided information about the percentages of people of different ages who claimed to have drunk a carbonated soft drink on they day before they were questioned. This of course is a different question to that asked in the other survey. In addition, the data relates to 1992–93, and there was a bias to female respondents. The results were:

Age group	Percentage of respondents claiming to have drunk a carbonated soft drink the previous day
2–4	4
5–9	10
10–12	7
13–15	8
16–20	12
21–24	9
25–34	17
35–44	12
45–54	8
55–64	6
65–69	3
70+	4

b   How does this fit the picture you obtained from the previous table?
c   What do you make of the result for the 25–34 year old age group?
d   What additional information – if any – does this result suggest you require?

Finally, a colleague in the office passes you a trade magazine containing another interesting table. It shows the consumption of unconcentrated soft drinks by household composition in 1991. The results were:

Household type	Consumption per head	Expenditure per head	Percentage of total UK consumption
	(index: all households = 100)		
Old age pensioners	49	46	4
All single persons	78	85	6
Other households without children	93	94	36
Households with 1 or 2 children	111	111	46
Households with 3 or more children	102	93	12

Source: *Retail Business* from NFS

e   How important are households with children in this market?

f   Which household types tend to buy the cheapest, and which the most expensive brands?

g   How does this data relate to your manager's perception of the national market?

YOUR TASKS

You must prepare to report back orally on your initial research to Mrs Dalgleish.

1   Summarise clearly the results of all the data you have obtained.

2   Identify any differences in research methodology and categorisation of which your manager needs to be aware.

3   Be ready to define the terms:

   a   beverage

   b   carbonated soft drink

   c   unconcentrated soft drink.

4   Outline proposals for further research you believe the company should undertake (if any) to better understand the relationship between age of consumers and product purchase.

CHAPTER 3

The role of market segmentation

Yuppies, Dinkies and Whannies

What is market segmentation?

Market segmentation is the analysis of total demand in a market into its constituent parts, so that different sets of consumers, with distinctive needs and behaviour patterns, can be identified.

This definition may be a bit of a mouthful, but the concept is really quite simple. The term *segmentation* is used to convey the idea that, just as a grapefruit is composed of a number of segments, so the total demand for a product or service type is made up of a number of component parts. The demand for banking services is a good example. Although in essence all the occupants of the total market want bank accounts, the reasons for wanting those accounts will vary enormously, depending on how much money people have got and what they want to do with it. These reasons may, in turn, be influenced by the age, social class, lifestyle and psychological make-up of the people concerned.

A market segment, therefore, is a discrete group of consumers enjoying common characteristics (e.g. buying habits, patterns and preferences), who with other groups of consumers (or segments) comprise the total market for a product or service.

Clearly, therefore, one of the key functions of market research (see Chapter 2) is to identify the existence of different market segments, and help organisations to understand the occupants of those segments – what they want to buy and why.

Why bother to segment markets?

Segmentation enables businesses to:
* define and understand their markets better;
* position their brands and product ranges more accurately to satisfy consumers; and
* identify gaps in the market for expansion and/or new product development.

Activity

Think for a moment about the value of segmentation to people who run small businesses. List the benefits of segmenting local markets to the following:
* garden maintenance contractor
* chimney sweep
* bureau providing temporary staff.

Why has segmentation become increasingly important?

Although it has always been important for a business to have a proper understanding of its customers, the process of segmenting markets has become much more important in the final quarter of this century. The factors which have influenced this development include:

* the increasing strength of volume suppliers – this has compelled smaller rivals to identify niche markets in which to operate;
* the growing control of multiple retailers in fast moving consumer goods (FMCG) markets – this has forced manufacturers to understand their markets better in order to survive; and
* technical advances – these have made it easier to produce variations upon basic products to meet the requirements of different segments.

However, arguably the single most important factor has been demassification.

Demassification

Demassification is a phenomenon of our post-industrial society. It refers to the fragmentation of demand for products which have conventionally enjoyed mass markets. It occurs as a result of increasing consumer affluence, and changing behaviour and taste. Canned fruit products provide an example of the challenge facing the supermarkets. One-time popular lines such as tinned prunes, peaches and mandarin oranges, have now been joined on the shelves by more exotic lines – guavas, mangoes and lychees. Fruit in natural juice (rather than syrup) is a popular healthy option. At the same time, improving husbandry, transport and storage has made previously seasonal fresh fruit available all year round.

All of this poses problems of space for the multiples who are required to stock increasing numbers of line-variants, even though the total amount of food purchased by individual consumers is unlikely to be significantly affected by the changes. The process of demassification in grocery markets had reached the stage, that, by the mid-1990s, an average sized Sainsbury's store has over 15,000 different product lines.

Segmentation and marketing strategy

Historically, organisations began by treating their markets as though all the people who occupied them were *homogeneous* (i.e. similar). As a consequence it was thought acceptable to provide them with a single product, considered suitable to all. However, in recent decades, evidence has shown that the occupants of markets are usually *heterogeneous* (i.e. dissimilar) and that the idea of a single product being equally acceptable to them all is unrealistic.

In the case of the motor car industry, for example, Ford has moved a long way from the maxim – 'They can have any car they like, so long as it's black!' – to the present position in which a wide range of models, and colours, is on offer.

Ford has learned that the total market for motor cars can be divided up in many ways – between private and fleet car buyers, between people looking for high performance and those seeking economy, between those people who need a family runabout and those looking for a second car, and so on. Accordingly, there is a depth and breadth to the Ford range which means that, whatever the consumer need, there is likely to be a suitable Ford product to meet it.

Selecting a target strategy

In selecting a suitable target strategy, organisations can choose between:
* undifferentiated marketing (i.e. convergence)
* differentiated marketing (i.e. divergence)
* concentrated marketing (i.e. target one market segment).

Convergence   Divergence   Concentration

Figure 3.1 – Convergence-concentration continuum

In positioning products for the market, organisations must choose between policies of convergence or concentration. *Convergence* involves presenting a single product to a variety of market segments, in the hope that the appealing claims made on its behalf will make it acceptable to a variety of different consumers (e.g. variety shows on TV, which claim to offer 'something for all the family').

A more *divergent* policy, however, recognises variation in consumers' goals, and involves modification of the product to a greater or lesser extent. When that reaches the stage of producing a product to appeal to a single market segment, perhaps even a single consumer, the policy is one of *concentration*. For example, British Rail operated a policy of divergence in marketing its rail passenger service. It offered transport by train between a fixed points at a limited number of times – which illustrates convergence. However, the use of branding such as InterCity, the application of first and standard class accommodation, the designation of some seating as non-smoking, and the use of OAP railcards, and Saver and Supersaver fares, all show evidence of divergence in positioning variants of the same basic product for particular segments.

Only a taxi service, conveying individuals or small groups ofpeople from unique points of departure to unique destinations is truly a *concentrated* transport marketing strategy.

Activity

Draw a convergence-concentration strategy continuum (see Figure 3.1) in your note-book. Along that continuum, mark the strategies you think each of the following products or services demonstrates:
a   local council's refuse-collection service
b   bespoke tailor
c   frozen food manufacturer
d   twenties' holidays
e   Royal Mail letter service.

DISCUSSION

Compare your placings with the following:

Convergence   Divergence   Concentration
(a)   (e)   (c)   (d)   (b)

It is difficult to determine the placings exactly but if you have them in a fundamentally different order, it might help to re-read the above section of this chapter.

Product positioning

The complementary activity to market segmentation is, therefore, product (or service) positioning. In this context, *positioning* refers to the way in which the product or service is presented to the market – who it is for; what it will do for them; how it is to be compared with other competing products. Decisions about the positioning of products will concern factors such as its performance, quality, packaging, price, advertising and more. Choices about the mix of these factors are dealt with fully in Chapter 5.

As organisations learn more about the needs of specific segments which they can satisfy profitably, so they are able to position their brands to meet those needs. For example, manufacturers of carbonated drinks have identified significant numbers of weight- or health-conscious consumers. As a consequence they have developed low-calorie or caffeine-free extensions of their brands, positioned to appeal directly to these market segments.

The retail chain BHS (formerly British Home Stores) had, since its relaunch, focused on middle to up-market consumers aged 25 to 45. In the early 1990s, however, the company decided to reposition some of its underperforming stores as a discount chain called 'One Up'. These stores are targeted at lower socio-economic groups than the company's conventional stores. They carry merchandise tested in BHS outlets, but generally one third cheaper than prices in the more upmarket stores.

Activity

From your experience as a shopper give examples of branded products which have been repositioned, or extended, in order to satisfy the needs of different market segments.

Methods of segmenting markets

Although the fundamental principles of segmentation are common to both consumer and business-to-business markets, different methods are appropriate. Those used in consumer marketing are dealt with below, while those for business-to-business segmentation are discussed later in this chapter.

For consumer markets, the methods of segmentation available are:

* by associative characteristics – geographic, demographic, psychographic, and geodemographic segmentation
* by direct consumer characteristics – occasions of purchase, usage patterns, brand loyalty, and benefits sought.

All the methods described here are used in the UK. Similar categorisations exist elsewhere in the world, although they will differ in detail. This can create problems in attempting to apply data from one country to another.

Market segmentation by associative characteristics

Some of the major methods of market segmentation are done on the basis of association; that is, on an assumption that purchasing patterns will be influenced by where people live, their age, sex, psychological make-up and lifestyle. Although there is considerable evidence to support the importance of these influences, the process can, at its worst, lead to sweeping generalisations, such as thinking that all US visitors to the UK are interested only in visiting Soho, Stratford-upon-Avon and Edinburgh Castle.

Geographic segmentation

This segmentation method divides up markets by area, for example, by country or region, or sales area, and so on.

The full list of methods of geographic segmentation is:
* trading blocks (e.g. the European Union)
* states/regions (e.g. Nielsen, TV, or Standard regions)
* counties/districts (mainly local government areas in the UK)
* urban/rural
* sales/distribution territories
* telephone exchanges
* postcodes
* electoral divisions (constituencies, divisions, wards)
* distance (e.g. radii from a location)
* drive times (i.e. time taken to reach a location by car).

The British Tourist Authority (BTA) views the overseas markets for tourism initially on a geographic basis. The single largest national market for UK tourism in terms of expenditure is – predictably – the USA, although people from France make an equal number of visits. For each country, not only is promotional material prepared in different languages world-wide, but different features are emphasised depending on different cultures and lifestyles in the target market.

Even within the UK, there are important regional differences. Although the average spend per person per annum on food is much the same in Wales and the North of England, the focus of this expenditure differs. The Welsh drink markedly less beer and cider, and eat less fish. On the other hand, they spend more on meat, fruit and vegetables, and sweet treats (source: *Supermarketing*, 15 October 1993). These regional variations are important determinants in the planning of marketing and advertising campaigns.

Demographic segmentation

Demographic segmentation divides the market by population characteristic. Marketers make great use of a system of socio-economic classifications based upon employment status (see Table 3.1), but sex, marital status and age are also used for categorising the population.

In demographic segmentation, the primary unit of measurement is the individual, the secondary one being the family or household in which the individual lives.

A full list of characteristics selected as the basis for demographic categorisation includes:
* gender (and sexual orientation)
* age
* marital or cohabitational status
* occupation
* educational level
* social class
* income
* ethnicity.

The most widely used of all the demographic categorisations is the classification of socio-economic groupings within the UK, based on that of the Director-General of Population Census (see Table 3.1).

Table 3.1 Socio-economic groupings in the UK, 1990

(Source: JICNARS National Readership Survey)

Social grade	Class status	Occupational range	Percentage of adult population
A	UMC	Senior managerial, professional group	2.7
B	MC	Intermediate managerial/professional group	15.1
C1	LMC	Supervisory or clerical	23.9
C2	SWC	Skilled manual workers	27.8
D	WC	Semi- and unskilled manual workers	17.8
E	Sub	State pensioners, widows, casual, lowest paid workers	12.7

Note: UMC = upper middle class; MC = middle class; LMC = lower middle class; SWC = skilled working class; WC = working class; Sub = subsistence class.

Data for these classifications is obtained from census returns, the Register of Births Marriages & Deaths, and from electoral registers.

Social class is not based purely on economic characteristics. The major determinants are education and occupation – not income because there can be significant overlap in income levels between groups, for example, between skilled manual workers and lower level professionals, such as teachers. Similarities in income may suggest that people have a similar *ability* to buy; that should not be confused with their *likelihood* to buy, for which other factors, such as social class, are better predictors. The 1980s cultural phenomenon known as 'Essex Man' (and later 'Essex Girl') demonstrates this point. Essex Man was an affluent, skilled working class male, resident in the south-east of England (not just in Essex), with a disposable income in line with that of the middle class, but whose behaviour was still largely determined by his working class roots.

Activity

In what ways might social class be an influence upon purchasing decisions? Try to think of some examples from your own experience. Can you think of exceptions?

DISCUSSION

You may have mentioned purchases such as meals out, entertainment, education, insurance, and holidays, all of which show the strong influence of social class membership. However, people can also act out of character. For example, middle class people may visit dockside pubs or transport cafes in order to be among what they perceive to be 'real' people.

Other demographic factors

Income levels are measured by the Inland Revenue. Wealth will influence both the nature and scale of purchases. In the food market, for example, the wealthiest 20 per cent of households spend above the national average right across the range of grocery products. This is only marginally so on sugar and preserves, but dramatically so – twice the national average – on wines and spirits, accounting for nearly half the UK market (source: *Supermarketing*, 15 October 1993).

Another factor influencing purchasing will be the consumer's age. For census purposes, ages are grouped into bands of five years, from 0–4, 5–9, and so on up to age 84. The final band is 85+ years. For many research purposes, these age bands are too narrow, and not all are relevant. So, for example, industry research on alcohol consumption, uses wider bands beginning at age 18.

Activity

Look at the table below. What conclusions do you draw about the influence of age on the consumption of alcohol?

Age group	Percentage drinking alcohol at least:			
	Weekly	Monthly	Ever	Never
18–24	67	82	88	12
25–34	63	80	88	12
35–49	62	77	86	14
50+	51	62	75	25

However, just as the influences of socio-economic groupings can be differentiated from those of wealth, so some researchers prefer life-cycle categorisations to simple chronological ones. These reflect different rates of maturation, and the influence of family formation on spending.

An example of such a classification system is the *sagacity life cycle model*. It assumes that people have different aspirations and behaviour patterns as they go through their life cycle. The four main phases are as follows:

* dependent – mainly under 24, living at home or full-time students;
* pre-family – under 35, have established own household, but have no children;
* family – head or joint heads of households, under 65, with one child or more in the household
* late – all adults whose children have left home, or those adults 35+ and childless.

Psychographic segmentation

The term *psychographic segmentation* was devised by Emmanuel H. Denby as 'a measurement of consumers' propensity to purchase under a variety of conditions, needs and stimuli'. As such, it represents a merging of demographic characteristics with psychoanalytical approaches to consumer behaviour.

Psychographics goes beyond age, sex and social class to assert that, beliefs, value systems and attitudes – all elements of an individual's orientation to his or her culture – will influence purchasing decisions just as they influence other aspects of behaviour. For example, an animal rights campaigner is unlikely to be a prospective consumer of air rifles and ammunition.

Some experts prefer to separate psychographic from lifestyle influences, on the grounds that the first is categorisation by attitude, and the second by an individual's behaviour. However, as the two are closely linked, this seems to be rather a hair-splitting distinction. It is far from clear-cut which comes first, attitude or behaviour (see Chapter 4).

The phenomenon of psychographics was, therefore, responsible for introducing terms like 'Yuppies' (young upwardly-mobile professionals), 'Dinkies' (dual income, no kids), and 'Whannies' (we have a nanny) to our language.

A classic example of a psychographic segmentational paradigm (or example) is the VALS – values and lifestyles system – devised by the Stanford Research Institute at Harvard University (Figure 3.2).

Case study

Categorisation	Claimed characteristics
Belongers	Patriotic, stable, sentimental, traditionalists, tend to be content
Achievers	Prosperous, self-assured, middle-aged materialists
Emulators	Ambitious young people – trying to break into the system
I-am-me group	Impulsive, experimental, inclined to narcissism
Experiential	People-orientated, inner-growth directed
Societally-conscious	Mature, successful, mission-oriented, supports causes
Survivors	Elderly, poor, little optimism for future
Sustainers	Resentful of condition, struggling to make ends meet
Integrated	Pyschologically mature, balanced, self-fulfilling

Figure 3.2 – Values and lifestyles paradigm

Activity

Do this with a partner. Using Figure 3.2, attempt to categorise yourself. Now do the same for your partner. Exchange your results. What do you conclude from this?

Categorisation of individuals is achieved by questionnaire. In these, individuals record their agreement or disagreement with statements, such as:

*   'I like to do all my own maintenance around the house.'
*   'It is better to pay cash for goods than to buy on credit.'
*   'I enjoy watching current affairs and documentary programmes on TV.'

The BTA produces research about the US market for European travel which relies heavily upon the use of psychographics to measure propensity for overseas travel. Clearly those who are adventurous, self-confident, pleasure-seeking, people-oriented, impulsive and inquisitive will be more likely to travel abroad.

The study used by the BTA identifies three major psychographic groups: life-enhancers, sunseekers, and play-it-safers. Each has different motivations for an overseas visit. Unfortunately, these categories differ from those of the system exemplified above. Indeed, it is this very lack of a commonly agreed standard system of psychographic segmentation which prevents it from achieving the prominence of demographics in segmenting markets.

Finally, because human behaviour is constantly changing, the validity of any particular psychographic paradigm is finite, and new ones constantly emerge. It is also fair to say that psychographics has many detractors in the business, who see it as an excellent way for unscrupulous market research consultants to fleece their gullible clients.

Geodemographic segmentation – a hybrid method

An increasingly important form of market segmentation uses postcodes. Strictly speaking, this hybrid assumes that people of similar social class frequently cluster in the same neighbourhood. For many purposes, the postcode provides an ideal means of categorising market segments, each unit being fairly small (around 20 homes) and relatively homogeneous.

In Great Britain, the first commercial system was called ACORN (A Classification of Residential Neighbourhoods), developed by CACI Information Services. ACORN categorises each postcode into one of 54 different neighbourhood units. It is still the leading system of geodemographic segmentation in Great Britain. Other similar commercial services are MOSAIC and PINPOINT.

The following figures show how postcodes in Great Britain (but not Northern Ireland) are used by ACORN. There are six major categories of neighbourhoods as follows (see Figure 3.3):

A: Thriving   B: Expanding   C: Rising
D: Settling   E: Aspiring   F: Striving

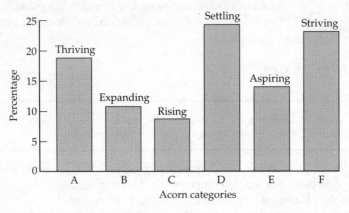

Figure 3.3 – Major ACORN categories as a percentage of GB households

These six major categories provide users with a readily accessible point of entry into the system. They are, in turn, broken down into 17 further groups (see Figure 3.4).

Finally, each of these groups is divided into 54 sub-units which can be precisely described (see Figure 3.5).

Postcode analysis

How is a postcode analysis built up? Assume that we are trying to build up an ACORN unit profile, using the postcode **WS12 5EZ** as an example.

* **Stage one** Use the postcode itself to locate the households.
* **Stage two** Find out the names of the people who live there. Such information is contained in the electoral register.
* **Stage three** Find out what sort of properties are contained within the postcode. The Council Tax Register and census returns are consulted for the property's rough value and type (a house, bungalow, or flat; how many rooms it contains; and whether it is rented or owned).
* **Stage four** Find out something about the type of people who live here. Census data gives the age, sex, social class, and occupational status of occupants, particularly useful for finding information on number of children – data that is unavailable from the electoral register.

Group		No.	Type	Type %	Description	%
A THRIVING	19.8%	1	Wealthy Achievers, Suburban Areas	15.1%	Wealthy Suburbs, Large Detached Houses	2.6%
					Villages with Wealthy Commuters	3.2%
					Mature Affluent, Home Owning Areas	2.7%
		2	Affluent Greys, Rural Communities	2.3%	Affluent Suburbs, Older Families	3.7%
					Mature, Well-Off Suburbs	3.0%
					Agricultural Villages, Home Based Workers	1.6%
		3	Prosperous Pensioners, Retirement Areas	2.3%	Holiday Retreats, Older People, Home Based Workers	0.9%
					Home Owning Areas, Well-Off Older Residents	2.1%
					Private Flats, Elderly People	0.3%
B EXPANDING	11.6%	4	Affluent Executives, Family Areas	3.7%	Affluent Working Families with Mortgages	2.6%
					Affluent Working Couples with Mortgages, New Homes	3.0%
					Transient Workforces, Living at their Place of Work	2.2%
		5	Well-Off Workers, Family Areas	7.8%	Home Owning Family Areas	1.5%
					Home Owning Family Areas, Older Children	2.6%
					Families with Mortgages, Younger Children	1.9%
C RISING	7.5%	6	Affluent Urbanites, Town & City Areas	2.2%	Well-Off Town & City Areas	1.1%
					Flats & Mortgages, Singles & Young Working Couples	0.8%
					Furnished Flats & Bedsits, Younger Single People	0.4%
		7	Prosperous Professionals, Metropolitan Areas	2.1%	Apartments, Young Professional Singles & Couples	1.1%
					Gentrified Multi Ethnic Areas	1.0%
					Prosperous Enclaves, Highly Qualified Executives,	0.7%
					Academic Centres, Students & Young Professionals	0.5%
		8	Better-Off Executives, Inner City Areas	3.2%	Affluent City Centre Areas, Tenements & Flats	0.4%
					Partially Gentrified Multi Ethnic Areas	0.7%
					Converted Flats & Bedsits, Single People	0.9%
D SETTLING	24.1%	9	Comfortable Middle Agers, Mature Home Owning Areas	13.4%	Mature Established Home Owning Areas	3.3%
					Rural Areas, Mixed Occupations	3.4%
					Established Home Owning Areas	4.0%
					Home Owning Areas, Council Tenants, Retired People	2.6%
		10	Skilled Workers, Home Owning Areas	1.7%	Established Home Owning Areas, Skilled Workers	4.5%
					Home Owners in Older Properties, Younger Workers	3.1%
					Home Owning Areas with Skilled Workers	3.1%
E ASPIRING	13.7%	11	New Home Owners, Mature Communities	9.8%	Council Areas, Some New Home Owners	3.8%
					Mature Home Owning Areas, Skilled Workers	3.1%
					Low Rise Estates, Older Workers, New Home Owners	2.9%
		12	White Collar Workers, Better-Off Multi-Ethnic Areas	4.0%	Home Owning Multi-Ethnic Areas, Young Families	1.1%
					Multi-Occupied Town Centres, Mixed Occupations	1.8%
					Multi Ethnic Areas, White Collar Workers	1.1%
F STRIVING	22.8%	13	Older People, Less Prosperous Areas	3.6%	Home Owners, Small Council Flats, Single Pensioners	1.9%
					Council Areas, Older People, Health Problems	1.7%
		14	Council Estate Residents, Better-Off Homes	11.6%	Better-Off Council Areas, New Home Owners	2.4%
					Council Areas, Young Families, Some New Home Owners	3.0%
					Council Areas, Young Families, Many Lone Parents	1.6%
					Multi-Occupied Terraces, Multi Ethnic Areas	0.8%
					Low Rise Council Housing, Less Well-off Families	1.8%
					Council Areas, Residents with Health Problems	2.0%
		15	Council Estate Residents, High Unemployment	2.7%	Estates with High Unemployment	1.3%
					Council Flats, Elderly People, Health Problems	1.1%
					Council Flats, Very High Unemployment, Singles	1.2%
		16	Council Estate Residents, Greatest Hardship	2.8%	Council Areas, High Unemployment, Lone Parents	1.9%
					Council Flats, Greatest Hardship, Many Lone Parents	0.9%
		17	People in Multi-Ethnic, Low-Income Areas	2.1%	Multi-Ethnic, Large Families, Overcrowding	0.6%
					Multi-Ethnic, Severe Unemployment, Lone Parents	1.0%
					Multi-Ethnic, High Unemployment, Overcrowding	0.5%

Figure 3.4 – ACORN targeting classifications

Type 14 Home Owning Family Areas, Older Children

These are established family neighbourhoods with relatively low levels of population migration. They are very evenly distributed all over Britain, but are present in above average proportions in the metropolitan counties. The highest concentrations are in Cleveland, Leicestershire and Warwickshire.

Figure 3.5 – Extract from an ACORN unit profile

*   **Stage five** Ascertain levels of affluence by integrating this data with information from other market surveys (see Chapter 2) and data about investments and credit ratings; all of which enable organisations to make very accurate assumptions about the occupiers of any postcode area.

Making use of geodemographic data

How do organisations make use of these commercial systems of postcode analysis in reaching marketing decisions? For example, a multiple retailer might be seeking sites which are suitable for the development of a new retail superstore. An analysis of postcode characteristics in the surrounding area will help with the decision. Likewise, where should a holiday tour company mail next year's holiday brochure? Taking a look at the categories of postcode areas of current customers will indicate fertile new areas for expansion. Manufacturers can use this method to define their sales territories. Research agencies can use the system to select representative sample areas with the desired consumer mix. Public authorities can target their services at the areas and people most likely to require them.

Activity

Identify the dwellings that make up your home postcode area. Are all the properties alike? Are they located in a single, or in several, council tax bands? What is the size and make-up of the households? Are there common characteristics, for example, of age, car ownership, holidays? To what extent are they homogeneous or heterogeneous?

How useful do you think your home postcode would be for market segmentation purposes? Based upon the sales material that is delivered to your home address, which organisations appear to be using postcode analysis?

Write up your answers in your note-book.

Criticisms of market segmentation by associative techniques

The very associativeness of the categories discussed above resulted in increasing criticism. Some marketing people argue that demographic categories are often so broad as to be meaningless. People frequently act out of character, it is claimed, so the doubters question the usefulness of psychographic or age-group categorisations.

This has led to greater attention being paid to direct consumer characteristics. However, when an organisation wishes to sell to people who do not yet buy, there is, as yet, no substitute for associative segmentation methods for predicting those who will be most susceptible to purchase.

Market segmentation by direct consumer characteristics

Each of the segmentary methods dealt with so far has been associative; that is, characteristics such as age, social class or lifestyle are assumed to be associated with particular forms of consumer behaviour.

However, direct consumer characteristics are argued by some experts to be more relevant in segmenting markets, and in deciding the consequential marketing mix for particular products. These consumer behaviour methods include:

* Occasions of purchase – knowing when and why products are purchased is important. For example, boxes of chocolates are frequently bought as gifts, so Thorntons confectionery is often sold in specialist greetings card shops.
* Usage patterns – commercial market surveys such as TGI make distinctions between 'heavy', 'medium', 'light' and 'non-user' segments. These are of obvious value in identifying target groups for marketing effort.
* Loyalty (i.e. the degree of commitment shown by consumers) – loyalty is measured in terms of those who insist on, prefer, recognise, are indifferent to, or are unaware of, brands. Understanding who is loyal and why, and who is not, is of great importance in shaping a strategy. Identifying a highly loyal market segment has great value for an organisation, and may justify initial inducements in order to be able subsequently to exploit that loyalty. The so-called 'lifetime value of a customer' is a calculation of how much a typical customer can be expected to spend with an organisation during his or her lifetime, and of how much it should be prepared to spend in promotional offers in order to secure the customer's loyalty.
* Benefits sought (or problems addressed) – it is important to know why products are being purchased. Although a motor car may get people from A to B, for most consumers it is also a portable status symbol. All products can be segmented according to the different benefits that consumers seek, and some benefits can be given greater emphasis. For example, toothpaste may be segmented by its benefits: it fights decay; it freshens breath; it makes teeth gleam; its taste; it tackles gum shrinkage; it cleans false teeth.

Business-to-business segmentation

Business-to-business marketing differs from consumer marketing in that companies are selling to other companies – rather than to private consumers. Many companies, however, straddle this divide. A company making cleaning products may sell them to both consumer and business-to-business markets.

The methods of business-to-business or *industrial segmentation* are less well-developed than those which apply to consumer markets. Nonetheless, the same basic principles apply.

The methods in use include:

* geographic
* industrial/business sector (Standard Industrial Classification)
* size of organisation, and
* industrial buying characteristics.

Geographic

As for consumer markets, segmentation by area occurs. The best examples are company's own sales territories covered by individual salespeople. There may be differences in prices, business culture, climate and technical standards between the segments.

Industrial/business sector (Standard Industrial Classification)

This is a method of segmenting markets according to the activity of the companies being supplied. Different industrial sectors will provide different opportunities and impose different requirements. For example, a metal-pressing company might supply companies in the automotive and so-called 'white goods' manufacturing sectors, each of which will have different expectations. An automotive company will expect to be supplied 'to order', with critical just-in-time requirements, while a white goods maker may still be prepared to take batch orders.

Hence a nationwide system of Standard Industrial Classification (SIC) is used to categorise companies by business sector. The first classification system was drawn up in 1948; the most recent appeared in 1992, as a result of an attempt by the European Commission to produce a Europe-wide classification which would also be compatible with international standards.

As with postcodes, the four or five digits of the SIC system have specific meanings. The first two numbers denote the division of business activity; the third denotes a group within the division; the fourth denotes the class within the group and a fifth number (where necessary – not all codes are this long) denotes the sub class.

Here is an example:

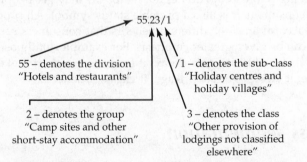

So, the SIC 55.23/1 is used to denotes businesses which are holiday centres or holiday villages.

Activity

1   Look up the SICs for the following types of business activity:
    a   Computer dating agencies
    b   Footwear manufacturers
    c   Haggis making
    d   Royal Air Force establishments
    e   Vending machine retailing.
2   Which SICs are important to the local economy of your own home area? You may restrict
    your research to identifying the first two digits of the SICs (i.e. divisions) if this seems more
    relevant.
Note: You will need to consult either *Standard Industrial Classifications of Economic Activity
1992*, or *Indexes to Standard Industrial Classifications of Economic Activity 1992*, both
published by HMSO, for this activity.

Size of business customer

The size of a business customer is important in terms of predicted potential usage
of a company's products. Another way of expressing this categorisation is by the
value of the business done with companies. Higher volume customers will expect
larger discounts, and better credit facilities. Owing to the scale of their purchasing,
they are worth nurturing to develop strong relationships.

Industrial buying characteristics

As we shall see in Chapter 4, individual companies display differing buying
characteristics. As a result of its dealings with its prospects or customers, a
business can segment those companies in terms of:

* the strategies employed (e.g. some companies require tenders for any order
  placed over a given value);
* the degree of responsibility for decisions accepted by customers;
* internal corporate influences upon buying policy (e.g. cultural pressure for
  aggressive price deals as a sign of a customer's effectiveness);
* level of technical development (e.g. few UK companies were using robotic
  technology in the 1990s, despite its availability); and
* differing performance preferences (e.g. rapid delivery response, supplier
  involvement in design, agreed quality systems etc.)

Activity

Which of these business-to-business categories are based upon associative characteristics, and
which upon direct customer characteristics?

Assignment 3

'Riot Grrrls'

Assume that you have taken a work placement in the marketing department of a
company making cosmetics. Your section head has passed you a press cutting
(Figure 3.6) dealing with the phenomenon of 'Riot Grrrls' and asked you to read it
to assess the implications for the company's markets.

YOUR TASKS

1   Write a memo to your section head explaining how you would categorise 'Riot Grrrls' using the major associative methods of segmentation.
2   Draw up a list of typical, widely-used women's cosmetic products. (Assume that your company makes these.) How attractive do you think the products will be for this new market segment?
3   Put forward proposals for market research to assess the likely extent of the 'Riot Grrrl' phenomenon and the changes the company will need to make to its product range or positioning.

Sweet little rock'n' snarlers

IT'S over-hyped and now, inevitably, it's over here. American Politically Correct Pop, where the music takes second place to the polemics, has arrived in Britain. Young feminists have taken the thrashing guitar sound of Grunge and injected it with some radical, Girls-Are-Best politics.

The result is Riot Grrrl, the name given to all female Grunge bands like Voodoo Queen and Bikini Kill, and their various fanzines, one of which carries the statement, "Reasons it's cool to hang out with yourself and not have a boy? Get more sleep. Have more friends, don't have to play mother and no boring phone conversations." Fed up with being leered at and constantly pushed to the back at rock concerts, these angry young women are now on the offensive against their acne-ridden male counterparts.

They wear the same torn jeans, baggy lumberjack shirts and woolly hats as the Grunge boys, and the music is just the same. But Riot Grrrls want to do it on their own. And that means forming their own bands – the teenage answer to everything – and attending the odd girls only meeting. It also means singing about menstruation and anorexia, and presenting what they call a "girl-positive" image.

In the case of Donita Sparks, lead singer with L.7, the Californian Grrrl band, this meant throwing a tampon into the audience at a recent concert and dropping her pants during a live performance on Channel 4's *The Word*. The British Grrrl group Huggy Bear followed suit by throwing a tantrum on *The Word*, shouting politically correct obscenities at presenter Terry Christian.

They are Kylie Minogue's worst nightmare. Riot Grrrls loathe the superslim models and girlie pop singers nearly as much as they despise their salivating male fans. Not that they don't get on with the boys. Courtney Love, the American lead singer of Hole, the all-girl band who inadvertently started the whole Grrrl craze, was married to Kurt Cobain, lead singer with Nirvana, the original Grungers from Seattle.

Courtney Love first achieved notoriety by dressing up in baby-doll clothes that were three sizes too small for her. More of a femme fatale than a feminist, she can out-tough even the toughest of male rockers, and in doing so, has become the first Riot Grrrl icon. The fact that she publicly snubbed Madonna, who is, for Riot Grrrls, about as fashionable as Elvis, only increased her status.

But a lesson all pop stars should learn, is that radical politics and pop are two elements best left apart. One is bound to outlive the other. And record sales can shrink quicker than any rain forest, as Sting found to his cost when he started appearing in public with a rather bewildered Amazonian native.

Riot Grrrls are obviously angry and are definitely PC, only in their case, PC stands for Politically Confused. The British Riot Grrrl band, Huggy Bear, recently performed at a "women-only" concert in London. But they had presumably overlooked the two men in their own band, so it was more of a "women-only-audience".

And when Courtney Love came on stage and called Linda Duff, the *Daily Star's* cellulite challenged pop columnist, "fat", sisterly solidarity collapsed. The audience were incensed by such fattist remarks, especially from a hitherto Riot Grrrl idol. After continual heckling, Courtney Love finally snapped, and shouted, "Look, I'm not politically correct. So f- you." At which point, the two men in Huggy Bear vacated the premises.

Riot Grrrls, like so many before them, want to make the world a better place by playing a guitar. But as Mick Jagger once sang, It's Only Rock'n'Roll.

Source: *Sunday Telegraph*

Figure 3.6

CHAPTER 4

Why and how do people buy?

Making your mind up

Buyer behaviour

Having information about the occupants of a market is not enough in itself. Organisations also need to know when, where, how and why those purchases are made. They need to know who is making the purchases, and what factors influence those decisions. In other words, organisations need to understand *buyer behaviour*. This can be defined as:

> 'Acts and decisions by individuals and groups, leading to the purchase of products and services.'

In particular, organisations need to examine buyer behaviour to look for patterns which may give a clue to future behaviour, as well as explanations for the existence of those patterns.

What is meant by a *buyer*? It may seem obvious, but the term refers not only to someone who is buying for their own consumption, but to anyone who buys on behalf of others. For instance, this could be an adult member of a household buying on behalf of a child, or it could be someone with a formal buying role for an organisation (e.g. a fashion buyer for a department store).

Buyer behaviour in consumer markets

Ability versus willingness to buy

In talking about buying behaviour, it is important also to distinguish between a consumer's *ability* to buy as opposed to his or her *willingness* to buy. This distinction was drawn by George Katona in his book *The Powerful Consumer* as follows:

* ability to buy – is dependent upon economic resources, i.e. income-level, availability of credit, disposable assets;
* willingness to buy – is a consequence of a buyer's motivation, his or her needs and wants, and expectations of the purchase.

Both conditions must exist before a purchase is likely to be made.

Activity

1   Jot down four items which you can afford, but are unwilling to buy.
2   Now do the same for four items you would like, but are unable to buy.
3   Could the providers of those products or services change them to make them more affordable or more desirable to you?

DISCUSSION

The ability of consumers to purchase can be increased by offering lower quality goods at cheaper prices, by offering trade-in discounts on more expensive items, encouraging leasing (e.g. of a car), or part-ownership (e.g. time-share holidays), and by providing credit facilities. Willingness to purchase can also be increased by imaginatively communicating a product's benefits.

Categories of purchase decision

There are three categories of purchase decision:

* **Straight re-purchase**   This is the most frequent type of purchase. The consumer repeat-buys a product or brand purchased on a previous occasion. This occurs most frequently in circumstances in which a consumer is loyal to a brand, and is reluctant to try an alternative.
* **Modified re-purchase**   This occurs when a consumer needs to change his or her behaviour. This might be because the habitual brand is out-of-stock and a near substitute is selected; it might be prompted by the changed needs of the consumer; it might be promoted by the updating of an existing product; it might be prompted by promotional activity by a competing product (e.g. a bank offering free services to accounts in credit).
* **New purchase**   This is self-explanatory. It refers to that category of purchase which is being made for the first time. Here promotion plays a key role in stimulating demand for products, notifying consumers of their availability, and in reassuring consumers about their purchases.

Activity

What is the significance of the above three classes in terms of the decision-making process of buyers? Jot down your ideas in your note-book, and then check them against the rest of this chapter.

DISCUSSION

You probably concluded that the most thought-about purchases were those being made for the first time, and that in these cases buyers would require the greatest amount of information before committing themselves to the purchase.

Influence of product type

Decisions will also be influenced by the type of product or service being purchased. There are broadly-speaking three types of product:

* **Consumables** – these include convenience products, which cost relatively little, are not expected to last for long, and are sold in very large numbers. (They are known as fast moving consumer goods (FMCGs) and examples include toothpaste, breakfast cereal, and daily newspapers.)
* **Durables** – these are products that are relatively expensive, and are expected to last much longer, perhaps for many years (e.g. electrical products, furnishings, and cameras).
* **Services** – these are less tangible than products and cannot easily be handled or inspected before purchase (e.g. a theatre visit).

Thus categories have their limitations. Most FMCGs are purchased routinely, and without much thought, but not always. A consumer who refuses to buy cosmetics that are animal-tested will take time to read the pack to check for details. Durables will normally require a longer decision-making process, both because of their higher cost, and because they will be owned for much longer. However, a busy person with little interest in soft-furnishings may simply order ready-made items. Some services can be seen as consumables (e.g. window-cleaning) while others are likely to be much longer-term (e.g. legal advice).

High and low-involving decisions

Limitations with the system of categorising buyer behaviour according to what is being purchased has led many writers on marketing (notably Engel, Kollat and Blackwell) to concentrate on the decision-making process instead, and to differentiate between high- and low-involving decisions. Whether a decision requires high or low involvement is not determined simply by whether the purchase is of FMCGs, durables or services but by the significance of the purchase for the consumer, and therefore the time which he or she invests in making a decision. Buying a new car is, for most people, a high-involving decision; buying petrol is not.

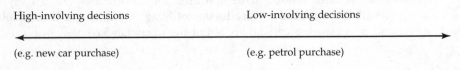

High-involving decisions   Low-involving decisions

(e.g. new car purchase)   (e.g. petrol purchase)

Figure 4.1 – High- and low-involving decision continuum

Although it is the behaviour of the decision-maker that determines whether a decision is one of high- or low-involvement, there are three common factors which increase the likelihood of high involvement. These are:
* the cost of the purchase relative to income,
* the amount of time for which the purchase will be owned,
* the extent to which the purchase reflects self-image.

Decisions about where to spend a holiday are good examples of high-involving decisions. Consumers will take time to gather considerable amounts of information about a prospective destination before committing themselves.

Activity

1   Are the decisions to buy the following, high- or low- involving decisions for you:
    a   buying new clothes
    b   selecting dishes from a restaurant menu
    c   deciding what to watch on TV
    d   buying a present for someone else's wedding
    e   choosing a university or college?
2   Is your behaviour fairly typical, do you think?
3   For one of the above, say what levels of help and information are provided for potential customers. Given your categorisation, is it enough, do you think?

DISCUSSION

Deciding what to watch on TV is probably a low-involving decision because it is inexpensive and takes up perhaps only minutes of your time. Choosing a university is more likely to be high on involvement, given that a stay there may last three or four years. The purchase of new clothes, which may be fairly cheap and be worn only a few times may still take a lot of time because many see clothing as making some form of personal statement.

Buying cycles

It is in the interests of all suppliers to know the likely frequency with which consumers will purchase their services or products. Buying cycles are a way of measuring the intervals between purchases, and the peaks and troughs in demand.

Some buying cycles may have only one purchase during a consumer's lifetime – for example, the hire of an academic cap and gown for a graduation ceremony. Others will show daily purchases – newspapers and household milk delivery, perhaps. The usefulness of such information lies in predicting future demand, and in identifying opportunities to decrease the length of time between purchases.

Many markets are highly cyclical. These cycles may be daily, weekly, monthly, quarterly, yearly or – worst of all – erratic. Copies of the *Independent*, *Times*, *Telegraph* and such like which have not been sold by 9.00 a.m. on a weekday morning will probably remain unsold. A Nielsen Homescan survey has shown Friday to be the day for heaviest shopping in Britain, both in volume and value of purchases. One third of all DIY products are bought at Easter, and 65 per cent of all greetings cards are sold at Christmas.

Activity

Reproduce Table 4.1 showing overseas visits to the UK by month and market area for 1991 as a graph. What patterns of demand emerge?

Table 4.1 Overseas visits to the UK: visits by month and market area, 1991

Month	Total ('000)	Area of residence		
		North America	Western Europe	Rest of world
January	992	171	586	236
February	769	80	565	123
March	1014	141	709	164
April	1288	178	924	186
May	1436	256	935	245
June	1463	316	893	255
July	1939	349	1223	367
August	2204	359	1458	388
September	1666	279	1019	367
October	1449	312	853	285
November	1272	187	881	204
December	1173	145	834	193
Total	16,664	2772	10,880	3013

(Source: BTA Annual Digest of Statistics, 1992)

Buying operations

How did you buy this book? From a bookshop? Did you have to order it? How far ahead of your course did you place the order? Did you buy it by mail order? Did a teacher or lecturer organise a bulk purchase on your behalf? Is it second-hand? Has it been lent to you by a library or academic institution?

In the overseas travel market, people can buy from package operators, through a travel agent, or make their own direct arrangements with ferry-operators, hoteliers, etc. A move away from the fully-packaged holiday is increasing the dependence of tourists on their travel agents for booking the component elements of an independent overseas holiday.

Knowing how people buy is of great interest to organisations. Increasing opportunities and reducing barriers to purchase, should increase an organisation's sales. For example, First Direct was the first entirely branchless bank, established by the Midland Bank in response to a growing number of customers for banking services whose only contact with their bank was electronic or postal.

Activity

Find out how changing buying operations are affecting a local business in your area. If this is difficult, focus on your college.

Ask how methods of enrolment have changed over the past decade. How far in advance of the course do people decide to study? How far in advance do they apply for a place? Have payment systems altered? What were the reasons for these changes? Are buying operations expected to change in the near future?

Buying readiness

Earlier you saw that ability was not the same as willingness to buy. The willingness of consumers to purchase is determined by a number of factors, some dealt with already. Other cultural, social, individual and commercial factors will be dealt with in the remainder of this chapter.

These influences will vary from person to person, so not all consumers will be equally willing to purchase at any one time. When new products enter the market, it is assumed that consumers will begin to purchase the product at different times, depending upon factors such as knowledge and acceptance of the product.

The process of acceptance of a product by consumers is represented by the product adoption curve (Figure 4.2) which charts the adoption process in terms of buyer behaviour over time. The model attempts to record the rate at which additional consumers start buying and using a product. Innovators are trend-setters who are looking for distinctive and unusual products. Early adopters are those who closely emulate these fashion-leaders. By the time the early majority begin to buy, the product has lost its rarity or cult-status and will probably be abandoned by innovators. The late majority are extremely cautious in their purchasing of this product, but the laggards arrive only when it is already considered out-moded.

Such a model enables an organisation to identify who should be the targets at each stage in the lifetime of the product (see *Product Life Cycles* in Chapter 5).

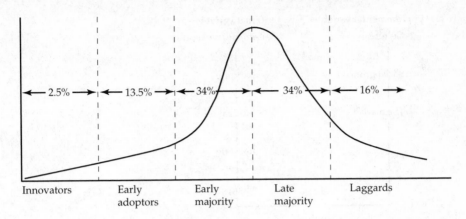

Figure 4.2 – Product Adoption Curve

When a genuinely new product is launched it is critical to attract innovators. Their purchasing will set a trend for the rest of the market to follow. Careful segmentation will enable consumers to be identified in terms of their propensity to adopt products, and the marketing mix for the product can then be adjust accordingly. Psychographic segmentation (see Chapter 3) is particularly helpful here, as it will identify groups in terms of their interest in material possessions, independence from routine, interest in new experiences, desire for gadgetry, willingness to take financial risks, and a host of other characteristics.

It is important to remember that the same consumers will not be innovatory purchasers in all product groups. For example, a laggard in fashion-wear may be an innovator within a specialist field such as personal computing. However, it is helpful to know the attitudes of consumers to previous, similar new products, as this can enable predictions to be made about the adoption rate for the newer product.

Models of buyer behaviour

There are two types of model (i.e. theoretical representations) of buyer behaviour. These are:

*   **stochastic models** – based on the assumption that earlier observed behaviour, forms a valid basis for predicting the future (e.g. a consumer who has bought Kellogg's Pop Tarts on six out of ten purchasing occasions will be assumed to have a probability of 0.6 of purchasing them on future shopping trips);
*   **behavioural models** – these are an attempt to map the inter-relationship of environmental and internal influences in order to understand the effect they have on consumers' decisions to purchase, or not to purchase. (These influences are called 'variables', as they vary from individual to individual.)

A behavioural model of buyer behaviour might contain the elements shown in Figure 4.3. Some of these variables (influences) are discussed below.

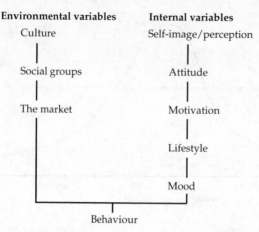

Figure 4.3 – Behaviouralist approach to modelling the influences on buyer behaviour

Environmental variables

Cultural influence

Human culture can be defined as:

> *a group of complex belief and value systems, and artefacts, handed down through the generations as determinants and influences upon human behaviour within a given society.*

Much of our behaviour is determined by our culture, but it may require contact with another culture, with different beliefs and value systems, before we become aware of this fact.

Examples of cultural influences upon human behaviour can be seen in social customs (e.g. weddings), in the roles accorded to people (e.g. the behaviour considered appropriate to the two sexes), and in the symbolic meaning attached to natural phenomena (e.g. the idea that black cats crossing your path bring good luck).

Social group influence

Social class

Social class can be defined as:

> *a system for stratifying society into homogeneous groups.*

The class system is itself a feature of human culture. Although under the law all women and men are believed to be born equal, for the remainder of our lives we are conscious of being ranked in a social 'pecking order'. Similar systems of social organisation are found in most countries; for example, in India it is more rigidly organised into castes.

Studies have shown that social class does influence buying. For example, middle class members are more willing to defer spending until they can afford exactly what they want. When membership of the desired social class has not yet been achieved, it will be aspirational membership which will influence spending. Although income is a factor, social class membership will exercise greater influence upon spending decisions. (See Chapter 3 for a more detailed consideration of this influence.)

Family influence

Of all the influencing groups, the family is considered particularly significant, although the traditional 'nuclear family' with a 'husband-centred' pattern of decision-making is rapidly declining and the number of one-parent families and single-person households is rising.

It remains the case that the stage of family-development (e.g. the arrival of a baby) will influence purchasing decisions. Early childhood purchases will clearly be much influenced by parents. As children age, the roles reverse. Children begin to influence parental spending, particularly in matters such as eating out, holiday destinations and day trips. The family may also have considerable influence over educational and career expectations.

Peer group influence

Outside the family, peer groups exercise great influence, though this may vary with the age of the individual. Teenagers are particularly susceptible to peer group influences on purchases of clothing, recorded music and other leisure pursuits. Other groups which have varying degrees of influence on consumer decisions include workmates, neighbours, religious and pressure groups.

Activity

How might social factors influence purchases of food and drink? How might they be used in promotional materials to encourage the trial of new, convenience home-cook meals, for example?

DISCUSSION

Social class may influence foodstuffs eaten at meal times, and where and how the meal is taken. Attitudes towards eating in front of the television, in the kitchen, or in the dining room are class-related. So too is interest in exotic foods, such as quail's eggs. The influence of the family can be seen in the need to make meals acceptable to each member. Cooking for others is an important feature of social relationships: invitations to meals in other people's homes are common.

Market factors

One major market factor is the state of the national economy. This goes beyond simple affordability. In the recession of the early 1990s, a big fall in house prices resulted in widespread negative equity in the property market – a situation in which householders owed more money on their mortgage than the house was actually worth. This had a crippling effect on consumers' confidence and thus on their willingness to spend money. A similar inhibition occurs during periods of high unemployment, when consumers defer spending in case theirs is one of the jobs to be cut. However, the opposite is also true. Buoyant economies contribute to a feel-good factor which encourages consumers to spend, even in some cases to over-extend themselves.

Other market factors which are likely to influence purchase decisions are much more under the control of suppliers. These include the level of promotional activity for a product or service, its observability in retail outlets or the homes of friends, and – for some high-involving purchases – the opportunity to evaluate the purchase in use (e.g. to test drive a new car).

Internal variables

Self-image

A person's *self-perception*, which can be defined as:

> *the individual's view of him or herself,*

will have a major effect upon purchasing behaviour. People with positive self-images will behave differently to those with low esteem. For example, men with low self-esteem who have trouble forming satisfying relationships tend to be the main consumers of pornography.

Self-image is frequently socially derived. During adolescence, peer group membership provides a self-image; later in life this may be provided by employment or family status. Self-image plays an important part in influencing the complexity of purchases, for example, holiday making in exotic overseas destinations. Those travelling are likely to regard themselves as adventurous, find new experiences and destinations stimulating, enjoy personal gratification, feel self-confident, and rate their social skills highly. Those staying at home on the other hand may see themselves as unadventurous, conservative, feel high levels of insecurity about personal relationships and their financial affairs, and be persuaded that they are unlucky in life and more likely to be a victim than others.

Attitude

It is generally assumed that a consumer's attitude towards a product will influence his or her likelihood of purchase. Attitudes towards products will be influenced by the way they are perceived; first, in terms of the attributes the product is perceived to possess, and secondly in terms of the importance attached to them. For example, in purchasing lipstick, a consumer might be looking for attributes which include colour, durability, non-allergenic, non-animal tested, low price, brand name, etc.

There remain three problems in attempting to establish causal links between attitude and behaviour. These are:

* attitude-formation may follow – rather than precede – a purchase (e.g. 'I didn't realise how good Cantonese food was until we went for the office outing at Christmas!');
* attitudes may change over time, and cannot all be assumed to be constant;
* the strong influence of social factors on attitudes held by individuals.

Motivation

Considerable attempts have been made to understand the intrinsic motivational influences within people. Rational models of consumer behaviour argue that people are usually looking for value for money, good quality, reliability, and sympathetic personal service, for example. However, this is a wish-list of good product characteristics: it does not explain underlying human needs and wants. Many writers have used Abraham Maslow's hierarchy of needs theory (Figure 4.4) to explain the goal-related behaviour of consumers.

How is Maslow's model helpful?

Maslow argued that human needs were met hierarchically – bodily needs before safety, safety before a sense of belonging, and so forth. He argued that once the basic physiological need (e.g. for food) has been met, people can begin to take

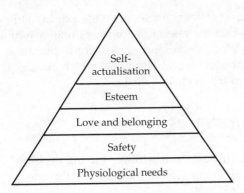

Figure 4.4 – Maslow's Hierarchy of Human Needs

more care of their personal safety (e.g. by eating the right kinds of food). This done, they then seek affiliation with others (e.g. family, workmates or school-fellows). When this is achieved, they then try to satisfy their need for esteem, or status. Self-actualisation needs (i.e. personal development) will only be satisfied when all others are met.

Activity

Few products are called upon to satisfy all the needs discussed above. An activity holiday resort is an exception.

Assume that you work for a company that organises activity holidays. How would knowledge of human motivation help you to provide the right atmosphere for consumers seeking to develop their proficiency in:

a   golf, and
b   tennis?

DISCUSSION

The differences between motivations can be summarised as follows:

Golfing holiday

* high social activity (affiliation needs)
* considerable social interaction during play
* limited physical demands – many players travel around courses on buggies (different physiological needs)
* associated with the good life – drinking and dining
* location and terrain of course important.

Tennis holiday

* highly competitive activity (esteem/self-actualisation needs are important)
* limited opportunities for conversation during play
* high levels of fitness and physical training required
* dieting and spartan regimes including early nights
* location of facilities relatively unimportant.

Other individual factors – lifestyle and mood

We have already seen in Chapter 3 how people's behaviour may be influenced by their lifestyles, and that this forms a valid basis for segmenting markets. One influence which it is more difficult to account for is mood, because so many things can affect it. However, the placing of souvenir shops at the exit to 'white-knuckle' rides in theme parks, suggests that the operators know a thing or two about the relationship between high levels of arousal and propensity to purchase. Salespeople are also trained to be alert to body language which can signal the right and wrong moment at which to try to close a deal.

Making decisions about purchases

What process do consumers go through in reaching a buying decision? Attempts to answer this question have led to descriptive models, like the one shown in Figure 4.5.

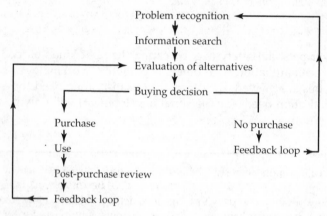

Figure 4.5 – Purchase decision-making process

In this model, the rational consumer identifies a problem: an unsatisfied want or need. The consumer then seeks information about what is available to satisfy the need, how it will perform and what it costs. Competing goods are evaluated. If an affordable and effective solution to the problem is available, it will be purchased. Once used, the rational consumer considers whether the product did in reality, resolve the problem. Where no purchase occurs, the rational consumer revisits the problem. Is the need really important? Could it be satisfied in another way? Are there further alternatives not so far considered?

Activity

Is this how you make purchasing decisions? For which, if any, of the following purchases do you think it might be true in your own case:
a   breakfast cereal
b   new shoes
c   carry-out meals
d   summer holiday
e   opening a bank account?

DISCUSSION

Your answers to this activity will depend very much on the sort of person that you are, the importance of the decision to you, and whether the item was being purchased for the first time. If you are impulsive, it may be that you are seldom aware of going through the sequence of events mapped out above. Even those who deliberate long and hard about spending their money might still not behave in the impeccably logical way described by the model. However, you may have felt that it came closest to describing your behaviour when you are making high-involving decisions.

The value of descriptive models

How valuable then are such models to marketing departments? The answer is that a universal model describes above is of limited value. Whilst it is true to say that on some occasions and for some consumers, some of the above stages will be gone through, there are many exceptions to the rule. What about those habitual purchases of branded goods for which no alternatives are sought? How does the model explain those purchases about which the consumer is indifferent? What does it say about impulse buying, which occurs even though the consumer was previously unaware that he or she had a 'problem'?

Buyer behaviour is learned behaviour

It is important to remember, in concluding this review of influences upon consumer behaviour, that purchasing behaviour is learned. Much of human knowledge is received indirectly, and not from personal experience. That applies to the information you receive from this book, of course. But the most telling learning is derived from direct personal experience. The important message for marketers here is that if a consumer buys and is in any way disappointed, it will take a great deal more effort next time to persuade them to repurchase, as they have already 'learned' that this product is not right for them.

Buyer behaviour in business-to-business markets

This is an area that has not been as well researched as consumer behaviour. Why is this? First, it is because these markets are often much smaller than consumer markets, and would not therefore justify the production of off-the-shelf data by commercial agencies.

Hence not as much research has been undertaken. Secondly, industrial buying decision-makers have been more difficult to research and categorise than consumers. However, interest is now growing in the subject.

Market types

For business-to-business purposes, there are three main types of market:
* **Commercial consumer markets**   These comprise organisations requiring products and services as an incidental part of other activities. For example, most organisations require office stationery, but only for purposes of internal or external communication.
* **Reseller markets**   These comprise organisations which then re-sell products to others. They are stockists and wholesalers. Stockists sell on to commercial consumers or end-user markets. Wholesalers sell on to retailers.

* **End-user markets**   These comprise organisations which require products or services as an essential part of producing their own; for example, a car plant requires components from other manufacturers. Demand from these markets is known as *derived demand*, because the level of, say, components demanded, is entirely dependent upon the number of cars being sold.

So a paper supplier may sell both to general office suppliers (in the reseller market), who in turn sell on to organisations whose need for paper is small, and directly in bulk to end-users such as printers.

Within each of these markets, there will again be three types of purchase decision, as was the case for consumer markets, namely:

* straight re-purchase
* modified re-purchase
* new purchase.

Activity

In which type of market would you expect each of the following to be principally involved:

a   electric heater element manufacturer
b   public relations agency
c   paint manufacturer
d   vitreous enameller
e   office furniture supplier?

DISCUSSION

The answers are:
a   end-user market
b   commercial consumer market
c   reseller market
d   end-user market
e   commercial consumer market.

Buying roles in organisations

It had for many years been assumed that commercial buying behaviour had little in common with consumer purchasing behaviour. Recent US research, however, suggests that as many industrial buyers are also consumers, they are susceptible to similar influences in both roles. It is even more likely to be the case that the model of decision-making (Figure 4.5) described earlier will hold true in commercial buying decisions because of the formal process by which decisions tend to be reached within organisations.

There is often also a clearer distinction between the buyers and users in organisations than in the case for consumers. The networks of people who influence or decide on purchases by business came to be known during the 1980s as decision making units (DMUs). An alternative term now in use is buying centres. Figure 4.6 gives a sample DMU structure.

The roles identified within this model are as follows:

* **Specifiers** are those who define the need for a service/product.
* **Users** are those who may be consulted for advice in setting specifications for purchases.

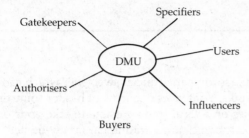

Figure 4.6 – A typical DMU for industrial purchases

* **Influencers** are those with a direct/indirect part in the decision; these may range from the organisation's MD who is in the same golf club as the supplying company's MD, to a transport driver who has heard that a supplier is about to go into liquidation.
* **Buyers** are the formal order-placers, frequently in a professional role, who also shortlist suppliers.
* **Authorisers** are those who actually take decisions; sometimes they will be buyers, but big orders may go as far as board-level for a decision.
* **Gate-keepers** are those who control the flow of information in organisations. For example, they may prevent unwanted promotional messages from other organisations reaching the buyers.

Each role may overlap with others on the list.

(**Source:** Cranfield Institute)

The extent to which each of these roles will be involved in purchase decisions depends upon the size of the organisation, and the importance of the purchase. Generally speaking, the bigger the organisation, and the more unusual, technical or costly the purchase, the more complex will be the DMU.

Commercial buyer motivation

Organisational buyers' rational requirements are similar to those of consumers, so in their purchasing buyers are likely to be looking for:
* value for money
* good credit terms
* a reliable, secure supply
* good quality
* technical support
* sympathetic support towards complaints
* compliance with legal requirements.

Where products or services to be purchased are substantially similar, the personal relationships between the organisational buyer and the company salesperson can be very important, especially as high levels of inertia are apparent on the part of organisational buyers. In some instances, organisations have identified 'preferred suppliers'. Such companies are then virtually guaranteed an agreed level of business, in return for meeting rigorous performance criteria on quality, deadlines, price and profit mark-up.

Assignment 4

Artificial Sweeteners

You work for a company manufacturing an artificial sweetener which can be used to replace sugar in food and drinks. Your sales department has for some time been trying to interest two companies on a local trading estate to take your products but without success. The two companies are a traditional family-owned confectionery business, and the UK subsidiary of a German company that manufactures carbonated soft-drinks. Tomorrow, a sales meeting will take place at which the sales team will review the progress made to date in attempting to persuade each of these companies to take supplies.

YOUR TASKS

1   Read the sales intelligence notes which follow on each company.
2   Sketch out in diagrammatic form the information held on each company's DMU.
3   Make notes from which you can explain to the meeting how your company should target its sales efforts at each member of these buying centres.

Horton's Confectionery

A family-owned firm started in 1951 by Jack Horton, who is still company chairman, although well into his eighties. He still visits the factory every day, arriving early, and being among the last to leave. It is his vision of an upmarket range of expensive chocolates which has sustained the company since its inception. The produce is sold through major department stores and delicatessens in select shopping districts, and his name is synonymous with self-made success in your district. However, he is increasingly wheel-chairbound, and your auntie, who is Horton's chauffeur's next-door-neighbour, says the old man is becoming very ill.

The sales file records several unsuccessful attempts to obtain appointments with the sales manager, Timothy Horton, grandson of the founder. He also acts as purchasing manager, although most purchases are made by a team of buyers. Tim Horton remains an unknown quantity as he seems to spend a lot of time away from the office, but local rumour suggests that he and grandfather do not get on.

However, there are dates for a few meetings in the last five years with their chief buyer, Sally Pertwee, related to the Hortons by marriage. She has said they would not be interested in replacing sugar in their lines unless there were plans for low-calorie items. She thinks they would sell well to the alternately indulgent and guilty customers who gorge themselves on Horton's chocolates. She claims the sticking point is old Mr Horton who does not believe in marketing because he thinks he understands Horton's customers well enough himself.

In 1995, the file recorded that Hortons had invested in new production plant, reputedly following the recruitment of Fran Koepler, as production manager. There is a press cutting, saying that Fran had previous experience in the industry in Belgium. It gives the date of her appointment as 1994, and says she has made a name for herself as a technological whiz-kid. Clearly, she has made an impact on the Horton's business, but there is nothing in the file on how strong her powerbase is, or how interested she is in product development.

The final active member of the company's management is Muriel Wainwright, Jack Horton's colourful daughter. She spent most of her life married to a rubber planter in Malaya, and then came home after his death to become a member of the board, and is now financial director. She is a local councillor, and has made a name for herself by making sponsored bungey jumps for local charities. She is believed to be the one member of the Horton family who has real influence over old Jack Horton.

Zitronegetranke A.G.

Within the last two months, this major German soft drinks company has begun production in the UK. Most of the ingredients are believed to be coming from existing suppliers on the European mainland, but there is tremendous enthusiasm to capture this company as a customer.

All the senior managers of the UK company are Germans, although the supervisory and production staff have been recruited locally. The managing director, production manager and sales manager of Zitronegetranke were recently received with formality at a meeting of the local Chamber of Commerce, when they were non-committal about the prospect of ordering more ingredients locally for their low-calorie drinks.

The sales manager has attached to the Zitronegetranke file some notes that she made at a seminar on selling to Germany. They read:

''German management teams are rigidly organised under a strong leader. Members are, however, valued more for their technical competence than for their charismatic qualities. Most decision-making takes place in formal meetings, with long leadtimes and agendas which are strictly adhered to. These are rarely forums in the way that UK managers understand them. Divergent opinions are not usually welcomed, and should either be resolved in advance or kept till later. Once decisions have been made, everyone is expected to implement them, regardless of personal feelings.

Communication is primarily from the top downwards in German companies. Mostly it takes the form of written communication, as Germans prefer to keep copious records, rather than rely on the phone to confirm earlier decisions.''

Informal contacts in the town are providing some useful information. The Germans have made an attempt to mix socially, and have a good grasp of English. They do not talk much about their work when in social settings. The comments of the workforce are also interesting. Zitronegetranke has made a favourable impression on its workpeople, paying fair wages, and offering a clean and well-run working environment. The German managers are a long way from their unapproachable and puritanical stereotypes.

Unfortunately, at this stage, there is no purchasing manager in place in the UK, although an appointment is imminent. The MD has suggested that this post may be advertised in the UK. At present, the production manager is responsible for the few items being bought locally.

CHAPTER 5

The marketing mix

Managing the mix

Introduction

Having examined the ways in which organisations can research and segment their markets to find out how and why consumers buy, it is now necessary to consider how that information can be used. This chapter will examine some of the ways in which the development, introduction, continuation and, if necessary, departure of products or services can be managed.

The make-up of the marketing mix

The *marketing mix* can be defined as the combination of elements in an organisation's offerings to the market; 'offerings' being either products or services. These elements were identified as Product, Price, Place and Promotion in early versions of the mix. As a result, they were known as the **Four Ps**. The relative importance of each element in the mix varies depending upon:

* what is being sold, and
* the state of the market.

For example, some products compete almost exclusively on price while others may have an emphasis on heavy advertising (i.e. on promotion). In each of these circumstances, the resulting marketing mix will be different.

Over time, commentators have expanded the original Four Ps of the mix to include further factors. The figure below shows one such expansion to include Positioning and People, with the original Four Ps identified with an asterisk (*).

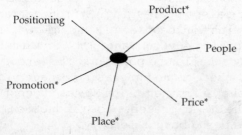

Figure 5.1 – The marketing mix (the Six Ps)

The six elements of the marketing mix

What follows is a brief indication of what is meant by each of the Ps within the mix:

* **Product** (or service) – any offering to consumers which either solves problems or provides benefits, including any 'add-ons' (e.g. guarantees).
* **People** – the influence on consumer behaviour exerted by the organisation's own employees.
* **Price** – the cost of the purchase to the consumer in cash, time, or pre-qualification for purchase.
* **Place** – the location at or channel through which the product can be ordered or obtained.
* **Promotion** – the means by which marketing messages about the product are communicated.
* **Positioning** – the process of identifying the specific market segments to which the product or service will appeal, enabling it to be targeted at each segment.

The significance of each one is discussed below in more detail. Remember, however, that it is the successful integration of these elements which make for successful products or services.

Product in the mix

In many cases, product will be the most important element in the mix. It lies at the core of successful marketing. The features of the product must match as closely as possible the benefits that consumers are seeking. Getting this element right will require an understanding of what consumers expect. This means not only that the product must do what is claimed for it and stand up well in comparison with rivals, but also that it comes in what the consumer considers to be the right colour, weight, and pack size.

Basic features of products may be extended by a variety of so-called 'add-ons' (added features). In the case of durables, these may take the form of after-market support (e.g. extended guarantees, and repair and maintenance services). Today, these features are taken for granted, but there was a time when they were unheard of. However, the competitive advantage offered by a product add-on depends on how quickly it can be copied by a competitor. In the early 1990s, one car manufacturer sought to add value to its product by offering customers the option to return a new car within one month if they were not delighted with it. On the same day that this initiative was announced, other manufacturers rushed to offer this benefit, too. This example illustrates how short-lived the advantage of offering add-on features to products can be.

People in the mix

For organisations to achieve a market-orientation, their staff must share the same philosophy. This applies whether the business is in the service sector or in manufacturing. The service sector is obviously affected because many services (e.g. hairdressing) are so dependent upon people for their delivery. The presence of other consumers also affects perceptions of a service. In the case of product marketing, the role of people in the manufacturing and distribution process is also crucial to ensuring consumer satisfaction. Organisations therefore need good training programmes, and quality assurance systems to ensure that their workforce understand the importance of being responsive to consumer needs.

Price in the mix

Price is quite simply what it costs people to acquire a product or partake of a service. However, to see this purely in terms of monetary value is unhelpful because what is expensive to one may seem ludicrously cheap to another, even though the monetary price is exactly the same. Economists prefer to talk about *opportunity cost*, by which they mean the cost of what people will have to forego by purchasing a particular item. This is an interesting concept because it makes the point that price is not purely monetary. It may also involve the consumer in foregoing time, for example, in queuing all night for Wimbledon Centre Court tickets. It might also involve an element of pre-qualification. For example, the price of membership of many professional bodies is not only the subscription, but also passing the necessary examinations.

Place in the mix

Some 'offerings' can compel people to travel – Blenheim Palace, Blackpool Pleasure Beach, The Edinburgh Festival are all examples where effort is involved in order to enjoy the offerings. In many cases, however, the benefit can easily be outweighed by the effort of obtaining the offering. In order that consumers can easily obtain goods and services, extensive time-critical distribution systems are developed. Effective management of these systems can make the difference between life or death for a product (see later in Chapter 8).

Promotion in the mix

Promotion is the means by which messages about a product or service's availability and suitability are communicated to the market. There are a multitude of available methods, which can be grouped under the following broad headings:

* public relations (PR) activity
* advertising
* point-of-sale (POS) materials
* packaging
* sales promotion
* field sales force activity
* sales support material (e.g. catalogues)
* direct marketing
* exhibition attendance.

Most of these activities are dealt with in more detail in Chapter 7.

Positioning in the mix

Positioning is the name given to the process of locating your product (service) as being distinctive from others in order to address viable market segments with different requirements and expectations. (The process of identifying these segments was dealt with in earlier chapters.)

The features which enable consumers to differentiate a product from those of its competitors are the elements in the mix which are modified as a result of the positioning decision. Most products today compete as brands, and consumers differentiate between products by brand identity. The make-up of the brand is a consequence of positioning and might include a distinctive pack, promotional message, price level and distribution network (the other elements of the mix). For example, the introduction of angled necks on toilet cleaner dispensers, enabled some brands to position themselves differently to rivals. They were targeted at a segment who were anxious about being able to clean under the rim of the toilet bowl, and who eagerly snapped up the new angled neck dispensers as being easier to use, and therefore more effective.

Activity

What positioning strategies have been adopted by the grocery retailers? Choose two from the following list for the purposes of comparison:

Tesco; Co-op; Sainsbury; Safeway; Keymarket; Morrisons; Presto; William Low; Aldi; Costco.

Discuss your conclusions with others in your group. Have these companies changed their positioning strategies recently?

Relative importance of the elements in the marketing mix

The importance of each of the above elements in the mix will vary depending upon the nature of the product (or service) and its market. For example, for a neighbourhood fish and chip shop, *place* will probably be crucial. It should be close to a main road, and other facilities such as shops or a pub, and with good parking nearby. *Product quality* will also be important, but less so if the shop enjoys a near monopoly of fast-food carry-out meals in the locality. *Price* will be critical if many of the shops' customers are in low income groups, and the influence of the shop's *people* in their dealings with customers – welcoming regulars and special consideration for the elderly and infirm – can enhance the shop's appeal. But how many fish and chip shops spend much on *promotion*? As the take-away food business matures, with increasing interest in ethnic foods and home delivery, *positioning*, which has hitherto been unimportant in this market, will claim greater attention.

Activity

For each of the retail businesses on the list below, decide which aspect of the mix you would expect to be the most and the least important:
a Marks & Spencer (variety stores)
b Kays (catalogue shopping)
c pet stall in a local market
d hot drinks vending-machine operator.

DISCUSSION

In the case of Marks & Spencer, product is arguably most important, whereas for Kays, promotion is clearly top of the list. The market trader will make price the most important element in that mix, whereas the drinks machine operator will want to be in the right place (and as many as possible).

Finally, it is important to remember that successful services and products are those which effectively integrate all the elements of the mix, in order to create a coherent offering to the market (see the example of After Eight Mints on page 112).

Product management

Earlier in this chapter we saw that within the marketing mix, often the most important element was the product itself. Many manufacturers recognise this by vesting the management of their products in people whose job title is that of *product manager* (or brand manager). Such people are not specialists. In fact, it is their role to co-ordinate all those internal functions which relate to the products (or product groups) over which they have control. At an operational level, product managers are concerned with day-to-day matters, such as monitoring production targets. At a strategic level, however, they are responsible for developing medium- to long-term plans for their products, within the framework of the organisation's corporate plans.

The scope of strategic product management is set out in Figure 5.2. It includes the development of new products – vital to secure the future market share of the organisation – and the modification of existing products to keep ahead of, or respond to competitor activity. From time to time, it becomes impossible to modify products any further, and they may need to be deleted from the organisation's catalogue. This is referred to as *rationalisation* in Figure 5.2. Costs and prices will also need to be kept under review to ensure that the product group delivers the profit target specified for it within the organisation's corporate plans. This will mean constantly seeking greater production efficiency and 'benchmarking' the organisation's costs and prices against those of rivals.

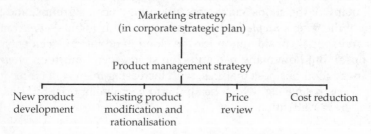

Figure 5.2 – Components of a product management strategy

Product planning

In order to ensure that an organisation continues to satisfy its existing customers, and will have the right products to acquire new ones, it is necessary to:

* anticipate the life cycle of current products,
* research and develop new and replacement products, and
* phase-out those which, in terms of their acceptability to the market, have passed their 'sell-by date'.

In doing so, product managers will have to take account of:

* the organisation's strategies
* legislative pressures
* competitor activity
* technical innovation
* changing consumer expectations.

For example, if an organisation requires all its products to make, say, a 40 per cent profit on turnover this will probably hasten a decision to discontinue an ailing product, and means there will be extremely high criteria for the selection of new ones.

Failure to manage a product range with adequate foresight allows competitors to gain market share. Between 1987 and 1993, General Motors' UK subsidiary company Vauxhall dramatically narrowed the gap in market share between itself and Ford, from over 14 per cent to just 4 per cent. Arguably, Ford failed to keep abreast of its competitor's activities and was slower with technical innovations. It was also caught out by Vauxhall's offer to convert existing models to unleaded petrol, and cuts in dealer margins to reduce new car prices. However, the launch of Ford's Mondeo model to replace the Sierra was expected to prove a turning point in Ford's fortunes.

Activity

Using market research sources (e.g. *Keynote*) or the motoring press, find out the present market share of Vauxhall and Ford. To what extent does product planning – as manifested in the current model range on offer from each manufacturer – seem to be playing a part?

The product life cycle model

In the product management field, one of the analytical tools that is used is the *product life cycle (PLC)*. This model of a product's life-span in the market assumes that all products have a finite life, and that each stage displays different characteristics. The assumed profile for a PLC is shown in Figure 5.3. Life cycles are assumed to be applicable both to generic product types (e.g. artificial sweeteners) and to specific brands (e.g. Nutrasweet).

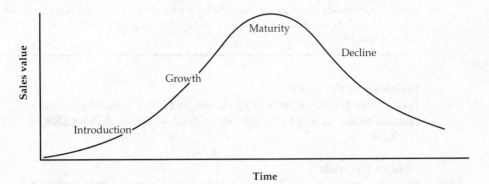

Figure 5.3 – Product life cycle

Characteristics of each phase of the PLC
The **introduction** is characterised by:

* high failure rates caused, for example, by over-optimism, and lack of proper development prior to the launch;
* lack of competitors, certainly for genuinely new products;

* limited distribution because retailers are waiting to see how the product performs before stocking it;
* the organisation trading at a loss, because of low sales volumes and the need to repay development and launch costs.

The **growth phase** is characterised by:

* rapid sales growth as the 'early majority' of consumers begins to buy (see Figure 4.2 – The product adoption curve);
* increasing competition as others hurry to place rival products in the market;
* less product distinctiveness as rivals emerge;
* profit growth as sales rise and development costs are repaid;
* organisation/product acquisition occurring by rivals who want to avoid the costs of developing their own products.

Maturity is characterised by:

* slow sales growth (only the laggards have still to buy);
* attempts being made to extend the product (e.g. by introducing variants to appeal to new/smaller market segments);
* an increase in price competition;
* heavy promotional spending to maintain brand loyalty;
* inventory rationalisation by retailers occurring with the least successful brands becoming de-listed;
* marginal producers retiring from the market.

Decline is characterised by:

* price-cutting being used in an attempt to retain market share;
* the introduction of replacement products;
* producers leaving the market.

Activity

In your note-book draw a product life cycle for your current college or correspondence course. You will need to find out how long the qualification has existed in its present form. Using the list of characteristics given above, and any figures for student numbers you can obtain from the college and/or the awarding body, try to identify the stage of the life cycle which the course has now reached.

Variations of the model

The regular profile of the model shown in Figure 5.3 seldom occurs. Three main variants of the model have been developed to reflect different life stories for products.

Fashion products

These are products which enjoy a period of brief popularity, but then fade quickly from public attention. They are characterised by a short introduction period, prolific growth, a brief period of saturation sales at maturity, and then rapid decline (see Figure 5.4). Fashion products tend to be associated with youth markets, but not exclusively so. Examples of fashion products include the Rubik Cube, a three dimensional puzzle which enjoyed phenomenal success in the late 1970s, and Teenage Mutant Ninja Turtle merchandise which enjoyed similar currency during the late 1980s and early 1990s.

The key message for organisations wanting to enter fashion markets is that the extreme brevity of these markets makes for very high risks.

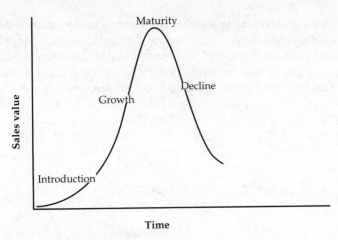

Figure 5.4 – Fashion product life cycle

Relaunch life cycle

In this variation, the decline phase of the cycle is arrested by product modification, and by relaunch. The sort of modification which might be made could affect the product's features or attributes; performance or reliability; style; design or packaging; or a combination of these. Such a strategy could be simply a reaction to the start of the decline phase, it could be a holding strategy pending the introduction of a replacement product (see *Leapfroging* below), or it could be a proactive policy of continuous improvement (see *Staircasing* below).

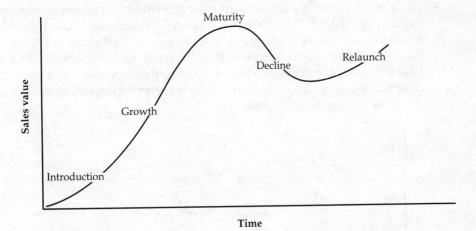

Figure 5.5 – Relaunch life cycle

Leapfroging

Leapfroging is the name given to a process whereby replacement products become available when the original begins to decline (see Figure 5.6). It is a very common pattern in the case of durable goods, where fashion and technological pressures mean that particular models have a limited life span. The motor industry provides an example of leapfrogging, with the Ford Mondeo replacing the time-expired Sierra in the company's product range. Occasionally, because of the enormous lead times involved in developing replacement models in the motor industry, the decline phase of the original may begin before the replacement is ready. In such circumstances, car manufacturers will frequently indulge in a cosmetic relaunch of the original as a stop-gap measure. This is done to limit the damage caused by customers who might desert the range for a rival marque whose products seemed more up-to-date.

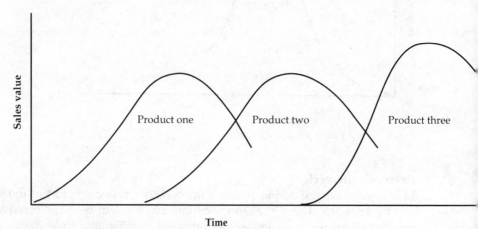

Figure 5.6 – Leapfroging life cycle

Staircasing

A further variant of the standard life cycle occurs, when by a process of continuous product improvement, an organisation avoids entering the decline phase of the cycle by stimulating further growth after a period of apparent maturity. By manipulating one of the product characteristics used to relaunch a product, some long-lived brands – Coca-Cola and Kit-Kat are examples – have been able to sustain enviable records of longevity in their markets. The result is a sequence of higher peaks of 'maturity' giving the appearance of a staircase when drawn as a product life cycle (Figure 5.7). This effect is difficult to achieve, and few products manage it successfully.

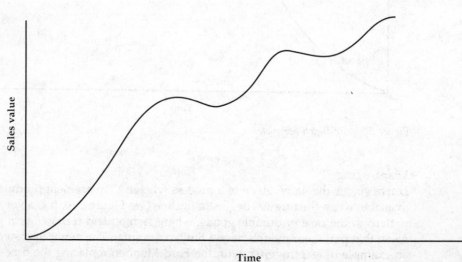

Figure 5.7 – Staircasing life cycle

Criticisms and usefulness of life-cycle models

There are three major criticisms of product life cycles. The first is that the models are too simplistic, and that products seldom – if ever – conform to the neat geometric profiles exemplified above. The second asserts that the cycles are not predictive, and that they can only be drawn with any accuracy in retrospect, by which time they are of only limited interest to a product manager. The third criticism contends that the supposed characteristics of each phase in a product's life are by no means inevitable, and that they are dependent upon the nature of the product and its market.

There is truth in all these points. However, those responsible for product management would be foolish to use the life cycle in the mechanical way implied by the criticisms. For example, few managers expect their products to conform rigidly to the curve; they would, however, expect such a pattern to emerge over time. The predictive value of life cycles lies in enabling managers to anticipate the conditions they may expect at any stage in the cycle, particularly where organisations can look back at the performance of their other products at a similar stage in their development.

Product life cycles remind all businesses that their products have finite life spans. They help them to calculate pay-back periods for the research and development of new products. They help to justify promotional support during the growth phase by showing the potential of the product at maturity. Finally, they can be used to stimulate innovation during maturity and to inform management decisions during the decline phase. Used with discretion, the life cycle is a valuable marketing tool, and its application to brand management is considered in Chapter 6.

Case study

The computer dinosaurs

In the computer industry, companies such as IBM (of the USA) and Groupe Bull (of France), which had grown rich in the 1970s and 1980s by supplying computer hardware had, by the 1990s, become as famous for their massive losses as they once were for their pioneering technology.

What were the reasons for this reversal of fortunes? First, there had been a decline in demand for larger mainframe computers in which these companies specialised, and a growth in the capabilities of small personal computers, at which the dinosaurs did not excel. Secondly, there had been a steep fall in the price of computer hardware, caused by fierce competition and technological advances. Between 1987 and 1991 it has been calculated that the proportion of organisations' IT budgets spent on mainframes, dropped by half (from 30 per cent to 15 per cent of total IT spend).

Belatedly, companies like IBM tried to compensate for the loss of their 'traditional' markets, by developing new services. They identified three main areas for development:

* consultancy – the provision of advice and guidance to organisations on installing and operating computer systems. The problem for IBM was that there were already well-established consultancies in this field. In addition, as a supplier of equipment, IBM was not considered sufficiently independent, and the fact that IBM's consultants were having to be retrained from other roles did not help.
* systems integration – the linking-up of separate machines to provide a complete service package for business users. As the dinosaurs' salesforce already provided this kind of service to customers, this was considered by industry experts to be a good prospect for growth.

* maintenance – the servicing and repair of computer hardware. This already contributed significantly to the turnover of hardware companies, but much of it was accounted for by after-sales servicing of their own machines. There were already specialist companies established in the personal computer market, who would bitterly contest the invasion of their markets by companies such as Groupe Bull or Olivetti.

The moral of this tale is that these companies were too complacent during the maturity phase of their mainframe systems. Had they been planning ahead, they would not have been panicked into seeking alternative sources of future income, but could have developed them in a planned and systematic way.

Activity

Update the story given above. Find out how well the 'dinosaurs' have done in attempting to diversify in this way. Check back to Chapter 2 for possible sources of up-to-date information about markets.

Product rationalisation

A key issue for product managers to emerge from a study of a product's life cycle is that of rationalisation. This is the process by which products in decline are amalgamated or withdrawn from sale. While it may be accepted that all products have a finite life-span, organisations may be reluctant to accept that it is time to part with an old friend. For example, the product may have been the great success story of the early days of the organisation and it may still be best known for that particular product. Someone on the board may still be waiting for the market to pick up again. Whatever the reasons for the reluctance to rationalise products, there can be drawbacks for those who are reluctant to withdraw. Apart from any damage to an organisation's image that may result from carrying an obsolete product, there may be tangible additional costs from carrying slow-moving stocks, and wastage of management time and resources in dealing with its protracted demise. On the other hand, too rapid a withdrawal can be equally damaging. If no replacement or alternative product is available, customers may switch to other organisations' products. The cost of stocking declining products has to be balanced by the contribution they make to meeting organisation overheads. Finally, image may be damaged by the demise of a core product, particularly if this was one which enjoyed a national reputation.

The issue for product managers, therefore, is to balance the need to rationalise products, with that of introducing new or modified ones. This is not easy to achieve.

New product development

The development and introduction of new products is an ongoing process – so much so that we, as consumers, are only occasionally aware that it is happening.

Activity

How important are new products? To answer this question, make a guess as to the length of time that the following products have been available:

a   mobile telephones
b   time-share holidays
c   air bags (safety restraints in motor cars)
d   duvets/continental quilts (in the UK)
e   Femidom (the female contraceptive).

Jot down any other recent innovations you can think of, and compare your responses with those of others in your group.

DISCUSSION

You may well have been surprised at the extent to which products you now take for granted were unheard of when you were a child. The mobile telephone, for instance, was not introduced into the UK until 1981! Your general conclusion from this activity should be that innovation – either in the form of new product development, or of modifications to existing products – is a vital ingredient of successful marketing.

Avoiding 'marketing myopia'

The absence of innovation is a key indicator of a product orientation on the part of a business (see Chapter 1). It was a factor that Theodore Levitt called 'marketing myopia' in his book. *Marketing myopia* was defined as 'the assumption that customer needs will continue to be met with whatever products or offerings are currently being produced'.

Was marketing myopia responsible for the demise of the famous piano-makers, the Bechstein Company? Bechstein made the pianos upon which Brahms, Liszt and Debussy played and composed. They graced many of the world's finest concert halls. However, during the 20th century they could neither match the technical improvements being made by their greatest rivals, Steinway, nor could they compete on price with the flood of good, imported pianos from the Far East. More than anything, the piano ceased to be a major form of family entertainment, and became just another relic from the Victorian period.

Types of new product

All 'new' products can be categorised as one of three types:
*   innovatory products (genuinely new)
*   modified existing products
*   'me-too' products (copy-cat versions).

In addition to new or modified products, however, innovation can lead to improved manufacturing processes – making better quality possible at the same, or reduced cost – or, more rarely, to the introduction of novel processes, making possible dramatic changes in cost and quality (e.g. robotic manufacturing systems).

Activity

The Mars Ice Cream bar (see Figure 5.8) was launched in the UK in 1990. In which of the above categories would you locate it?

Figure 5.8 – Mars ice cream bar

DISCUSSION
Although it has spawned many copy-cat products, the Mars bar was the first confectionery to ice-cream product. Whether it was simply a modification of an existing product or a genuine innovation is a matter of opinion, but it must be viewed as an inspired example of brand extension.

The pressures for change

Activity
Look back at the list of new or improved products that you drew up in the activity on page 83 and think about what prompted those innovations.

The principal causes are as follows:
* changing consumer tastes or behaviour (e.g. for 'green' products);
* changing legislation (e.g. the toy safety directive);
* competitor activity (e.g. chocolate bars to ice-cream);
* spotting a market opportunity based upon market research (e.g. Frish toilet cleaner);
* technical innovation, either externally or internally (e.g. the Sinclair C5);
* creative inspiration (e.g. the safety pin);
* overseas markets (e.g. Smirnov vodka made in Warrington).

Activity
New products or brands are particularly associated with part-work magazines – those which build up into a reference work over several months – and, in recent years, with bottled lagers (of which there were more than 400 in the UK in 1992). Why might this be so, do you think? Discuss this question with others in your group.

Choosing what to run with

Deciding which proposals for product modification or which wholly new products to adopt is remarkably difficult. Product modification looks less risky, as it represents less radical change. However, there is always the worry that any change will upset existing customers without winning over new ones. Exactly this problem has faced BBC Radio 1 in recent years. Many of the teenagers who tuned in during the 1970s and 1980s remained listeners – yet their musical tastes differ markedly from teenagers of the 1990s. Attempts to reformat the station risk driving away older listeners, and depressing audience figures still further. Yet without change, Radio 1 risks losing its younger audience to the plethora of national, regional and independent stations serving this age group.

Ideas and suggestions for modifications, or wholly new products, are not difficult to come by. This is particularly so if a specialist research and development (R&D) department exists within the organisation. Existing stockists, customers, advertising agency people, the organisation's own workforce and even holders of unused patents may also make proposals. The real difficulty lies in deciding which of the innovatory ideas is a likely winner. So a very careful screening process is essential for slimming down the proposed ideas to those finally selected for test marketing, and full launch. In general, the ratio of suggestions for wholly new products to those actually launched is about 100:1. Figure 5.9 illustrates the elimination process through which any new product will have to pass before launch.

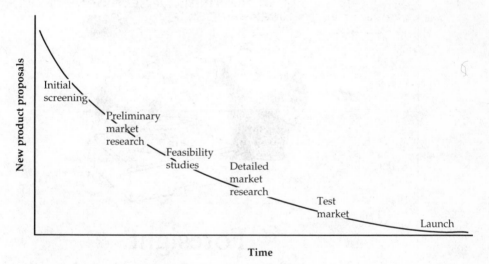

Figure 5.9 – New product proposal elimination process

The first stage is an *initial screening*; this will concentrate on three key questions:
* Does a sufficiently sizeable market exist to make the product profitable in the future?
* What would the competition do in response?
* Are resources of finance, plant, personnel and know-how available for this development?

The next stage of the screening process is some *preliminary market research* with those consumers thought to be likely purchasers. These will be asked to respond to the product concept in terms of its appeal, the features and benefits they would expect, their likely attitude to purchase, and what they would be prepared to pay.

Any product idea which survives stage two will then be subjected to a *feasibility study* by the R&D department to see whether it is feasible to make the product in a consumer-friendly form within the likely budget. Those few product ideas still alive by this stage will now be subjected to a more *detailed market research* exercise. Mock-up packs and advertising will be shown to small *test market* groups; they will be asked to handle, use and/or taste the product, if necessary at home. Their reactions will be carefully studied, mainly with the intention of modifying the product, if necessary, but always with the option of aborting the launch if the product performs badly in research.

If all is still well, the product is ready for *launch*, either into a small test market, for final checking, or into a national market, depending upon the organisation's strategy (for a full account of test marketing see Chapter 6).

Not only are many product suggestions discarded, but many products which are launched do not survive for more than five years; estimates vary between 60 and 90 per cent for new product failure rates.

Why do new products fail?

Source: Advertisement for Foresight research services

There are many marketing directors who will ruefully tell you that their new product flopped because the advertising was wrong, or the distribution was not right, and so on. Most academic research on new product failure, however, points to the following causes:

*   too hasty an introduction;

* inadequate screening and lack of test marketing, symptomatic of a scramble to place products in the market;
* excessive established competition;
* many products competing with little difference in quality, function or appeal;
* a high level of capital investment is necessary, thus requiring a high volume of sales – failure to achieve rapid sales growth and a significant market share in a short time lead to the product being pulled.

A critical factor in the longevity of new fast moving consumer goods (FMCGs) is the speed with which they penetrate their markets. Nielsen studies in the USA in the 1960s showed that the greater the initial penetration, the better the chance that the product would survive. For this reason, organisations introducing new products use a battery of devices to encourage trial, in an attempt to achieve the highest possible sales.

The importance of market share and market growth

Two indicators of enormous importance to a product manager are market share and market growth. *Market share* is a term which refers to the proportion of total sales for one product group which is enjoyed by an particular brand. For example, Coca-Cola enjoyed a 58 per cent share of the total sales of cola drinks in the UK in 1992. Market share is important because it is a measurement of the success of a product or brand within its market. Yet so tough is the competition in consumer markets that few of even the most successful brands achieve more than one-third of total sales within their markets. Winning just a few extra points of market share is often the focus of managers' attention, and organisations that do not set such targets can become complacent, ultimately rendering them vulnerable to those with more aggressive strategies.

Porter's matrix

In his book on competitive strategy, Michael Porter identified two key factors for attaining the competitive advantage which wins higher market share. These two factors are low costs in relation to other suppliers, and a high degree of product differentiation. These two aspects of competitive positioning form the axes for Porter's matrix.

		Relative costs	
		High	Low
Degree of product differentiation	High	Niche market	Outstanding success
	Low	Disaster	Cost leadership

Figure 5.10 – Competitive positioning matrix

Porter's case was that an organisation whose costs are high in comparison to competitors, and whose products are undistinguished against its rivals is heading for disaster. The recipe for success, according to Porter, is to achieve the opposite characteristics: low costs and high product distinctiveness. Some organisations with high costs may survive with marked product differentiation in a niche market, for example, BMW cars or Bang and Olufsen hi-fi systems. Others may trade with run-of-the-mill products so long as they have tight control of their operating costs.

Market growth on the other hand is a measure of changing demand in the market. Such change can be negative as well as positive. Growth of total demand for a product group can be measured either in cash value, or in volume. The latter is often a better guide as a rise in market value may be caused by inflation, rather than genuine growth. Given the difficulties that face an organisation trying to increase its market share, many settle for a steady share of a growing market, achieving increased turnover by this means instead. Equally, a declining market can still be attractive to an organisation which is able to increase its market share as marginal producers stop supplying the market.

Marketing managers therefore need to be able to assess a market's potential for growth. Product life cycles can help here. Those markets least likely to grow are those which have reached maturity or are already in decline.

The Boston matrix (product portfolio)

The two key factors – market share and market growth – come together in a useful tool for managers called the Boston matrix. The *Boston matrix* measures the relative strength and potential of the portfolio of products/services offered by an organisation. Each product is scored for its share of the total market – small or large – and then by the growth rate of the total market – low or high. As a result, each product is placed in one of four categories – dogs, question marks, cash cows, and stars. Each category expresses a judgement about the worth of such products to the organisation, and suggests appropriate actions.

		Market growth Low	High
Market share	Small	Dogs – deserve to be kicked out	Question marks – have potential, but is it achievable?
	Large	Cash cows – to be milked	Stars – top performers, but open to attack

Figure 5.11 – The Boston matrix

Stars

These sound as though they should be the most successful, enjoying a large share of a growing market. However, they are also most vulnerable to attack by rivals seeking to increase their share. Maintaining a star's position can often be at the expense of product profitability. These products are suitable for 'harvesting' – a short-term strategy to increase turnover and thus profitability, but at the risk of sacrificing the long-term position. Such behaviour should only be contemplated in exceptional circumstances.

Cash cows

Occupying a large share of a static or declining market, these products are less vulnerable to competitors, because the market affords little potential to a new entrant. As a consequence, the market may well bear higher prices, enabling these products to make significant contributions to the organisation's profitability. These products can be expected to finance the development of new products during their introduction phase in the life cycle.

Question marks (also called 'problem children')

Such products, occupying small shares of expanding markets, could be regarded as having potential for growth. But before resources are committed, organisations need to ask why these products are only achieving small sales volumes, what level of investment would be required to increase sales, and whether they would still be profitable as a result. They may equally be suitable for extinction.

Dogs

The dog's role in human society has been – among other things – to get kicked when things go wrong. Here then are the brands to be dumped during rationalisation of the portfolio. However, organisations are often emotionally attached to such products. (Or else why have they been allowed to survive this long?) For example, such a product may have been the first one the organisation ever made.

The matrix also assumes that small shares of static markets cannot be profitable, which, as we have seen, may not be the case. However, if a significant number of the organisation's products are clustered in this quarter of the matrix, urgent attention needs to be given to new product development.

Activity ───

Copy the matrix into your note-book, and then locate the following products within this fictitious organisation's portfolio. What strategies could the organisation consider for these products?

Product A	10% share of a growing market
Product B	5% share of a static market
Product C	3% share of a declining market
Product D	34% share of a slowly growing market
Product E	4% share of a rapidly growing market
Product F	25% share of a declining market
Product G	2% share of a collapsing market.

DISCUSSION

		Market growth	
		Low	High
Market share	Small	Dogs -- B,C,G,	Question marks – A, E
	Large	Cash cows – F	Stars – D

The matrix clearly classifies products B, C and G as dogs; A and E as question marks; F as a cash cow; and D as a star. (If you did not consider any of these products to have a large market share, look back at what was said on this subject on page 85.)

Logically, all three dogs should be withdrawn, but it was pointed out in the previous section that injudicious rationalisation can be damaging. As between them the dogs account for three-eighths of the organisation's range, it may be sensible that they should be phased out in the order G, C, and then B, but not until new products are ready to take their places. Product F as the sole cash cow will have to provide funding for this process. However, this will not be possible indefinitely as the market is in decline. With only one star product, the organisation should give urgent attention to its question mark products, notably E, which is in a rapidly expanding market.

Criticisms of the Boston matrix

As with all simple marketing tools, it is possible to criticise the Boston matrix for what it does not do. For instance, it makes no reference to the value of products to the organisation. Product B may have a small share of a market with no growth, but it could still be the organisation's most profitable product. The matrix takes no account of this. Its other assumptions are not always valid. For example, cash cows are supposed to be suitable for price rises for greater profitability. However, if demand for these products is very elastic, price rises would only depress sales. It is not always easy for organisations in small or specialist markets to be very accurate about the total size of their markets or their share in them.

Despite these failings, the Matrix still commands a place in the marketing armoury. It is not intended to be the sole arbiter of product management decisions, merely one tool in the process of analysing and planning an organisation's product range. Therefore, it needs to be viewed in that light.

The differences between products and services

So far the terms *product* and *service* have been used almost interchangeably. But is there in fact a difference between them? And if so, do they affect the make-up of the marketing mix? Read the following section and then make up your own mind.

The first point to make is that products are things, whereas services are activities (e.g. education, transport, banking). However, many service providers call their activities products. Lloyds Bank, for example, refers to its different types of account as a range of products between which its customers can choose. However, many writers on marketing continue to draw distinctions between the two (see Figure 5.12).

Products	Services
Tangible	Intangible
Permanent	Transient
Production and consumption separable	Production and consumption inseparable
Easily replicable	Not easily replicable

Figure 5.12 – The differences between products and services

The distinctive characteristics of services

Intangibility

Services lack a tangible physical form. They are, after all, activities. Products can be handled, and sometimes sampled, before purchase; with many services, this is impracticable. Set against this is the argument that many services take place in a tangible setting. For example, a holiday with Twentys in Ibiza will take place in a tangible enough resort.

Transience

Whereas products are to some extent durable, services expire at the moment that they are consumed. There can thus be no pleasure in ownership for the consumer – an important point to remember in promoting services. Restaurateurs, leisure centre and package holiday operators emphasise the quality of the experience they offer, and stress the creation of memories, which can, of course, be owned, in order to overcome this.

Inseparability

Whereas the creation and consumption of products occur at different times, the very opposite is true for services. The performance and viewing of a live musical show such as 'Miss Saigon' take place simultaneously. As most services – though by no means all – require people to produce them, this places considerable emphasis on the people element in the marketing mix. The attention given by a waiter or waitress may greatly influence enjoyment of an evening meal.

Replicability

Mass production techniques in manufacturing virtually guarantee that one item of the line will be identical to any other. When the service is highly dependent upon people for delivery, it is much more difficult to produce service to a consistent level. One night's performance of 'Miss Saigon' will never be quite the same as another. It is unlikely that a solicitor will ever make two identical appearances in a magistrates' court.

However, the development of franchised services (e.g. Prontaprint, and Wimpey) suggests that this difference is not as marked as it once was. Standardised routines for production, presentation and customer-handling have gone a long way to achieve this.

Activity

At the beginning of this section, you were asked whether it was worthwhile distinguishing between products and services in determining the marketing mix for each. What is your view now?

DISCUSSION

Strictly speaking, the answer is 'Yes'. In general, products are tangible, durable, produced separately from consumption, and easily replicable. The distinction is not always helpful, however. Think about a pre-recorded video cassette. If purchased for home use it is clearly a product, but how would you define it if you hired the same pre-recorded cassette from a local video library? Technically, this is now a service because the item is only on loan to you.

So, while it is possible to distinguish products and services, it is important to remember that what people actually buy are **benefits**, and both products and services can provide these.

Implications for the marketing mix

The component elements of the marketing mix are exactly the same for services as products. However, there will be differences in the importance attached to them in service marketing.

The product in the service mix will be intangible, and less easy to replicate than mass-produced goods. Positioning is just as important for services, but whereas a product itself can provide clues about the target market for which it is intended (e.g. a diamond tiara), place, promotion and people will be more important in communicating this positioning in the case of some services. Price considerations are not affected by the product-service distinction.

The two areas of greatest difference are place and people. Some services are both produced and consumed at the consumer's own home (e.g. a carpet cleaning service), whereas in other cases, location is a vital ingredient in the consumer's perception and enjoyment. For example, the design and decor of modern leisure pools is vastly different from the fish-tank atmosphere of the traditional public baths (see the case study, 'In at the deep end', in Chapter 1). The design and decor of a night club will be a vital element in the creation of its character.

There are also growing numbers of electronic services, such as those provided by telephone (e.g. catalogue retailing) and by computer (e.g. cash dispensers). The key point about their development is that they make take-up of the service easier for the consumer, and therefore more likely to occur.

The other key difference is in the people factor. In service-businesses, people are important both as representatives of the business, and as the focus of business activity.

Under those circumstances it is important to think carefully how consumers may encounter employees. For example, in an open-plan insurance office, some staff in the office may never appear at the counter. But if they can be seen across the counter, their dress, behaviour and manner can influence callers' perceptions of the organisation.

The other people who influence service-delivery are the other consumers present at the same time, the so-called 'co-consumers'. Their presence – or lack of it – can have an impact on other consumers' perceptions. For example, a show that plays to a nearly empty theatre may be less enjoyable because of an apparent lack of 'atmosphere'. A night out at the pub can be spoiled if the bar is filled with the 'wrong' sort of people. The problem can be avoided by properly targeting services at suitable market segments, and communicating the positioning in promotional material. For the most part, consumers will then self-select, choosing those activities at which they expect to meet people sufficiently like themselves in age, class, attitude or behaviour, while rejecting those where very different co-consumers are likely.

Activity

Read the following extract from a Twentys' Holiday Brochure. What is the positioning of the holiday packages described? How have the elements of the marketing mix been combined in order to reflect that positioning? (Note: prices have been omitted because of their complexity.)

'For the exotic and outrageous, I betcha can't better Ibiza! Every year beautiful people from all over the world make their way to this international playground. Naturally, we're permanent residents here – but then Twentys are beautiful people, right? If you're seeking a crazy lifestyle, you won't be disappointed. We are talking totally barking! For a start, Ibiza just doesn't sleep. The place is fit to bust with bars, clubs, cafes and restaurants and Twenty's larger than life presence ensures a larger than life atmosphere. No wonder that locals claim that other resorts eat Ibiza's shorts.

The beaches are absolute peaches – which makes daytime chillin' out all the more pleasurable.

Add to that seriously wicked skies, bustling street markets and fashions that are light years ahead of the time warp back home and you've got yourself one hell of a hardcore holiday.'

Facts you need to know

Resort	San Antonio
Beach	Sand
Bars	150+ in the 'West End'
Clubs	6 in San An (12 on the island)
Restaurants	You won't starve!
Watersports	Scuba, Waterskiing, Bananas
Airport transfer	30 mins approx.
Summary	Every possible taste catered for.

DISCUSSION

The intangibility of holidays requires promoters to use purple prose to bring the features and potential benefits to life. That this is done in a particular vocabulary (e.g. We're talking totally barking!) confirms the other clues about the positioning of the service and its target market. The very name 'Twentys' identifies the target age group, and its lifestyle is no less clearly specified – 'exotic', 'outrageous', 'beautiful people'. Those outside these categories are implicitly warned that they would not enjoy such a 'hardcore' holiday – there are no references to facilities for children or to cultural events. The importance of place – the holiday destination – is emphasised by the reassurance that other resorts 'eat Ibiza's shorts.' All of these impressions are reinforced by a glossy and well-illustrated promotional brochure.

Customer care: responding to rising expectations

The late 1980s has seen a rash of customer service departments and care policies instituted in all types of organisations. At the worst end of the scale they have resulted in little more than cliched elements like 'Have a nice day' at the end of phone calls. At their best they have revolutionised consumers' experiences of services by making the customer the key focus of all business activity.

Such innovations are a response to generally rising consumer expectations and a corresponding decline in the reputation of many businesses, such as banks. Higher expectations are a consequence of improved living standards and rising levels of affluence. In addition, these trends have been reinforced by the growth of the consumer lobby, tougher consumer protection legislation, the publication of consumers' and citizens' charters, and a more sympathetic attitude on the part of organisations towards consumer complaints.

Those features of organisations' activities which are the focus of customer care programmes will vary from business to business. Many are wary of defining the notion of quality service, arguing that it must be defined by the consumer, not the provider. Common quality issues raised by consumers include:

* incomplete performance,
* poor handling of enquiries and lack of information,
* causes of delay,
* unsympathetic handling of complaints.

Staff attitudes towards customer care

Early attempts at customer care programmes were often treated with scepticism if not outright hostility by staff in service organisations. Many still hold the view that 'This job would be alright if it weren't for the customers', and in the face of these attitudes, management platitudes such as 'The customer is always right' seem naive and even wrong.

Monitoring customer care

The success of customer care procedures can be assessed using performance indicators which include:

* repeat purchases (good indicators of satisfaction),
* numbers of complaints received from customers,
* numbers of items returned,
* suggestions received from customers,
* quality system audits (for organisations with a Quality Assurance Standard, such as BS 5750),
* customer satisfaction surveys.

Activity

Read the accompanying article from the *Independent* (Figure 5.13), dealing with the receptiveness of building societies to complaints in 1993. If, as the author alleges, organisations fail to disclose details of complaints procedures, number of complaints are not a useful indicator of the success of customer care programmes.

Survey the customer care programme for organisations in your locality. Start with your college. Does it publicise its complaints procedure? What about your own bank or building society? If you undertake this activity as a group, you might produce a survey of interest to a local paper or radio station.

Building societies 'dodge complaints'

BUILDING societies and banks are failing to disclose details of customer complaints schemes, arguing that they only "encourage" people to complain, according to a survey published today.

Among the worst offenders are the Woolwich and the Alliance and Leicester, two of the five largest societies. Nearly 500 branches of banks and building societies were surveyed.

Neither the banks nor the societies are doing enough to publicise their schemes, it found, but the societies are the worst culprits, with fewer than a quarter displaying customer service leaflets and nearly two-thirds unable to give customers a leaflet on their ombudsman. Some societies may be in breach of the Code of Banking Practice.

The survey is reported in the *Consumer Policy Review*, published by the Consumers' Association, which criticises the building societies' performance as unsatisfactory.

A relatively high number of societies refused to give any information at all. In other cases details of complaints schemes were presented in "microscopic print" or in the least noticeable position in the branch.

The authors, who include Cosmo Graham, Professor of Law at Hull University, argue that publicity about the ombudsman schemes is crucial because awareness of them is low: a survey by the Office of Fair Trading in 1991 found that fewer than a quarter of respondents were aware of their existence.

The survey found that the Halifax and Leeds Permanent provided most publicity, the Woolwich and the Alliance and Leicester the least, with the Nationwide coming about midway. Among the banks, Midland and NatWest performed best and the smaller banks worst.

It is argued that publicity encourages complaints, the authors say, adding: "This is to look at the problem from the wrong perspective: publicity does not *create* complaints – they arise when the service provided does not match the consumer's expectation. Publicity simply encourages customers to voice their complaints."

The Building Society Ombudsman said yesterday the issue was causing concern but no action has yet been taken.

Source: *Independent*

Figure 5.13

Assignment 5

Life and death of a holiday camp

Scenario

As someone who enjoys living and working at the seaside, you were delighted to gain a job in the sales office of Maplin's Holidays (a fictitious company), an operator of a small chain of holiday camps.

The company was started by Joe Maplin immediately after the Second World War, using ex-military bases near the coast to provide cheap, regimented holidays for working class people. Over the years, there has been considerable investment, and the present camps provide activity-related holidays, mainly for families. Camps are located at Paignton, Cleethorpes, Ayr and Prestatyn.

YOUR TASK

Produce a product life cycle using the data summarised in Table 5.1. How does it conform to the standard product life cycle? What phase do Maplins seem to be in at present? What options are open to the company now?

Table 5.1 – Maplin's Holiday Camps: visits and revenue 1947–92

Year	No. of camps owned	No. of visits (excludes day visitors)	Customer spend	Estimated market share (volume)
1947	1	6,123	60,450	3
1952	3	27,985	570,800	2.5
1957	6	88,000	2,068,250	5
1962	8	95,000	2,390,600	4.5
1967	8	118,000	3,290,150	6
1972	8	101,250	3,587,000	6
1977	8	98,600	4,435,400	7
1982	8	87,000	4,590,000	9
1987	6	48,000	4,620,700	7
1992	4	45,000	6,870,500	8

CHAPTER 6

Brands in the marketing mix

Building successful brands

Introduction

Chapter 5 dealt with the importance of the product or service as an element in the marketing mix. In particular, it examined the role of properly implemented product management in developing new products and rationalising those in decline. Throughout that chapter, products and services were referred to almost exclusively as if they were generic items, and not, as is more commonly the case, as branded goods. This chapter will redress the balance by drawing a clear distinction between products and brands, and explaining the importance of effective branding in successful marketing.

What is a brand?

A *brand* may be defined as:

'a marketing identity created for a generic product in order to distinguish it from its competitors'.

Brands differ from *generic products* – that is the product group to which the brand belongs – in so far as a personality has been created for the brand by the organisation which markets it. So the generic product group of national daily tabloid newspapers, included (in 1993) the following brands : the *Sun*, the *Star*, the *Daily Mirror*, the *Daily Mail*, the *Daily Express* and *Today*. Each of these is a newspaper (generic product) but each has its own distinctive character and is thus a distinct brand.

Activity

Draw up a list of distinctive characteristics possessed by each of these papers. How easy is it to tell them apart? How does the branding of these papers influence consumer purchases?

DISCUSSION

It would be very surprising if you could not distinguish each of these papers from the others. The *Daily Mail*, the *Express* and *Today* are mid-market papers. The *Daily Mirror* is slightly left-wing in its treatment of news and editorial attitude, the *Sun* is perceived to be right-wing. The *Star* carries a lot of sports coverage, and more advertisements for personal services. The *Mail* is targeted particularly at women.

All of them have distinctive 'mast-heads' and layouts to symbolise the brand. So well-known are these characteristics that consumers can quickly identify their favourite paper at the counter early in the morning. When their normal choice is not available, knowledge of the alternatives then enables another choice to be specified.

Added values in branding

The additional elements of a brand – over and above those of the generic product – are known as *added values*. These may be functional features, such as the angled neck on toilet cleaner dispensers to make it easier to clean under the rim of the toilet bowl, or a fuel consumption efficiency gauge on a car instrument panel. Additional functional features are known as 'bells and whistles'.

A brand's added values may appeal also to the senses or the emotions, and are related to how the consumer feels about the brand. These may be created in part by specific functional features, but also, and more often, by the brand's image, name, design and promotion. Some have argued that the benefit to the brand of the added values is disproportionate to their costs.

Any added values must correspond to the satisfactions which consumers are seeking when they buy those products.

Activity

Look at the magazine advertisement for the NEC P4 mobile phone (Figure 6.1).

What added values are claimed or implied for this brand over and above the generic product? Which of them are functional features, and which are sensory and emotional ones?

DISCUSSION

There are three aspects of a brand's appeal to customers. With some brands only one or two aspects appeal to a customer, but with others all three aspects simultaneously appeal. The aspects are:

* rational appeal (i.e. appealing to reason)
* sensory appeal (i.e. appealing to the senses)
* emotional appeal (i.e. appealing to emotions).

The appeal of the NEC P4 as distinct to other mobile phones can be summarised as follows:

* to reason – effectiveness, compactness, add-on and internal functions
* to the senses – shape, colour, weight, balance, feel
* to the emotions – high-tech image, boosts self-image, rewarding to own and use.

Did you identify any other aspects of this product's appeal? Which of these – to reason, the senses or emotions – do you consider the most and least important?

Advantages of branding to consumers

You may be surprised to find the advantages to consumers of branding are here listed first. It is true that producers and distributors gain most from branding, but they will only do so if consumers of the products gain as well.

THINGS TO COME

QUITE SIMPLY, THERE'S NO PHONE LIKE IT - ANYWHERE IN THE WORLD

When you own a P4, you demonstrate that you're not prepared to settle for the ordinary. As you would expect from NEC, the P4 is an extraordinary achievement. Both internally and externally, it represents a breakthrough in portable phone design.

AT HOME IN YOUR POCKET - AND IN YOUR CAR

The P4 is an engineering triumph. It packs a wealth of advanced features into its compact and lightweight body and slips easily into a pocket or handbag. Its revolutionary shape makes it easy to grip, gives it natural balance in your hand and enables you to enjoy clear conversations while holding the phone in a natural position.

Wherever you are - whether you're out and about or using the P4 as a powerful hands-free car phone in conjunction with its optional car phone kit, you'll find the P4 the ultimate phone for staying in touch.

ADVANCED COMMUNICATIONS

The P4 doesn't just do its primary task supremely well. You can also use it to send and receive faxes by plugging the phone directly into the NEC i300 portable fax - one of the world's smallest fax machines.

And that's just the start of a long list of innovative added value functions. You can use the P4 to access remote banking facilities and to transmit and receive computer data*. Use it totally hands-free in conjunction

with NEC's voice recognition unit or to call up your answering machine. Take advantage of its speed and auto-dialling facilities. Even use it as an alarm clock. The choice is yours.

A NEW WORLD STANDARD

The P4 takes product design in portable phones to a new level. Light, compact and remarkably sophisticated, it represents the ultimate communications concept.

Why settle for the ordinary when you can have the extraordinary? There's never been a phone like the NEC P4.

* when used with an in-car kit with the NEC Versa portable computer and a cellular modem.

A MOST REMARKABLE PHONE
Return this coupon now for a full information pack to NEC (UK) Ltd., Radio Division, FREEPOST (BS-4335), Bristol BS1 3YX, or call 0800-100105

Title (Mr/Mrs/Miss) _____ Initials _____

Surname _____

Address _____

_____

_____

Postcode _____

☐ Professional use ☐ Personal use Please tick

ND1

THE ULTIMATE COMMUNICATIONS CONCEPT

NEC

Figure 6.1 – Advertising the NEC P4 mobile phone

Consumers benefit in four main ways:

* branding encourages quality – consumers will only repurchase the product if they are satisfied with it;
* branding enhances customer satisfaction levels – where a brand is perceived to be the leader in its market, or is otherwise considered to be of high status;
* branding provides reassurance about purchase – when consumers are presented with a range of alternative purchases about which they lack much information; and
* branding saves time – consumers in a hurry do not need to spend time assessing purchases.

How consumers buy brands

Chapter 4 dealt extensively with buyer behaviour. In doing so, a model of rational buyer behaviour was considered which, it was argued, was most likely to represent high-involving decisions.

It was argued, at that stage, that the model exaggerates the deliberation that is likely for habit-buying of branded goods. In these circumstances, consumers will spend little or no time in searching for information or evaluating alternatives. They will simply make their selection – almost absent-mindedly perhaps – as they rush round the supermarket on a Friday evening. A strong, easy-to-recognise brand image can therefore provide time-saving reassurance about a purchase for consumers.

Figure 6.2 – *The decision-making process for a purchase*

However, when a purchase is being made for the first time, or when it constitutes a high-involving decision, the existence of brand identities is also important at the stages of information search, evaluation of alternatives, and post-purchase review (see Figure 6.2). It is dangerous to assume that all consumers will want to minimise the information search stage of the purchase – there are those who like to shop till they drop! Yet, in many instances, consumers will possess neither the technical competence nor the motivation to search extensively for product information. They will rely on their own existing knowledge and the advice of social contacts including shop sales staff, just as much – if not more – as on objective product data (e.g. from the consumers' magazine *Which*) or sales literature (see Figure 6.3).

In making their evaluation, the status of a strong brand may provide a powerful influence in favour of one product rather than another. Interestingly, that evaluation may be based on subconscious influences on the consumer's existing knowledge absorbed from brand advertising long before purchase was contemplated. Even the advice of family or friends may be derived from this same source if consumers lack personal experience of the brand.

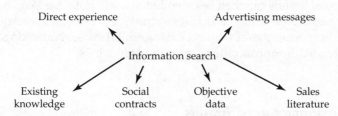

Figure 6.3 – Sources of brand information

It is quite possible that people may begin to doubt the wisdom of their purchases – not because they are actually dissatisfied, but because they are plagued by nagging doubts that an alternative brand might have actually been better. This state of discomfort is called *post-purchase dissonance*. To dispel these fears, some organisations indulge in advertising specifically to reassure their existing customers, by congratulating them on their taste or good sense. It has been claimed that many of those who read the advertisements for new cars are people who already own one, and are seeking this kind of reassurance.

This model of brand-buying by consumers, therefore, emphasises the importance of providing regular information in order to inform both high- and low-involving decisions and to counter the effects of post-purchase dissonance.

Advantages of branding to manufacturers

There are significant advantages to manufacturers in supplying goods to the market as their own brands. To begin with, the added values of a brand provide consumers with reasons to buy the company's products over and above those of the generic item. As a consequence, the company has an opportunity to increase its market share – even perhaps to achieve market leadership. In either case, increased profitability should result.

The existence of a brand also reduces the impact of price competition by rival products because consumers are choosing the brand for reasons other than low price. Additionally, frequent repurchasing of the brand creates a kind of inertia in the consumer. So, when a brand faces competition from a new, potentially more attractive rival in the market, consumer inertia gives the established brand time to respond.

Some of the advantages which big name brands enjoy over their rivals have nothing to do with a brand's performance, and everything to do with image. This is clearly shown by the battle between Coca-Cola and Pepsi. On blind product testing, when people do not know which cola they are drinking, there is often little difference in satisfaction levels recorded by testers. However, in open tests, where people are told which product they are drinking, the stronger brand image of Coca-Cola pushes its satisfaction ratings well ahead of those of Pepsi.

These advantages may seem obvious, but there are others that are less so. Possession of a successful brand increases a company's leverage in distribution channels – for example, by making it difficult for wholesalers and retailers to refuse to stock the brand, and by securing prime positions on supermarket shelves. Successful brands can then be extended. For example, the Mars bar is now available in a number of different formats – drink, ice cream, presentation box – each of which is an example of a brand extension. Likewise, Nintendo's Super Mario was extended from computer gaming to soft drinks.

The vulnerability of manufacturers' brands

Many brands continue to enjoy high market share – particularly if they are established ones. However, brands are vulnerable, and threats do exist. They come from:

* the buying power of multiple retailers who may refuse to stock brands which do not meet their performance targets, or demand increased discounts in return for continuing to stock manufacturers' brands;
* the success of retailers' own-brands, which has occurred largely at the expense of manufacturers' brands;
* the demassification of markets (already dealt with on page 41) which has lead to fragmenting demand for former mass brands; and
* the associated emergence of the 'connoisseur-consumer' who is looking for speciality purchases.

The power of the multiples

Of all the problems facing fast moving consumer goods (FMCG) manufacturers, the growth of the power of multiple retailers has been the most acute. Some sectors, such as confectionery, have felt this less acutely as much confectionery is still sold through independent retailers or those without their own brands in competition.

In other sectors, however, brands which do not enjoy market leadership have often been forced to accept lower returns on their goods from the multiples just to ensure that they are not de-listed. In effect, these brands have been buying space on the shelves by reducing their margins. In turn this has left such companies with less money to invest in product development and in promoting their brands. Over time this has further weakened consumers' perceptions of the difference between the manufacturers' and the retailers' own products. Shoppers choosing on the basis of price, then switch to own label products, reducing sales of the manufacturers' brands still further and renewing the pressure from multiple retailers, who may threaten to stop selling the brands altogether.

The potential dangers for manufacturers' brands are illustrated in Figure 6.4.

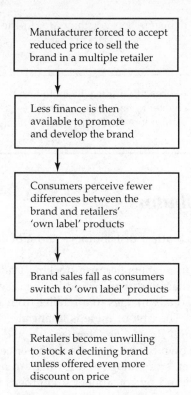

Figure 6.4 – The potential decay stages for manufacturers' brands (based on Chernantony and McDonald)

Such a downward slope is not easy to escape from. It can only be done by committing resources for investment in the brand's performance and image so that the multiple retailers will be anxious to stock it. This is exactly what leading brands have done.

Advantages of branding to service businesses

It is possible to put forward the case that branding is by no means as well developed in the service sector as it is in the supply of consumer goods. Many professions – accountancy, the law, education – have only the most rudimentary brands, if at all. In other cases, branding is arguably of limited value. People will not hire a video, for example, simply because they recognise the name of the distribution company.

Yet many of the advantages to manufacturers apply equally to services. Branding can go a long way to help the standardisation, replication and promotion of services. Franchising (see below), in particular, has brought strong brand identities to service businesses – take the examples of McDonalds, Burger King and Kentucky Fried Chicken in the fast-food sector.

A *franchise* is an agreement under which a branded, standardised service is operated under a form of licence by someone other than the owner of the brand name. The name and its associated image reassures customers about the nature of the service and the standards they can expect wherever they are. In the case of McDonalds, even in Moscow!

Activity

Your college is a service business but is it also a brand? You may want to turn back to the definition of a brand at the beginning of this chapter to help your reasoning.

Discuss this question with other people in your group. What advantages – if any – can branding bestow on educational institutions?

Advantages of branding to distributors

There are two categories of brands which affect distributors – those of manufacturers and retailers' own brands.

Manufacturers' brands are attractive to retailers because stocking leading brands results in a more rapid stock turnover than would be the case with generic, unbranded goods. There are also advantages to a retailer from the development of its own branded goods. The first of these is financial.

In their excellent study *Creating Powerful Brands*, de Chernantony and McDonald claim that profit margins on own branded goods are 5 per cent better than on manufacturers' brands. However, store image and loyalty are powerful benefits as well. Acceptance of a store brand by consumers strengthens their loyalty to a particular retailer. Reports in the *Grocer*, the trade journal for the retail food industry, show that most of the multiple stores are increasing the share of sales which are attributable to own brands (see Figure 6.5).

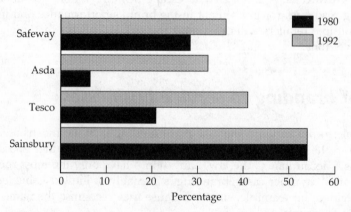

Figure 6.5 – Trends in own label share

(Source: AGB Superpanel)

The great success story of retailers' own brands is that of St Michael products in Marks & Spencer (M&S) stores. M&S sells its own brand exclusively, and this strategy has been copied by rivals British Home Stores (BHS) and Littlewoods. Other retailers have a mixed strategy. Boots, for example, carries both manufacturers' products and its own brands – including electric and photographic products.

In grocery, where own brands are now very strong, it was in the years after World War II, at a time of increasing dominance by manufacturers' brands, that some retailers resurrected generic (or unbranded) products, offering cheaper-priced alternatives to the leading brand names. What began as generic items have evolved into the powerful own brands of the chain stores.

The evolution of own brands

It is possible to characterise the evolution of own brands into roughly three phases:

* **phase 1 – the bargain basement phase:** where retailers are offered a low-cost alternative to existing brands without trying to match them on quality;
* **phase 2 – the me-too approach:** where retail brands are moved as near as possible to the brand-leader on performance while maintaining a favourable price differential for the consumer;
* **phase 3 – the classic phase:** some own brands have become distinctive, even unique, market offerings. Examples of this include Sainsbury's carbonated soft drink Gio (a brand in its own right) and several of its breakfast cereals which are not copied from existing manufacturers' brands.

Not all own branded products have moved through these development phases; there are still many examples of products still in the first phase. Indeed, one of the achievements of retailers has been to run products from all three phases simultaneously, without damaging the image of those at the other end of the spectrum!

Clearly, small independent retailers can easily be disadvantaged in terms of the greater customer loyalty and better profit margins which flow from having own brands. To combat this, a number of wholesaler brands have been introduced, some on the basis of voluntary chains (e.g. Spar and VG). These give the independent retailer the option of selling what seems to be an own brand. Some of these initiatives have been remarkably successful. Spar stores sell on average 20 per cent of own label goods, and the group has plans to increase this percentage.

Manufacturers are often faced with the dilemma of whether to produce retailers' branded goods on behalf of the chain stores, knowing that they will compete directly with their own. Kelloggs for example, takes an uncompromising stand, reminding customers in its advertising that if it doesn't say 'Kelloggs' *on* the packet then it's not Kelloggs *in* the packet either!

Those manufacturers that have decide to produce on behalf of retailers include some which had so far achieved only limited market share. A manufacturer may take the view that making both its own brand, and a leading retailer's brand, is a much easier way of increasing revenue than by trying to increase sales of its own brand. Competition dictates that if a manufacturer does not make a retailer's brand, one of its competitors will.

Activity

Chox Box is a fictitious small but growing retail franchise chain, with about 2 per cent of total UK confectionery sales. It specialises in good quality lines, particularly boxed confectionery which is bought as gifts. The stores have similar decor and fittings, displaying only a limited number of products. At present these are all manufacturers brands, but the franchise company is toying with the idea of introducing a small number of own branded items into branches.

1   What advantages, if any, would you expect own brands to bring to Chox Box?
2   What advice would you give about its first products if it decides to go ahead?
3   What general advice would you make about the choice of a product brand name?

DISCUSSION

1   While there is no single correct answer, it would be strange if you had not referred to the opportunity for developing store loyalty by creating an exclusive brand. The potential problem for the chain will be the response of existing manufacturers; these enjoy a stronger position in relation to retailers than other food manufacturers because much confectionery is still sold by independents. With only 2 per cent of the market, Chox Box may lose its purchase discounts as a reprisal by angry manufacturers. There may also be difficulties in finding a reliable manufacturer for its own brand lines.
2   In terms of which products to select for own brands, the least-risk strategy is to copy existing strong-selling lines (e.g. chocolate peppermint creams). The market is already familiar with these products, whereas the development of new products would involve much greater uncertainty and substantial promotional support. Finally, the company will have to decide between using a corporate brand, or a number of individual product brands, or a combination of the two.
3   A corporate brand need not be the name of the retailer; Dunnes uses St. Bernard as a brand name in homage to Marks & Spencer.

Brand equity

In his book *Managing Brand Equity*, David Aaker argues that a brand is more than a name and symbol, and uses the term *brand equity* to refer to the assets bestowed on an organisation by ownership of a brand (see Figure 6.6).

Figure 6.6 – The components of brand equity

(Source: *Brand Equity*, David A. Aaker, 1991)

The components of brand equity are:
*   loyalty – this creates inertia on the part of consumers, buying time for a brand to respond to challenges from competitors:

* awareness – a familiar brand will usually be purchased in preference to an unknown alternative;
* perceived quality – consumers' perceptions will not normally be based on a technical assessment of detailed product specifications, so assumptions such as 'I've just bought a well-known brand, so it ought to be okay!' are of enormous value, and can be used to support a premium price;
* associations – these are the symbolic values of a brand that add to its enjoyment (e.g. driving a Jaguar may be more satisfying simply because it is a Jaguar)
* other assets – these include patents, trademarks and licences (e.g. Cadbury desserts are produced and marketed under license by St. Ivel Chilled Foods), and channel position (e.g. Marks & Spencer stores often occupy prime or anchor sites in shopping districts).

The first two of these elements of brand equity are now considered in more detail; the others have already been dealt with elsewhere in this chapter.

Brand loyalty

The ladder of brand loyalty (see Figure 6.7) is a device for ranking customers according to the degree of loyalty they show to a particular brand. In terms of calculating the value of a particular brand, it is important that as many customers as possible should be located towards the top of the ladder. The movement of customers up the ladder should be an objective for product (or brand) management, if only because the retention of existing customers is much more cost effective than winning new ones. Any evidence that customer loyalty to a brand is poor, or declining, should be investigated and the cause remedied.

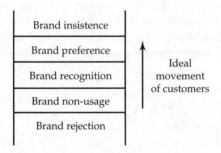

Figure 6.7 – Ladder of brand loyalty

Brand awareness

Just as brand loyalty is important, so too is brand awareness. Certainly the former cannot be achieved without the latter; however, brand awareness does not of itself create loyalty. As with loyalty, organisations should aim to have the greatest number of people towards the top of the pyramid (see Figure 6.8). This does not mean that consumers will inevitably purchase a brand that is, for them, 'top of mind'. Sellotape, for example, may enjoy that status as a brand, but a consumer may happily settle for an alternative.

Figure 6.8 – Brand awareness pyramid

Activity

Carry out an assessment of brand awareness to see whether it appears to correlate with purchasing behaviour. Take one product group likely to be used by other students at college, or people at your workplace. Ask individuals to name one branded product within the group. Then ask them how often they purchase that brand, and to what extent they buy or use rivals.

This is *not* a scientific way to undertake the research, but your results may nevertheless be interesting. Compare them with those of another student.

Branding components

It has already been demonstrated that the difference between a generic product (or service), and a brand, is the market identity – or personality – that is created for it through the values that are added. Although the added values will differ in each case, there are a number of brand components that are common. These are:
* added features
* the brand name
* corporate branding
* packaging and design
* fulfilment
* image and reputation.

Added features

Most brands have at some stage added benefits or features to the core product. Even if these are copied, or become taken for granted by consumers, they remain added features. Sometimes the features will be *tangible*, such as the self-feed facility for the plastic cutting wire on a Black and Decker Strimmer, or the provision of an Aerialator container in packets of Aerial powdered detergents. The added features may also be *intangible*, and are mainly services. In the case of durable goods these commonly include guarantees, after-sales service, and the availability of finance or deferred payment. Intangible features are often based on consumers' sensory experience of the product in use. For example, Kellogg's Rice Krispies claim a distinctive auditory effect.

The brand name

Some brand names themselves become generic; that is they become identified with the product type, either because they are brand leaders, or because they were first in the field. Examples include Biro, Hoover, Nylon and Sellotape.

Activity ————————————————————————————————

Can you think of any other brand names that have become generic? How big an advantage is this?

DISCUSSION

Other common examples include Tipp-Ex, Polaroid and Lycra but you may have thought of several more. Clearly, to have a brand name which is also a generic name is a major advantage. However, it is still necessary to ensure that a brand has other advantages over competitors other than its name.

Brand name check-list

A brand name should have the following characteristics:

1   It should be distinctive, easy to say and remember, for example, OXO, Vim, the *Sun*. Could this explain why Pampers are the brand leaders in the UK for disposable nappies and Peadouce is not?
2   It should say something about the product, for example, Jet (petrol), Rapport (perfume), Mr. Sheen (polish) and Ready Brek (instant porridge). So, where does that leave Death (a cult cigarette brand)?
3   It should be versatile. Organisations need to consider the possibility of brand extensions, particularly for corporate brands. Sony (electrical products) is a versatile name; Frigidaire is not. It is ideal for fridges, but not so good for other electrical products. Imagine a Frigidaire electric blanket!
4   It should be international. With the growing importance of global brands, names also need to be versatile enough to work all round the world. For example, Rover cars have trouble in the USA, where the name is perceived to have something to do with dogs.
5   It should complement the other elements of brand image, for example, Mr Kipling (cakes), provides associations with the Edwardian era when afternoon tea was enjoying its heyday.
6   It must be registered to prevent poaching, including any abbreviation (e.g. Coke is registered as another version of Coca-Cola).

Corporate branding

Another issue for organisations is whether to put the emphasis on the individual product brand names, or on the whole organisation as representing the brand. This last option is known as *corporate branding*. In some cases, the choice is straightforward. British Coal, for example, has a range of fuel products which are difficult to distinguish from each other. In such cases, strong corporate branding is the primary aim.

Organisations also need to consider whether the individual products are strengthened or weakened by the backing of a corporate brand. On the one hand, strengthening can come from favourable associations with the organisation-as-brand being transferred across all the products in the range, as happens with Cadbury's confectionery products, or with supermarket own brands. In the case of Cadbury's, the company is usually the primary brand (e.g. Cadbury's Dairy Milk chocolate), and the individual products are the secondary brands. On the other hand, individual brands may lose credibility by association with other unrelated brands or with a corporate image at odds with the brand's claimed personality. This happened when Cadbury's over-stepped the mark in the 1970s by adding its name to non-confectionery brands (e.g. SMASH instant potato), thus damaging its credibility and losing its distinctive position as a chocolate manufacturer.

Activity

What is the strategy of the frozen food manufacturer Birds Eye? Does it use a corporate or an individual brand strategy? Think about this for a moment, and note down your response.

Figure 6.9 – Birds Eye corporate logo

DISCUSSION

Birds Eye is an example of a strong corporate brand, with five product groups each with secondary branding. The well-known Birds Eye *logo* (see above), epitomising freshness, quality, and family appeal, is used to back up the identity of its five individual brands – Steak House, Country Club, Captain's Table, Menu Master and Healthy Options – each with its own discrete group of products, and different market segments.

Packaging and design

In some cases the design of the package is virtually the same as the design of the product. The aesthetic qualities of dispensers for toilet cleaners, for example, are clearly integral to a consumer's perception of the brand, in a way that is not true for durable goods, where the stylistic elements of the product itself, rather than the box, is more important to the consumer. The shape of the Toilet Duck dispenser is integral to the very identity of the brand; tins of Heinz food always have the same geometric design on the label; petrol brands are communicated almost entirely through design, whether by corporate logo, fuel pumps or filling-station architecture.

You will be familiar with logos of all shapes, sizes and colours even though you may not have known their correct name. A *logo* is a visual symbol that represents the full brand identity.

Activity

Make a list of design elements that you associate with well-known FMCG brands. If possible, cut out some examples from magazines and put these advertisements into your note-book. What common elements are there between brands?

DISCUSSION

No doubt you will amass quite a collection of logos. (For example, if you had been doing this exercise for political parties, you would have found that the Labour Party uses a red rose, the Conservatives a torch and the Liberal Democrats, a bird of liberty.) Mostly logos are associated with corporate brands. You may also have a substantial number of registered trade marks. These differ from trade names in that they are a particular way of printing the name – the curly script style used for Coca-Cola is a good example.

Other design elements that you may have noticed in FMCG pack design are the consistent use of shape, colour and packaging material.

Packaging check-list

Packaging should have the following characteristics:

1   It must protect the product during transit.
2   It should enable inspection to occur (where appropriate).
3   It should promote the product by acting as point-of-sale (POS) advertising.
4   It must reflect the needs of the market segment at which it is targeted (e.g. an economy pack for large households).
5   It must reflect consumer and legislative pressure to reduce packaging, and use recycled materials.
6   It may be used to stimulate repeat purchases: for example, the sale of re-usable packs and refills increases the likelihood of repurchase.

Another issue in pack design is the use of labelling. Although much of its use is purely functional – describing the size, weight and contents, providing instruction on how to use or clean the product, and meeting health and safety requirements – it also has important promotional aspects. First, labelling ensures recognition of the brand. This is particularly important for unpackaged goods, such as fruit, which may simply carry stickers. Secondly, the use of visibly branded goods by other consumers is an endorsement of the product, so sports wear and carrier bags frequently carry brand names. Thirdly, labelling can increase the likelihood that the brand will be reselected when the time comes for repurchase.

Fulfilment

Fulfilment is a term used to refer to the sense of satisfaction that should be experienced by consumers following purchase. This should begin at the moment of purchase, and continue through use of the product, and beyond. For more expensive items, high-quality carry-home packs are used by manufacturers and retailers to ensure pride in the purchase immediately following purchase and before use of the product. Advertising which emphasises the shrewdness of the purchase is then used to reassure existing customers that they have made the right decision, as much as to attract new ones. Organisations go to these lengths because fulfilled customers are those who will be most loyal to the brand.

As consumers' expectations and needs change over time, it is important to ensure that the brand image is also changed in order to provide continuing satisfaction.

Fulfilment check-list

In order to ensure fulfilment the following should be checked:
1   Brands must not raise expectations in their promotion that can not be realised – this should influence advertising, public relations and on-pack claims.
2   Packaging should be used to ensure fulfilment occurs between the moment of purchase and eventual use of the product by the consumer.
3   Effective distribution systems must exist. Unavailability of, or delay in, obtaining a brand, is a likely cause of dissatisfaction for customers.
4   Effective quality assurance systems must exist (e.g. BS 5750) or defective items will reach customers.
5   As part of such a system, an effective complaints procedure must also be in place, to ensure that complaints are treated as an information resource (to prompt improvements).

Image and reputation

If all the above requirements are complied with, then the *image* (that view of a product, service or organisation created by the owner) and its *reputation* (that view of the product or service held by consumers) should be substantially similar and favourable to continued success. However, problems can sometimes occur which are completely outside the control of the brand's managers. This happened when some of the springs supplying Perrier water were discovered to be hazardous to health (see Chapter 9). In such circumstances, a brand's reputation can collapse very quickly, and short- and long-term remedial action become imperative.

Image check-list
1   The brand must be a coherent entity. Every element in the brand's personality must compliment and reinforce the others. For example, with After Eight Mints, the product's delicate wafer-thin shape, name, packaging (including a silver dispenser available by mail order), advertising, and pricing are integrated into an image of refined indulgence).
2   The brand must possess a unique selling proposition (USP). An USP can be defined as one element of the brand's make-up that is exclusive to that brand and represents a distinct advantage over the competition (e.g. Centre Parcs holiday centres claim to be the British holiday that the weather cannot spoil, a reference to the dome at each park providing all-weather entertainment). A few brands possess selling propositions which are really unique; other brands have little that is really distinctive from the competition. The weaker the USP the stronger the communication required to sustain it.

Activity

Choose five brands of which you consider yourself a loyal customer. Can you identify each one's USP? Sometimes, these are contained in an advertising slogan: for example, Sainsbury claim they are the supermarket 'Where good food costs less', thereby trying to convince their customers that Sainsbury can provide quality goods at cheaper prices.

How unique are the selling propositions you have identified? Discuss your findings with others in your group.

Test marketing a new or modified brand

In Chapter 5, the process of developing and screening new product ideas was dealt with in detail.

When a new or modified branded product has run the gamut of organisational testing and user market research, it can either be launched direct to the market, or can go through a final filtration stage known as *test marketing*. This can be defined as:

'the partial launch of a product to a limited, representative part of the total market, to evaluate its performance'.

With a new product, some of the elements of the marketing mix might be tested. For example, a new washing powder might be tested to see whether it performed well in the water supplied to that region of the country. A variety of prices might be charged to assess reaction. Different promotional strategies can be experimented with. Problems with distribution can be ironed out.

With an established product, public reaction to a new pack design, product feature or advertising campaign can be evaluated before being 'rolled out' to the whole market.

To test or not to test?

It is not inevitable that a new or modified brand will be test marketed first. The usual objections to testing are that:

* competitors will catch on during the test, and introduce a rival at the same time as the roll-out (the launch to the whole market);
* competitors will attempt to sabotage the test (e.g. by saturation promotion and distribution in the test area to nullify the results);
* it is very expensive to test market, so an organisation may choose a national roll-out straight away; short-life products (e.g. fashion, novelties, books and audio recordings) often need to be produced in a hurry as demand may already be declining by the time the test is concluded.

All of these objections require marketing people to exercise their judgement. The key question to ask is 'How much would we lose if a national launch of a new product failed?' When that cost is judged to be much higher than that of test marketing, then a test market is desirable.

Activity

Read this list of potential new branded products. Which of them would you consider sensible to test market, and which to launch direct to the larger market:

a   low calorie chocolate selection box
b   fashion designer's spring collection
c   saloon car
d   cosmetics range for young males
e   environmentally friendly concentrated cleaner for automatic dishwashers?

DISCUSSION

Those products that would certainly not be test marketed are the fashion designer's spring collection and the saloon car. The fashion products depend upon reaching a large market very quickly, and garments that do not achieve this are swiftly pulled with no long-term damage to the designer. Saloon cars, on the other hand, take so long and cost so much to get to market, that there is no scope for a conventional test market. Even though, before the launch of the Ford Mondeo, 115 advance models had been placed in service with customers in Britain, Germany and Finland as part of an intensive quality evaluation programme, this is very different from testing the car competitively in one part of its intended market. To do this would allow competitors more time to catch up with technical or design innovations.

However, the low calorie chocolate box, male cosmetics and dishwasher liquid are all products with long-term potential but possible difficulties in gaining acceptance. Each offers scope for testing. Is the selection and pricing correct for the chocolate market? Are all the cosmetic lines equally acceptable, and does the brand proposition need refinement? Does the dishwasher work equally well with all makes of machine and in all water areas?

Check-list for organising a test market

Here is a straightforward check-list that can be used to organise a test market once the decision to test – rather than to go straight to launch - has been taken. Each of the items in the list is then explained in more detail later.

1   Decide which features of the brand's marketing mix need to be tested.
2   Choose an appropriate area for the test market.
3   Agree an appropriate length of time over which the brand will be tested.
4   Decide how the results will be collected and analysed, and what outcomes are anticipated.

Deciding which features to test

Before test marketing begins, there needs to be a clear understanding of what exactly it is that will be measured during the test. The factors under the control of the testers are known as the *independent variables*; the measured results are called *dependent variables*; and those factors that may change during the test, but are outside the control of the tester are known as the *exogenous variables*. (You met these terms in Chapter 2.)

Here is an example of how to use these terms. In testing a new lager, the sales figures or results of awareness surveys are the dependent variables. However, changes to the packaging, pricing or advertising made by the manufacturer during the test are independent variables. The weather and competitor reactions would be exogenous variables – the company would have no control over these.

In designing the test market, it is thus important to begin by identifying the dependent variables that the test will measure. These may include features of the product itself, its price or the effectiveness of different types of special offer. The full list of variables which may be tested is as follows:

* **Product** – Does it meet customer expectations? Does ordinary use show up technical shortcomings?
* **Positioning** – Is the basis of the product's positioning understood by and attractive to the target market?
* **Packaging** – is the design attracting sales? Does it adequately protect the product?
* **Purchasing** – Which customers are buying it? How frequently? In what quantities? What level of sales has been achieved? How do they compare with targets? How have competitors reacted?
* **Pricing** – How much are people prepared to pay? How susceptible is demand to price changes?
* **Distribution** – Are products reaching customers? Where do delays/rationing occur? What stock levels are needed?
* **Promotion** – How aware of the product is the target market? Which media have been most effective in reaching the target market?

Activity

A test was organised to find the most effective media for communicating a district council's summer activity scheme for school children. This required leisure staff to place advertising material in local public buildings, free weekly newspapers, a regional evening newspaper and local commercial radio. During the test period, one of the local free newspapers being used for advertising ceased circulation, and one of the scheme leaders was suspended amid considerable media attention. The results were then presented to the council's Leisure Services Committee.

Identify the independent, exogenous and dependent variables in the test described above.

DISCUSSION

The independent variables are those under the control of the staff (e.g. decisions about which media to use in what proportions), the exogenous variables are those over which they have no control (in this case, the closure of one paper, and the scandal surrounding one of the workers on the scheme), and the dependent variables are the results.

Choosing a test area

There is no absolute guide to the size of a test market. In the UK there is a tendency to use the ITV regions because most FMCG products are advertised on TV, and the advertising can be bought on a regional basis, station-by-station. Many consumer magazines offer the ability to target press advertising fairly closely to specified ITV regions. Two points to bear in mind about this apparent precision are:

* ITV regions frequently overlap (approximately 10 per cent of viewers can receive two or more such stations);
* ITV regions and magazine distribution areas do not exactly coincide.

However, it is possible that, for a multi-national organisation, the UK itself might seem an appropriate test market, while at the other end of the scale, 'mini-area' tests can be carried out, in small towns, or even in a single, albeit significant outlet (e.g. a retail superstore).

The factors that should determine test area choice are the similarities which exist between the test area and the final intended market in terms of:

* geodemographic characteristics
* product usage characteristics
* distribution network
* media buying/viewing behaviour
* strengths of other brands
* relevant technical characteristics.

Individual regions of the UK do differ markedly. For example, disposable income per head varies: in the West Midlands in 1989, it was £6898, while in the South East it was £9086. The West Midlands has a higher proportion of its population living in older housing than most others, and a smaller proportion in higher status, non-family housing. Visiting wine bars is most popular in Greater London, visiting licensed clubs is strongest in the North, but pub-going is most popular in Yorkshire and Humberside. Hypermarkets and superstores are not uniformly distributed – Morrisons is almost exclusively based in the North, Asda is dominant in Scotland while Sainsbury had only one branch there. TV viewing is highest in Scotland, and lowest in London. Sales of the *Guardian* are fairly uniform by region, but vary enormously within them. Not all households have gas supplies. Water softness varies from place to place, and so on.

Activity

Using government statistical sources, or a publication such as the *NTC/Advertising Association Regional Marketing Pocket Book*, compare your own region's characteristics with the rest of the UK. Do you notice anything interesting?

For many organisations cost will be a factor in determining the size of the test market area. The larger the test market, the more representative the results are likely to be for the full market. However, a larger test market means higher costs. This explains the growing popularity of mini-area tests, particularly as the availability of computer modelling makes for greater predictive accuracy, and smaller test markets make the brand less conspicuous to competitors.

Determining the length of a test market

The trick in assessing any test lies in allowing a sufficiently lengthy period for the test to avoid 'fluke' results, and in being able to establish a reliable causal relationship between changes in the independent and dependent variables. However, the longer a brand is being tested, the longer competitors have to catch up.

Analysing test market results

The results of a test marketing exercise are more likely to be reliable if:

* there were clear ideas about what was being tested,
* the area for the test had been carefully chosen to be representative,
* the data had been collected frequently and accurately,
* the number of exogenous variables affecting the results was limited, and

* the results have been analysed carefully by a market research agency or others experienced in test marketing.

Even after committing time and money to a test marketing exercise, an organisation may still feel that the results are far from conclusive. After all, a test market is not a laboratory experiment; there are too many factors outside the control of the organisation for that.

It is important in assessing results not to take a superficial view. For example, good sales returns might simply demonstrate over-enthusiasm by the trade. It is also important to know how much of consumer purchasing is attributable to repeat buying, and how much is occurring because people are just trying the product once, and then reverting to their former brands.

Fortunately, statistical models have been devised to enable organisations to evaluate the reliability of results and to make projections from them. For instance, it is often helpful to know what impact a new product has made on existing products in that market. If 5 per cent of an existing product's share is gained in the test, it is reasonable to assume that a similar share might be won nationally.

Case study

Breeze Detergent (Lever Brothers) – test marketing

Breeze was a new detergent test marketed in the Central TV region in l986 by Lever Brothers. The USP claimed that Breeze would preserve fabric colour during the wash while still getting clothes 'nice 'n clean'. This apparent opportunity had been shown up by gap analysis, a process for identifying gaps in the market. Central TV was chosen because its area closely reflected overall national consumer and trade profiles, it had representative levels of washing machine ownership, water softness, and established sales of liquid detergents. On the basis of the test, Lever decided not to go national. However, the advertising and product (under a new name) were tested again in 1989 in France and the product is now selling in continental Europe.

Case study

The gladiators for our laundry – branding

No UK market is perhaps so obviously dominated by just two equally matched competitors as that for fabric washing soaps and detergents. In one corner is the US-owned Proctor and Gamble. In the other corner is Lever Brothers, now part of the Dutch-based Unilever group, but originally a UK company based at Port Sunlight on Merseyside. Between them, these two companies command 90 per cent of sales volumes (1992 figure). Their dominance is illustrated by the following tables:

Table 6.1 – Shares of the market for low-suds powders in Great Britain 1990–92 (by value)

	1990 %	1991 %	1992* %
Proctor and Gamble	45	42	45
Lever Bros	42	45	43
Other	2	3	3
Own label	11	10	7

Source: Keynote Report, *Soaps and Detergents* (1993)

Table 6.2 – Shares of the market for liquid fabric cleaners in Great Britain 1990–92 (by value)

	1990 %	1991 %	1992* %
Lever Bros	43	46	47
Proctor and Gamble	44	41	42
Other	2	3	3
Own label	11	10	8

Source: Keynote Report, *Soaps and Detergents* (1993)

The fabric washing market is a mature one, with front-loading automatic washing machines in nine out of ten households in Great Britain. Despite the supply being concentrated in the hands of these two companies, this is a highly competitive market, characterised by heavy advertising support for brands, and frequent product modification. Competition on price, however, is less intense.

Both companies also operate multi-brand strategies. Lever Brothers and Proctor and Gamble own a number of brands which compare with other products in their own portfolios as well as that of the rival conglomerate. For Lever Brothers, Persil is flanked by the 'shoulder brands' – Surf, Radion, Lux, Stergene and Wisk. In the Proctor and Gamble portfolio, Ariel is flanked by Daz, Bold, Fairy Automatic, Dreft and Tide. Each of these brands is managed separately, in order to ensure competitiveness, and each is positioned differently in order to appeal to a different segment. Daz and Surf, for example, are sold on the basis of economy, while Lux and Dreft compete on the promise of safeguarding delicate garments. Bold emphasises its dual role in both washing and conditioning fabrics.

The two companies have mirrored each other's behaviour very closely. Both companies are highly secretive, but are unlikely to be caught out by new developments by their rival. While Lever Brothers has opted for the introduction of new brands into this market – notably Wisk (the first liquid fabric cleaner), the unsuccessful Breeze (see *Test marketing a new or modified brand*, above) and Radion (a brand emphasising the fresh smell of the wash) – Proctor and Gamble countered by the development of the washball which was filled with liquid detergent and placed inside the drum of the machine, to go 'right to the heart of the wash'. It also extended existing brands into new concentrated and colour-protecting formulations.

The only serious challenge to the dominance of the big two in this market had come from supermarkets own-brands. However, as Tables 6.1 and 6.2 demonstrate, own label products had been losing market share (probably because they lack the advertising support given to Proctor and Gamble's and Lever's brands), although the introduction of the strongly branded Novon products by Sainsburys appears to have arrested that decline.

The trends that existed at the time of writing suggest that there will be further decline in the older, high suds products, which predate the days of automatic washing machines. This will call into question the future of some of the shoulder brands such as Surf, Tide and Daz, which are still associated with these product types. However, multiple brands will continue to be an important tactic in the battle for market share between these two giants.

Assignment 6

Assume that you work in the marketing department of a successful company that manufactures household cleaning products. For years the company has toyed with the idea of extending its product range into the fabric cleaning sector. You are asked to assess the relative strengths of the current players in this market.

You will need to gain access to market research sources, such as Keynote or the Mintel Reports, the Target Group Index, and retail or pantry audits (e.g. Nielsen or AGB Super Panel) if possible. There will also be frequent references to major FMCG brands in the trade press, including *Marketing*, *Marketing Week*, the *Grocer*, and *Supermarketing*.

YOUR TASKS

You should try to find out:

1   In how many variant forms are each of the two major brands (i.e. Persil and Ariel) now available (e.g. non-automatic powders, automatic powders, liquids, concentrates, colour protective etc.)?
2   Which of the two companies is more successful in terms of market share?
3   Do differences exist in the market segments at which the brands are aimed?
4   What are the current USPs for these brands?
5   In what ways do these brands currently appeal to the reason, emotions and senses of consumers?
6   Is it still possible to talk about coherent identities for these two brands in view of the extent to which they have been extended?
7   How have the multi-brand strategies of the two soap giants developed since the situation described in the case study 'The gladiators for our laundry'?
8   What are the likely future trends in this market and how will they affect these two brands?

Arrange to present your findings as both a written informal report, and a presentation to your manager using computer generated graphics (where appropriate).

CHAPTER 7

Pricing and financial controls for marketing

The price is right

Introduction

The setting of the correct price is of enormous importance in marketing – both in getting the product accepted by the target market, and in generating sufficient revenue for the organisation. This chapter deals with the various elements that constitute the price paid by the consumer, examines the economic determinants of price levels, looks at how organisations make decisions about what to charge, surveys the battleground for price wars, and explains why it is necessary for marketers to have a good understanding of company finance.

What is a price?

You will remember that *price* is one of the six factors which make up the marketing mix (see Chapter 5). We can define a price as:

that which people have to forego in order to acquire a product or service.

The list of elements that might make up the price of a purchase are:

* monetary price (including any discount offered),
* taxation (e.g. VAT),
* cost of borrowing/credit for expensive items,
* time required for search, shopping and delivery,
* delivery cost,
* installation cost,
* costs of the product in use (e.g. electricity, spare parts etc.),
* servicing costs,
* expected life span of the purchase before replacement,
* depreciation,
* pre-qualifications required (e.g. licence to purchase a gun; GCSE certificates to enter college course).

Activity

If someone is contemplating the purchase of a new car, which elements of the price (listed above) would be likely to be relevant? Jot down your response in your note-book and then compare it with that below.

DISCUSSION

To begin with of course, there would be the net cost of the vehicle, a calculation which would involve any car being part-exchanged for the new one; and whether or not the price quoted is the 'on-the-road' price. Some dealers reduce the apparent price for a product, by quoting a basic price and then adding a number of 'extras' – such as delivery, seatbelts, number plates – which are really essentials. By the time the customer discovers this, he or she is more or less committed. It would also be prudent to calculate the depreciation (or loss of value) that the car will attract over the time it is owned – some cars go down in value more quickly than others. What will the cost of spare parts and servicing be? Is the insurance premium going to be high? (Racy cars can often be bought surprisingly cheaply because of punitive insurance premiums.) What will it cost to run? Can the repayment costs of a loan be afforded? Does the customer possess a valid driving licence? (Although not obligatory for purchase it is if you want to drive it on a public road!) How easy is it to find the model that is particularly desired? Is there a long delay between ordering and delivery? (There certainly is for some sports cars or if you want a particular colour.)

The moral of this activity is that there are other 'prices' to be paid than just the one on the showroom ticket.

The laws of supply and demand

Scarcity lies at the root of pricing. Nothing illustrates this more clearly than the paradoxical attitude adopted towards the prices charged for gold and water in the UK. Which of these is essential for life? And which is merely decorative? Which is normally available in abundance? Which is in limited supply? The answers to these questions explain why people will happily hand over a small fortune for gold jewellery, and then write a letter of complaint to a local school that charges children for a glass of water to drink with their sandwich lunch. On the other hand, after two days in the Gobi Desert the price of one gold ring for a bottle of water might seem quite a bargain.

It was not until the nineteenth century that the laws of supply and demand were formulated by Marshall. He showed diagrammatically how a fall in price results in an increase in demand for a product because people buy in increasing quantities. Conversely, as prices fall, fewer suppliers would wish, or could afford, to supply the market, so fewer goods are available. Price is determined by consumers' willingness to buy, and suppliers' willingness to supply. The prevailing price in the market is the point at which the level of demand exactly equals the level of supply.

Figure 7.1 (overleaf) represents these laws diagrammatically. The two axes represent price and sales volume. The demand curve (marked D–D) beginning in the top left corner, and moving down into the lower right of the graph, represents the volume of goods that are demanded at any given price level. It shows how a fall in price is reflected by an increase in demand, as consumers switch their spending from alternative products to buy this one. The supply curve (marked S–S) on the other hand, rises from the bottom left corner to the top right, showing the level of goods that are supplied at any given price level. Not surprisingly, it shows that as prices rise, more goods will be supplied. The point at which the demand and supply curves intersect (X) marks the point at which the level of goods demanded exactly equals the level of goods supplied, and determines the price level in the market (P1).

However, in circumstances in which consumers' incomes rise, the total demand at any given price is argued to be likely to increase, resulting in a new demand curve D2–D2 to the right of the original curve. With more items being demanded, the price is likely to rise in response, thus stimulating higher levels of supply. The new higher price (P2) is again determined by the equilibrium between demand and supply.

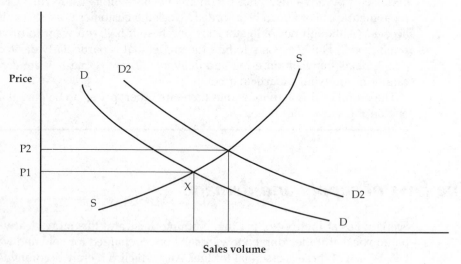

Figure 7.1 – Supply and demand curves

Activity

Copy Figure 7.1 into your note-book. Assume that new suppliers are now entering the market, increasing the quantity of goods supplied at any given price. A new supply curve needs to be drawn marked S2–S2 to the right of the existing one. Draw that curve and use it to work out the new market price (P3). Will it be above or below P2?

DISCUSSION

The new price (P3) should be below the old one (P2). This is because the number of goods supplied at a given price has increased because of the arrival of new suppliers – hence the need for a new supply curve. In turn this has reduced the scarcity of items created by the increased demand represented by the demand curve D2–D2 in Figure 7.1.

Elasticity of demand

Demand for some products is not much influenced by price. Under those circumstances, demand is said to be *inelastic*. Most products with inelastic demand are necessities, as opposed to luxuries, demand for which is more elastic. So, it is argued, increases in the price of bread would not reduce demand significantly because it is a staple item in the diet of many consumers. Higher prices for bread would be met by a reduction in the number of non-essential items purchased in the weekly shop. Equally, a fall in the price of bread would be unlikely to increase demand by much. Consumers would now spend the money previously spent on bread, on more delicacies instead.

Products with *elastic* demand, on the other hand, will be much more affected by price changes. Falling prices bring the product within the reach of those who could not afford it before, thereby increasing demand. However, a rise in price forces consumers to spend their money on essential items. These two patterns of demand – inelastic and elastic demand – are shown in Figure 7.2.

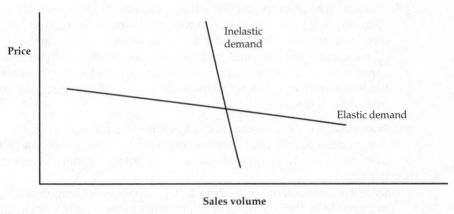

Figure 7.2 – Inelastic and elastic demand curves

Demand elasticity has considerable implications for an organisation's pricing decisions. Can you see what these are? Suppose a bakery cuts the prices it charges for its loaves in the hope of increasing sales. Unless it can gain market share from its rivals, the inelasticity of bread prices means it will probably be disappointed. On the other hand, a manufacturer of electronic goods who decides on a price cut may be overwhelmed by demand because of highly elastic demand for the product type. If this has not been anticipated, there may be rationing and delays for consumers – leading to dissatisfaction with the brand.

Activity

Rate the products listed below for their elasticity of demand. Copy the elasticity continuum (below) into your note-book and then place the product types along the line. The position of bread is marked as an example.

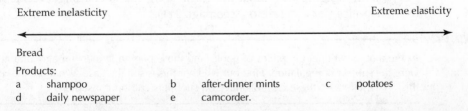

Products:

a	shampoo	b	after-dinner mints	c	potatoes
d	daily newspaper	e	camcorder.			

DISCUSSION

The line should show – left to right (inelastic to elastic) – potatoes; shampoo; daily newspaper; after-dinner mints; camcorder. However, individual differences, particularly in the acceptance of substitutes for the products listed may have influenced your ratings.

Not-so-free markets

The laws of supply and demand assume the existence of perfect competition, as defined by Adam Smith in his book *Wealth of Nations*. Smith, influenced no doubt by the commodity-based markets of the small mining and fishing towns of his native Fife, assumed that:

* all markets dealt in commodities (i.e. not in brands) and consumers perceived all goods in a particular generic group to be much the same;
* there was complete freedom for suppliers to enter the market;
* all consumers and suppliers had complete knowledge of the market;
* consumers would act in their own best interests and that of the economy – in Smith's own phrase 'led by an invisible hand to promote an end which is no part of his intention'.

But how valid are these assumptions? Consider the following points:

* few markets now deal in commodities or unbranded goods, and consumers do not necessarily perceive all goods in a particular generic group to be much the same;
* there are considerable difficulties facing suppliers wishing to enter particular markets. Even though competitors may act independently, their combined effect may persuade a newcomer that it can no longer afford the unequal struggle, forcing it to withdraw. Oligopolistic companies (i.e. those belonging to a small group which dominates a market) frequently set very low prices – and thus accept lower profits – on any products or services which might otherwise have attracted new providers;
* consumers and suppliers may have difficulty in obtaining complete knowledge of a market; whilst it is still possible in a street market, such as that in Kirkcaldy where Smith was born, for consumers and suppliers to know what all of the other suppliers of similar items were charging, mass markets are nowadays so vast that few people can have more than a vague impression of what is going on elsewhere;
* Smith's idea of an 'invisible hand' that would lead consumers to act in their own best interests, and those of the economy and society, now looks like wishful thinking, as the ailments of affluent societies will testify.

In circumstances where the operation of the free market has failed completely, governments and other bodies have intervened. This can be seen in the competition policies of the European Commission, and the anti-trust laws in the USA – both designed to combat the abuse of the market by oligopolistic suppliers or monopolies (for a definition, see page 211).

Activity

At the time of writing, the prices of books and those paid to farmers for agricultural products were the subject of regulation. Find out whether this is still the case. What are the reasons for this? What effect do these controls have on suppliers and on consumers?

Public perceptions of prices

Prices will also be influenced by people's perceptions of what is a reasonable amount to pay. This may bear absolutely no relationship to the cost of the product or service. For example, bottled spring water, which simply flows from under the ground, costs more to buy than concentrated orange juice, even though juice manufacture involves a process of fruit-growing, picking and crushing!

The equation by means of which consumers make judgements about whether they are getting value for money includes the cost-benefit elements shown in Figure 7.3.

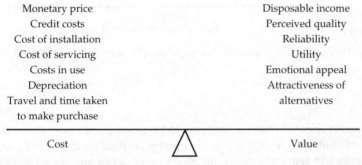

Monetary price	Disposable income
Credit costs	Perceived quality
Cost of installation	Reliability
Cost of servicing	Utility
Costs in use	Emotional appeal
Depreciation	Attractiveness of
Travel and time taken	alternatives
to make purchase	

Cost △ Value

Figure 7.3 – Consumers' perceptions of price/value

We have already seen in Chapter 4, how social class influences what consumers buy. It will therefore also influence what they perceive to be valuable, and that will in turn affect what they are prepared to pay. Disposable income also affects price perceptions. The more money people have to spend, the less sensitive they will be to 'high' prices. Steadily increasing affluence in society, the availability of hire purchase, and the widespread use of credit cards have reduced consumers' sensitivity to price, but not removed it altogether! Many consumers have in mind a range of acceptable prices when they embark upon a purchase, and any price above the expected range will lead the purchase to be reconsidered, if not abandoned.

Price breaks are an accepted way of communicating product quality and performance; for example, carpet prices are commonly charged at prices per square metre ending in 99p, with price breaks being at intervals of a pound – £7.99, £8.99, £9.99 and so on. This makes for easy comparisons between rival products.

The influence of branding upon prices

It is generally the case that branded goods can command higher prices than generic alternatives. The influence that branding plays on price is shown in Figure 7.4 (overleaf). The more distinctive a brand's image and appeal, the higher the price differentiation there will be between the brand and generic substitutes (though not necessarily against other strongly branded lines). The price curve at this point is in the top left of the graph, implying a premium price for the strong brand, which consumers accept as a fair reflection of the brand's added values. However, where the differences between alternative products are non-existent – as in commodity markets – the price differentials between products will be low.

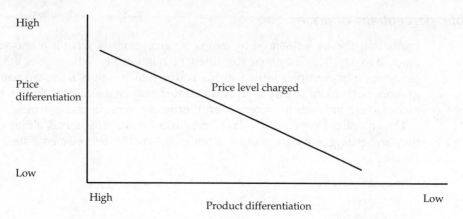

Figure 7.4 - The relationship between strong brand identity and price differentiation

Figure 7.4 also shows what can happen to branded goods over time: they may enter the market with a strong branded image, but as all the brands copy each other's distinctive features, the brand images will decay and revert to the status of generic products. In those circumstances price differentials will fall.

What is the significance of this? Firstly, it is in the interests of organisations to create strong brands, for they will then be able to charge higher prices than for generic alternatives. If those price differentials are to be sustained, the brand must constantly be refreshed.

Activity

Test the claim that high product image differentiation leads to generally higher prices. Either on your own, or with others in your group, examine a number of product groups containing well-known brands. You might choose canned cola drinks, jeans and washing powders. How do the strongly differentiated brands' prices compare with those of generic or weak brands?

Making pricing decisions

Broadly speaking, there are two alternative approaches to pricing open to any organisation: cost-driven pricing, where the cost of supplying a product is the major factor in determining its price, or market-driven pricing, where the major factor determining price is what the customer can be expected to pay.

Cost-plus (cost-driven) pricing

The approach to pricing which is driven by costs is known, for obvious reasons, as *cost-plus pricing*. It is a method which involves calculating all the costs of supply (e.g. production, promotion, distribution and overheads) to which is added an amount to provide an acceptable level of profit. This method is associated with product- or process-oriented organisations, and is still common in business-to-business transactions.

Calculating break-even point

One of the attractions of cost-plus pricing is that it is reasonably easy to calculate the price to be charged. As a first step it is necessary to calculate the break-even point for any product. The concept of break-even point can be represented diagrammatically, as in Figure 7.5.

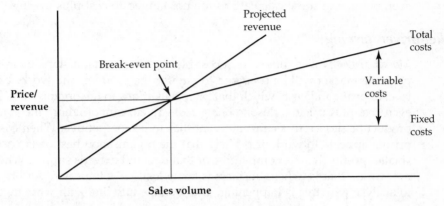

Figure 7.5 – Diagrammatic representation of break-even point

The break-even point is that at which total revenue from sales is exactly equal to the cost of supplying the volume of goods sold. Break-even point is expressed in terms of the sales volume necessary to achieve equality of revenue and costs. A street trader might say 'As soon as I've sold ten of these silk ties, I've paid for the whole case, and every penny after that is pure profit!' In other words, she assumes her break-even point to be the sale of ten ties. However, her analysis is short-sighted. She is only costing in the price she has paid for the ties. How long can she wait for the eleventh sale? Has she allowed for travel? Does she have to pay for the pitch?

Most organisations would say that this was too simplistic an analysis. They know that, generally speaking, the more that they produce of a product, the less it costs them to make one individual item, because of the economies of scale. Ford cannot afford to build the Mondeo at current prices in ones or twos, but in thousands, it is a different story. It is necessary, therefore to distinguish between fixed and variable costs in production.

Fixed and variable costs in production

Fixed costs are those that remain constant regardless of the volume of goods produced. They include rent, rates, loan charges and depreciation, and to an extent, heating, lighting and labour. Fixed costs are represented by the horizontal line in the break-even diagram (Figure 7.5). *Variable costs* are those which are directly related to the volume of goods produced, which is why they are shown rising from left to right in the diagram as output increases. Examples of variable costs are raw materials, packaging, and sometimes promotion. Fixed and variable costs when added together constitute the *total cost of production* for any given level of output.

Break-even point on the graph occurs when the line representing revenue from sales intersects with that representing total costs. When sales are below break-even point, the product is selling at a loss; when sales climb above break-even point, the product is now in profit. Graphs such as Figure 7.5 help to show that break-even point is not a simple fixed point, but a moving target that varies according to the quantity of items being produced, and the price at which goods are sold.

It is also important to understand that, although cost-plus pricing is driven by the calculation of break-even point, all pricing methods need to be aware of break-even point, and these calculations are not limited to cost-plus pricing.

Market-driven pricing

Market-driven pricing differs from cost-plus pricing in that it starts by asking what price the market will be prepared to pay for the product, and works back to the level of profit and costs which that price will afford to the organisation. However, even cost-plus pricing, despite being cost-driven, cannot ignore the value of the product or service to a consumer, and has to be competitive. When cost-plus pricing appears to work, it is likely that the organisation has lower costs, takes smaller profits than its competitors or that demand exceeds supply. Where it does not work – that is, where business is being lost – it is important for organisations to analyse why this is happening, and to come into line with what their competitors are charging.

Setting prices

Setting prices is not easy. It involves making a number of guesses about the future. In an ideal situation, an organisation should proceed as follows:
* Identify the target market segment for the product or service, and decide what share of it is desired and how quickly.
* Establish the price range that would be acceptable to occupants of this segment. If this look unpromising, it is still possible that consumers might be educated to accept higher price levels, though this may take time.
* Examine the prices (and costs if possible) of potential or actual competitors.
* Examine the range of possible prices within different combinations of the marketing mix (e.g. different levels of product quality or distribution methods).
* Determine whether the product can be sold profitability at each price based upon anticipated sales levels (i.e. by calculating break-even point) and if so, whether these profits will meet strategic targets for profitability.
* If only a modest profit is expected it may be below the threshold figure demanded by an organisation for all its activities. In these circumstances, it may be necessary to modify product specifications downwards until costs are reduced sufficiently to produce the desired profit. You will see that this is the complete opposite to the cost-plus approach to pricing.
* Anticipate the likely reaction of competitors (actual or potential).

The influence of the product life cycle model on pricing decisions

As was argued in Chapter 5, the phase that a product is passing through in its life cycle will affect pricing decisions. Figure 7.6 summarises the likely pricing behaviour of organisations during the four phases, each of which is then considered in more detail below.

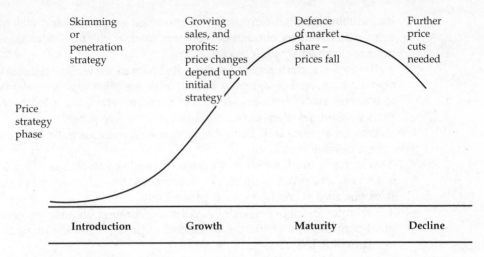

Figure 7.6 – The influence of the product life cycle model on price

Pricing during the introduction phase

At the moment that a product reaches the market, an organisation is forced to choose between two alternatives in determining a price for its new 'baby'. If there are already comparable products in the market – i.e. if it is a copy-cat product – the decision will, in reality, be made for the organisation. It will have to charge at most a comparable price. However, if it is a new product, the organisation will have much more freedom. Then the decision will depend on whether it wishes to aim for rapid penetration of the new market, or whether it prefers to 'skim the cream off' first.

In 1979, Dean identified the three objectives that all organisations shared when pricing a new product:

* to get the product accepted by the market,
* to be able to maintain market share in the face of competition from later entrants, and
* to produce profits.

He then memorably categorised two strategies at opposite ends of the spectrum to achieve this (see Figure 7.7).

Figure 7.7 – Pricing strategies for new products

The features of a *skimming strategy* are as follows:

* it is a high (or premium) price strategy;
* it aims for modest sales volumes but with high profit margins;
* it seeks to position the product as a prestige offering, perhaps as market leader;
* it can be used to discourage the 'wrong' type of consumer (e.g. the tariff for an exclusive hotel);

* it is suitable for high-tech products, protected by patents and well ahead of competition, but encourages competitors to enter the market to share in the bonanza created by high prices;
* it affords the opportunity to reduce prices later in the face of competition, or to open up new market segments. For example, mobile telephones were sold first to business customers, then consumer markets were penetrated by price reductions; today they are sometimes given as free gifts!

The *penetration strategy* is at the opposite end of the spectrum. It can be said to have the following features:

* it seeks rapid market growth through increasing volumes of sales;
* it delivers low profit margins per item – thus, the achievement of very high sales volumes is crucial to good profitability;
* it is therefore a higher-risk strategy than skimming, because the break-even point is further away and the likelihood of paying back the original investment is less certain;
* if successful, it can discourage newcomers from entering a market because of low returns;
* it is less easy to start from penetration strategy and move to skimming, than it is to do the opposite.

Penetration strategies are common at the launch of new fast moving consumer goods (FMCG) products, in order to prompt trial, without which there can be no repeat purchases. This may be done by coupons, on-pack offers (e.g. next purchase free) or two for the price of one (a common approach used for partworks). Yet price alone may not be sufficient to achieve rapid penetration of a market, and a 'push and pull' marketing strategy may be necessary (see page 155).

Activity

Assume that the following new products are about to be launched. Which strategy (skimming or penetration) would you expect to be chosen for each of them?
    The products are:
a   personal micro-helicopter
b   chocolate flavour corn flakes
c   speciality imported African beer
d   combined car shampoo and polish
e   robotic automatic lawn-mower.

DISCUSSION

Discuss your answers with others in your group. Reread this section if there is marked disagreement.

Using marginal pricing to achieve market penetration

One way of offering the low prices necessary to achieve market penetration is to opt for marginal pricing. In such a situation the market price covers only the variable costs, the fixed costs being charged to other products or other consumers. This can only happen in circumstances in which an organisation has surplus capacity. It is how many coach companies charge for daytime private hire. They have regular contracts to perform in the rush hours, but during the middle of the day, the coaches and drivers are not being used. The contract work is covering the fixed costs of running a coach, so a private hire need only cover the extra costs of the driver's wages and the fuel.

When an organisation wishes or needs to end its policy of marginal pricing, there may be negative consumer reaction at being suddenly asked to pay full price.

Pricing during the growth phase

Pricing strategy during growth in the product life cycle will be influenced by the choice that was made at launch between skimming and penetration strategies, and by the general level established in the market.

For products that followed the skimming route, prices will probably need to fall during the growth phase. The reason for this might be the arrival of more competition, causing over-supply to the market and putting downward pressure on prices. Alternatively, the market segments able to afford the higher prices may now be saturated, and the only way to maintain or increase sales is to open up the market to less affluent consumers.

For producers who chose penetration, the growth phase represents the best opportunity to increase prices. This is because the market is now growing in size, and even with the arrival of additional competitors, there may still be sufficient demand to justify rises.

There is also a third way – the adoption of a *mixed-price strategy*. This allows a new product to benefit from a skimming strategy at introduction, and then cut its price to see off the competition during the growth phase and into maturity. When this has happened it may milk the benefits of its strategy by raising its prices again. The three strategies are shown in Figure 7.8.

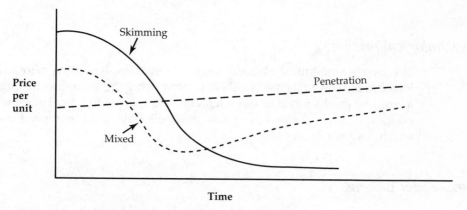

Figure 7.8 – Skimming, penetration and mixed pricing strategies

Pricing during the maturity phase

As demand reaches its plateau, the pressure between organisations supplying the market increases. One way in which an organisation can achieve sales growth is by means of price reductions, hoping thereby to drive the least efficient competitors out of the market. This can lead to damaging price wars, a subject dealt with later in this chapter. Consumers are not easily fooled and there is the danger that a brand that is always the subject of price discounts will be perceived to be in trouble, causing a consequential switch to alternative brands. This is a serious problem for manufacturers of FMCGs, who frequently come under pressure from chain retailers to provide sales promotions, including discounts.

Pricing during the decline phase

The perceived differences between brands are likely to be low as a process of regression to generic status occurs, while there will be only very limited opportunities to reduce costs. As a consequence, both prices and profitability can be expected to fall during this stage, although the fact that a product has now fully repaid its initial development and investment costs may still make it profitable.

Pricing tactics in consumer markets

Single price or variable price decision

FMCG and consumer durable suppliers tend to opt for single prices; variable pricing is much more common for services.

Variable prices for identical services may be charged to different market segments, depending upon their disposable incomes. For example, to secure the family trade, some restaurants advertise 'Kids eat free!' when accompanying their parents, unemployed people are often entitled to reduced fees on college courses, and old aged pensioners are offered cut-price hairdressing. However, they can also be used to discourage people outside the target market from buying (e.g. fares for cruises on luxury liners).

The circumstances in which products are offered at variable prices are often associated with bulk or regular purchases (e.g. economy-sized packs of detergent).

Psychological pricing

This covers a multitude of tactics, each of which involves using price to create an image in the consumer's mind likely to prompt buying. Examples are high pricing to suggest product quality or exclusivity, '£X.99p' pricing (i.e. 1p below a whole pound) to reduce the perceived cost, and bulk-buy prices to imply a discount which may not in fact exist.

Loss-leader pricing

This is widely used in retailing to encourage traffic in the store, when a few well-known brands are marked down to lure in consumers.

Price lining

Organisations use the tactic of lining prices at common intervals (e.g. £9.95, £11.95, £13.95, etc.) within their own product ranges to communicate the quality and image of products in relation to each other. If organisations discount higher-priced products in the range to try for increased sales this may damage the high standing of those products which may be thought not to differ very much from their cheaper counterparts.

Pricing solutions in business-to-business markets

Although the fundamentals of pricing do not differ for business customers, some of the tactics do differ, as the customers this time are professional buyers, not consumers. To begin with, prices for these markets will be quoted differently using terms such as:

* ex-works – this price excludes transport and is suitable for customers who will collect;
* cost and freight – price includes delivery;
* product price and delivery costs shown separately.

Some markets purchase on the basis of tenders, where competitors make bids against each other, not knowing what their rivals' prices are likely to be.

In other markets, the practice of haggling for discounts is common. Sometimes these are offered for volume or regular purchases, or to customers who pay either in advance or promptly upon invoice. In other cases, the price list may simply be a starting point with both buyer and seller seeking to do the best deal for their own organisation. Sometimes, the negotiations for purchase may be protracted, for example, an airline purchasing aircraft.

Activity

Can you think of any consumer markets in which haggling is acceptable?

DISCUSSION

How about second-hand car buying? Or bargain-hunting at car boot sales? Holiday souvenirs purchased in an eastern bazaar may have been bought after protracted negotiations.

Price wars

Price wars occur when competition between suppliers takes place primarily on grounds of price. Such conditions are obviously of benefit to consumers, at least in the short term. They usually occur in circumstances in which supply exceeds demand.

The outcome of a price war is by no means certain. An organisation that begins one may do so unwittingly, and may not be the best equipped to ride out the subsequent conflict. It is for this reason that many businesses use a combination of factors in the marketing mix – rather than concentrating mainly on price – in order to gain competitive advantage.

The major causes of price wars are either over-capacity during the maturity phase of the product life cycle, or attempts by innovative organisations to frighten off competitors from the marketplace during the growth phase. Whatever the cause, organisations need to know how to cope. A number of possible responses exist:

* **reduce supply** – by cutting back on production it may be possible to stabilise the market to the point at which demand and supply are again in balance at a

price that is satisfactory to the supplier; the problem with reducing supply is that an organisation may simply lose more market share to its rivals;

* **stimulate demand** – an increase in demand may restore the former price, and this might be achieved by spending more on advertising; but in mature markets, significant increases in demand are difficult to engineer and sustain;

* **reduce costs** – it is possible to endure a price war if an organisation's costs are significantly lower than those of rivals; short-term solutions, such as staff reductions, are however invariably problematical;

* **raise prices on other items in the range** – this option, while attractive, is available only if market conditions for other products will permit it;

* **reduce the basic price, but charge for extras** – this is easiest to accomplish in markets where it is not easy to compare actual prices between competitors (e.g. hotel accommodation or new cars);

* **attempt to influence other suppliers** – because price wars hurt all suppliers involved, there has sometimes in the past been collusion to avoid competition on grounds of price (e.g. by means of cartels); modern restrictive practice legislation has made such attempts illegal, but it would be idealistic to think that this has stopped the practice altogether.

Activity

You are the editor of the *Glutterworth Evening Chronicle*. In recent months, there has been a steady fall in revenue from display and classified advertising, resulting in space sometimes left unsold. Now your problem has been compounded by the policy of your rival, the *Glutterworth Star*, which is virtually giving away classified space for private advertising, and has daringly cut display rates to suicidal levels.

Choose one or more tactics that you might use to protect your position.

DISCUSSION

The newspaper could both reduce the supply of advertising space and cut its costs by slimming down the number of pages. Other cost-cutting options might include printing on a cheaper paper, using fewer photographs and cutting the number of staff. However, readers might perceive this as providing declining value for money.

Some of the better supported advertising sections of the paper, such as the TV page, might support a price rise, but there is little scope to raise revenue from other sources. However, it might be possible to start charging for design and layout work while cutting the lineage rate to match that of the rival paper.

Finally, you may have suggested promotional activity to increase the revenue from sales of the paper, but this would be very difficult to achieve in the short term.

Activity

Pricing of compact disc recordings

Read the article reproduced from *Marketing Week* (Figure 7.9). It outlines an investigation of the pricing of compact disc recordings by a House of Commons Select Committee. The investigation followed complaints of overcharging by the record companies.

The pain of a slipped disc

Compact discs, according to the record companies that market them, are a premium product – and one for which they charge a premium price. It is, after all, a free market, and if consumers are willing to pay the higher price for perceived higher quality, what's the problem? If they want something cheaper they can always opt for the pre-recorded cassettes.

Yet a Commons committee concluded that record companies are over-charging for CDs, dismissing the arguments of both producers and retailers that their prices are perfectly justified, and effectively writing off several years of canny marketing by the record industry as a spectacular own goal.

Simplifying brutally, the *prima facie* case against the record industry is this. CDs are up to £2.50 more expensive than cassettes, even though they cost about the same to make. And full-price CDs are more expensive than in the US, although mid-price CDs cost about the same and budget CDs are actually cheaper.

On this basis, the price in the UK is therefore "too high", and record companies are variously accused of profiteering, greed, profligacy, protectionism and operating a price-fixing cartel (either among themselves or in association with leading retailers – WH Smith/Our Price and Virgin between them have 28 per cent of the market).

The critics point to the fact that US consumers buy around twice as many CDs per head as in the UK as evidence that the high prices have provoked consumer resistance and that a price cut would result in an increase in sales.

This point is one the record companies vigorously dispute. If sales of recorded music were really price sensitive, they say, CD sales would not be rising (up 17 per cent year-on-year to 75.1 million units in the first quarter of this year) while cassette sales fall (by 11.7 per cent to 56.3 million in the first quarter).

Cutting CD prices would not increase sales by enough to make up for the revenue lost because of reduced margins. CD prices have declined in real terms since 1983, but if forced down further would result not only in smaller profits for the companies themselves but also in less to spend on unprofitable releases of minority-interest music and on developing new talent.

Furthermore, the industry resents the comparison with prices in the US – a market five times as large as the UK with economies of scale to match and where record companies customarily offer a much narrower range of titles – when CD prices in Europe are, it says, higher than in the UK.

The Heritage Committee under the chairmanship of classical music buff Gerald Kaufman, heard all these arguments, but took little account of them.

Its skimpy 20-page report issued at the end of an inquiry lasting barely three weeks, incensed the record companies, who called the report "shoddy" and the inquiry "a witch-hunt".

The committee decided that the major record companies and retailers were "interlocking cartels", and one of the questions is whether a so-called "complex monopoly" (in effect a cartel) exists in either the production or retailing side.

Source: *Marketing Week, 21 May 1993*

Figure 7.9 – The pricing on CDs

1   What does the article illustrate about the ways in which prices are determined?
2   How does an understanding of skimming pricing strategy help you to understand the behaviour of the record companies?
3   Has the stage in the product's life cycle affected pricing?
4   What has happened to compact disc prices since this article was published?

Marketing and company finance

It is impossible for people in marketing to ignore the financial consequences of their actions for their businesses. Indeed, the definition of marketing which appears in Chapter 1 makes it clear that making a profit is at the heart of the marketing philosophy.

There are three reasons why it is imperative that you must understand a company's financial and accounting functions:

* so that you know how the business is financed and how extra resources can be raised for new projects;
* so that you understand what constitutes a company's costs and how revenue flows into the business;
* so that you appreciate how financial performance is monitored and its importance to the company's owners.

The remainder of this chapter will help your understanding of these points.

How are companies financed?

All companies need money to get going and to sustain activity. The money which is used to fund business activity is called *capital*, and it is lent to the business as a form of investment in the expectation that it will provide a good rate of return. There are several sources of capital available, as discussed below.

The owners' personal equity (i.e. their investment)

Equity comprises the amounts originally invested by the owners of the business. This is expressed as holding 'shares', effectively in the net assets of the business, and is therefore the most exposed form of investment in a company because if the business fails, the owners only get their money back after everyone else – employers, creditors, bankers and other lenders – have received their legal entitlement.

However, the owners of a business will expect it to thrive and pay a good rate of return. If it does not they may switch their money to where they can earn a more lucrative return.

Should a business require additional capital for expansion, it can approach the existing owners to increase their equity stake in the business. Where this is not practicable, alternative sources of equity, such as venture capital, may be used.

Venture capital

This is provided by external investment trusts, so-called 'business angels' (i.e. wealthy individuals), government agencies, or merchant banks, in return for a stake in the business.

The Alternative Investment Market (AIM)

For small companies, or more substantial businesses without a track record, the Alternative Investment Market of the UK Stock Exchange allows them to raise capital from external investors. It is more lightly regulated than the full stock exchange list (see below) and offers tax incentives to investors. AIM was established in 1995 to replace the former Unlisted Securities Market, which had helped nearly 900 companies progress to full listing, and raise capital of over £6 billion, since it was established in 1980.

The Stock Exchange

When both company and investors feel the time is right, a business can raise money on the Stock Exchange. Access to this market in 1995 was possible for companies with a minimum equity value of one million ECU (£700,00) and where one quarter of its shares were to be publicly traded.

Raising money in this way dilutes the original owners' control of a business, and could ultimately lead to a take-over.

Profit retained from earlier activity for re-investment

This is, in effect, interest on the owners' investment earned from earlier trading activity which they have foregone in order to put money back into the business.

Although in a start-up company this source of finance will not be available, it is prudent for established companies to retain profits in this way as it is a cheaper and much less risky way of funding new developments.

Commercial borrowing

As an alternative to increasing equity, a company may choose to borrow money. Borrowing can take the form of:
* bank loans, or
* debentures or loan stock (i.e. loans secured on specific fixed assets).

Borrowing is more expensive as a means of financing investment; on the other hand it avoids the dilution of the existing owners' equity and can be quicker to arrange. However it is significant to the 'gearing' of a company (see *The balance sheet* on pages 143–4).

Sale of other company assets for re-investment

This is a way of providing new assets by selling off old ones. When investment in new production capacity is required, obsolete or under-utilised plant may be sold to provide some of the capital required. However, there are two points to bear in mind. The first is that elderly and worn-out premises and equipment are not worth as much as new equivalents. Secondly, they may not be available for sale until after their replacements are in operation.

In putting forward proposals for new marketing initiatives, such as the launching of a new brand, it is important to be aware of the extent to which these initiatives will require capital investment, where that money will come from, what it might cost, and whether it would lead to the dilution of the present owners' control over the business.

Managing cash flow

Cash flow can be defined as:

> *'the movement of cash in and out of companies to finance their operations.'*

Potentially profitable companies can still fail if they do not manage their cash flow. In other words, they can simply run out of cash to pay their way, even though their longer-term prospects might be very good.

However, it must also be emphasised that companies with highly seasonal markets (e.g. for Christmas decorations) may have negative cash flows for ten months of the year, and still earn sufficient revenue in the other two to compensate.

Components of cash flow

The purpose of a cash flow table is either to predict or to monitor the net movement of cash in and out of a company's bank account on a month-by-month basis.

The key components of that cash flow will be:
* opening cash balance
* receipts
* payments
* net movement of cash in/out of the account
* closing cash balance
* overdraft facility.

A cash flow forecast
Figure 7.10 shows the likely cash flow for a start-up company, ABC Engineering, whose two partners are each investing £25,000 of their redundancy money in this business, as well as a bank loan towards the purchase of a tiny factory unit.
The cash flow shows that initially, despite the partners investment and the loan, the business will be trading at a loss and require overdraft support from the bank.

1994	January	February	March	April
Opening cash balance	0	17,700	−100	−10,400
Capital invested	50,000			
Loans	20,000			
Cash sales (1)		2,000	14,000	24,000
Asset sales				
Total receipts	**70,000**	**2,000**	**14,000**	**24,000**
Wages	9,000	9,000	9,000	9,000
Raw materials		6,500	4,000	4,000
Overheads (2)			3,500	3,500
Distribution		1,000	2,500	2,500
Promotional costs			2,000	1,000
Premises	25,000			
Equipment	15,000			
Interest	300	300	300	300
Drawings	3,000	3,000	3,000	3,000
Total payments	**52,300**	**19,800**	**24,300**	**23,300**
Movement in cash	+17,700	−17,800	−10,300	+1,000
Closing cash balance	+17,700	−100	−10,400	−9,400
Overdraft facility	10,000	10,000	10,000	10,000
Additional requirement			400	

Notes:
1   The cash from credit sales is only recorded when it is actually received.
2   Includes rent and rates, post and phone charges, heating and light.

Figure 7.10 – Specimen cash flow forecast for a four-month period, January to April 1994

This reflects, in part, the fact that ABC Engineering have to pay most of its own suppliers within 28 days of purchase, whereas the partners will have to allow up to two months' credit for their own customers.

A cash flow forecast can then be compared with subsequent cash flow statements in order to monitor actual performance in comparison with that which had been expected. Marketing managers would require access to such data in order to assess the effectiveness of the strategies adopted by the company.

Activity

Assume that you and a group of friends are thinking of starting up your own business. Choose a business activity, and then guesstimate how long it would take between your initial investment, and the moment at which the business would move into a positive cash flow (i.e. when the business is receiving more income each month than it is paying out). Try to imagine what costs you would incur and anticipate delays in receiving income.

Monitoring company performance

Annual reports are used to monitor the performance of companies: these contain a profit and loss (P&L) account and the annual balance sheet.

Investors, analysts and managers will want that data to answer specific questions, such as:
* how efficient is this company? – i.e. measuring profit against turnover, administrative costs, capital employed or shareholders' equity;
* what trends are apparent? – i.e. deciding if this company's performance has improved or deteriorated during the recent past (say, a five-year period);
* how does this company compare? – i.e. 'benchmarking' the company against a general standard (e.g. interest payable on deposit accounts) or against other companies in the same business sector.

Profit and loss accounts

Companies are obliged by law to prepare a set of financial statements each year; one of these is a profit and loss account. Its purpose is simple – to show how much profit or loss has been made in any accounting period (usually a year).

The process for drawing up a profit and loss account is in essence, very simple:
* first add up all sales,
* then add up the costs of those sales (i.e. purchases + expenses),
* finally calculate the difference, which can be either
  – a surplus (i.e. a profit), or
  – a loss (i.e. a deficit).
Figure 7.11 shows a simple profit and loss account.

One word about depreciation. It is a non-cash outflow; in other words, funds are set aside to provide replacement for the future. In the short-term it can be omitted in order to improve profitability. However, to do so is very unwise. Eventually, plant, premises, vehicles and equipment will wear out and there will be no cash for replacements. A lack of this item in a profit and loss account should alert you to the fact that profitability is actually worse than would appear.

DG Engineering
Profit and Loss Account 1994/95

	£000s	£000s
Sales		61.00
Cost of goods sold		(33.00)
Gross profit		28.00
Operating costs		
Distribution	11.00	
Central overhead	6.00	
		(17.00)
Operating profit		11.00
Interest charges		(1.00)
Profit before tax		10.00
Tax		(3.00)
Profit after tax		7.00
Depreciation charges		(1.00)
Net profit		6.00
Dividend payable		(2.00)
Retained profit		4.00

Figure 7.11 – A specimen profit and loss account

What sort of profit?

Profitability is spoken about generally as simply meaning that a company is making money. However, the way that the term profit is used in profit and loss accounts is potentially confusing, and requires explanation. When accountants talk about:

* *gross profit* they mean the difference between turnover and the costs of those sales (excluding central overheads, transport costs, etc.);
* *operating profit* they mean the surplus after also deducting the exempted items above (e.g. central overheads, transport costs etc.);
* *profit before tax* they mean the operating profit, less interest charges;
* *profit after tax* they mean the before-tax profit, less corporation tax (a tax similar to income tax levied on companies);
* *net profit* they mean profit after tax, less an amount for depreciation (i.e. sums of money set aside to replace ageing assets in the future);
* *retained profit* they mean net profit, less dividends paid to shareholders.

The importance of profitability

Profitability certainly is important; without it, investors will take their money away and morale within a company will suffer. For a publicly quoted company, the Stock Market may get jittery, leaving the company open to predatory takeover. Raising additional capital becomes more difficult. Even customers, sensing a business in trouble, may begin to switch to rival products.

There are three ways in which a company's profitability can be expressed:
* simple profitability
* profit margin
* return on capital employed (ROCE).

Simple profitability

This expresses net profit simply as a raw score. As such, the figure may look impressive. No attempt is made to relate it to the scale of the company's activities or to investment in the business. A net profit of £4 million might seem impressive until you hear that the company has a turnover of £400 million or assets of £900 million.

Profit margin

This expresses profit as a percentage of turnover. Profit after tax is divided by sales then multiplied by 100 to give a percentage score. The previous example of a £4 million net profit on a turnover of £400 million now becomes a profit margin of 1 per cent – decidedly less impressive than the figure quoted in isolation.

Return on capital employed (ROCE)

This figure expresses profitability in relation to all the assets employed in the company. This performance indicator is of great interest to actual or potential investors. It is calculated by using information contained in a company's profit and loss account, and balance sheet:

$$\frac{\text{Net profit}}{\text{Net assets}} \times \frac{100}{1} = \text{ROCE}$$

where *net assets* are the total value of the company's assets, less any liabilities outstanding at the time of preparing the accounts. This figure can be obtained from the balance sheet.

However, this calculation can sometimes give a partial view of performance, because it ignores short-term factors such as an increase in research and development, or new plant and equipment, which increase the asset base but initially may reduce profits.

Here is an example:

	Year one	**Year two**
$\dfrac{\text{Net profit}}{\text{Net assets}} \times 100$	$\dfrac{10,000}{100,000} \times 100 = 10\%$	$\dfrac{8,000}{200,000} \times 100 = 4\%$

Although ROCE has fallen in year two, the long-term value of this company is made more secure by virtue of the rise in the value of the assets. Stock markets, however, are notoriously short-term in their valuation of companies.

Earnings per share (EPS)

Some profit and loss accounts will also show an earnings per share ratio, calculated as follows:

$$\frac{\text{Net profit}}{\text{Total number shares}}$$

EPS are usually more than the actual dividend paid to shareholders because of profit retained for future investment. Dividend itself is not an accurate assessment of profitability, as many companies will take money from their reserves during periods of poor profitability, in order to try to prevent a disastrous slide in the value of the company's shares.

The balance sheet

The purpose of the balance sheet is to show the theoretical value of a company.
  To draw up a balance sheet, the simplified process is:
*   first add up all the assets (i.e. what the company owns);
*   then add up all the liabilities (i.e. what the company owes);
*   finally the difference between the two is the owner's equity.
The balance sheet is in effect an equation in which the company's assets must balance with the amount of money owed by the company and the shareholders' equity added together:

$$\text{Assets} \quad = \quad (\text{Liabilities} \quad + \quad \text{Capital})$$

$$\qquad\qquad\quad \text{External debt} \quad\ \text{Shareholders' equity}$$

Assets are composed of two main groups – current assets and fixed assets.
Currents assets include:
*   raw materials
*   work-in-progress
*   unsold goods
*   debtors
*   short-term investments and
*   cash.
Current assets are calculated at their net realisable value. So, if a debtor cannot repay in full, the lower figure must be given.
  Fixed assets are those which are assumed to have a beneficial life greater than one year. They include:
*   land
*   buildings
*   plant
*   equipment
*   motor vehicles
*   brand names owned/goodwill.
The value given in the balance sheet (see Figure 7.12) will not necessarily reflect the actual market value, but probably the historic cost of the asset. Sometimes revaluation will take place. This increases the owners' equity in the company, but will require an increase in depreciation charges in the profit and loss account. The inclusion of brands as a fixed asset has proved a contentious issue, mainly because their value to a company is difficult to quantify objectively. However, for the owners of really successful brands, these may be their greatest assets.

Activity

Using the information contained in the D G Engineering profit and loss accounts and balance sheet, calculate the company's profit margin, ROCE, and earnings per share (there are 10,000 shares) for 1994/95.

DG Engineering
Final Balance Sheet 1994/95

	£000s	£000s
Net assets		
Fixed assets		10.00
Current assets:		
Stock	14.00	
Advance payments	5.00	
Trade debtors	13.00	
Cash	8.00	
		40.00
Current liabilities:		
Trade creditors	14.00	
Accruals	2.00	
Tax payable	3.00	
Dividends payable	2.00	
		(21.00)
Long term liabilities		(13.00)
Net assets		16.00
Shareholders' equity		
Share capital	12.00	
Retained profit	4.00	
Total		16.00

Figure 7.12 – Specimen balance sheet

DISCUSSION

D G Engineering's profit margin is 11.47 per cent, return on capital employed is 37.5 per cent and earnings per share are 60p.

Significance of balance sheets

The significance of the fixed assets in the balance sheet lies in indicating the attractiveness of the company to a potential lender. These assets provide security against default of the loan and will mean that companies with poor (or questionable) profitability but a good asset base will be able to attract capital, whereas those with limited fixed assets but good trading prospects will have more difficulty.

Apart from helping to assess the suitability of a company for a loan by indicating the level of security (i.e. fixed assets) against which the loan can be made, the balance sheet will also indicate the level of gearing in the company. *Gearing* refers to the ratio of long-term borrowing to owners' equity in the financing of the company. Any such borrowing will be shown as a long-term liability on the balance sheet. Where a company is highly-geared, this means that there is a high proportion of external debt; where gearing is low, there is little debt.

The problems with high-gearing occur when profitability falls and it becomes difficult to repay the high level of borrowing. Some notable instances of this problem in recent years have been the Saatchi and Saatchi empire, and the former Australian millionaire, Alan Bond.

Activity

A family-owned regional motor dealership wishes to expand by acquisition into areas of the country in which it is not at present represented. Negotiations for the purchase of a small chain of garages in South Wales is at an advanced stage. Would you expect the purchase to be funded by an increase in equity, or by borrowing?

Discuss the issue with other members of your group.

DISCUSSION

This is a family-owned business, so it may not be keen to dilute its ownership. However, the kind of expansion it envisages (of which the South Wales acquisition is merely a first step) is unlikely to be capable of being financed either by the present family members increasing their shareholding, or from retained profits.

You should have discussed the possibility of venture capital or entry into the Alternative Investment Market, both of which offer the least dilution of the family's ownership and control of the business. A long-term borrowing deal would increase the company's gearing quite substantially, and could leave the business exposed in the event of a serious recession or more intense price competition in the motor trade.

Assignment 7

A pricing hot-spot

Scenario

Congratulations! You have just been appointed as Marketing and Sales Manager of the Newbar Heating Element Manufacturing Company, which is based in North London.

This is a small company, with around 60 employees and an annual turnover of £1.4 million. It is an entirely family-owned business, the majority shareholder being an elderly woman who takes no active part in the running of the company. The only other shareholder is her grandson, an unambitious and talentless individual who works in the transport department, and has no management role.

There are at present two main product types which the company makes. The smallest, and declining, group is 'spiral' heating elements of the type used for hot-plates on electric stoves, and in electric kettles. The largest group is a range of 'bent' heating elements for use in fan heaters, and hair driers. The market has grown in recent years thanks to the products' suitability for hand-driers in public toilets. Both product types are made on a jobbing basis; that is, to the customer's specification, rather than to a standard type for general sale.

On your first day, you were asked to attend a meeting of the management team. The General Manager, Production Manager and Company Secretary were also present.

From them you learnt that the company has commissioned some product development research. This has developed a very low-energy form of element which would dramatically reduce energy use (and thus costs in use), of the 'bent' elements in particular. The challenge will now be to finance the development of the element, and of the associated new manufacturing technology.

You also discovered that the pricing system is the cause of friction because the responsibility for setting prices is not clearly laid down, and has traditionally involved several people.

It became clear that the Production Manager favoured a cost-plus approach to pricing. He prefers to tell your office what it costs to make the goods, and then determine a price to allow a reasonable profit. (This is particularly common in business-to-business marketing where short-run orders and even 'one-offs' are common.) He was also very critical of your predecessor as Marketing and Sales Manager. 'Bert used to promise customers all sorts of unrealistic prices, and delivery times. Sometimes we couldn't buy the raw materials at the prices he quoted them, let alone manufacture the elements! Then the so-and-sos had the cheek to complain when the stuff was late.'

Your discomforture grew when the Company Secretary joined in. 'Bert wasn't tough enough with his people,' she said. 'You are going to have to stop them giving ridiculous discounts just so they can get a bit of commission. Sometimes we've just been buying work. I think we should charge a 40% mark-up on everything we do. What we lose on sales we will more than compensate for in increased profits.'

The Production Manager shook his head. 'That's going too far the other way, Sheila. We'd lose half our contracts straight away. You would certainly have to change the way you charge overheads arbitrarily to different products.'

At this point, the General Manager looked at you. 'I think this might be a job for our new recruit. I'd like you to put forward some proposals on how we might sort out these wrangles over pricing. You needn't go into the figures at this stage, just make some suggestions about what our pricing policy should be, and where responsibility for fixing prices should be located within the company. We'll discuss it at our next meeting.'

Finally, he turned to the Company Secretary. 'Sheila, with your major holiday to Australia and the Far East coming up shortly, you are going to need a hand in researching our options for raising capital for the development of the new heating element.' He smiled at Sheila.

'I think this is another job we can leave with our new colleague. What does everyone else think?'

YOUR TASKS

1 Write a memo for the General Manager outlining a new pricing policy for Newbar.
2 Write a second memo suggesting the sources of capital likely to be open to the company. The initial requirement is thought to be for £750,000. The most recent balance sheet shows net assets of £160,000, of which share capital accounts for £40,000, and retained profit the remainder. The fixed assets are almost certainly undervalued.

CHAPTER 8

2000
I 489

Effective distribution

Getting it to the customer

Distribution in the marketing mix

Distribution is the process by means of which goods or services are made available and accessible to consumers. As such it falls under the 'place' heading in the marketing mix.

At one end of the scale are those offerings which are both widely available and easily accessible (e.g. fresh water 'on tap'). There are few occasions when consumers in the UK do not have as much running water as they could possibly need. This is because the suppliers ensure, through the distribution system of reservoirs and water mains, that it is always available. Furthermore, as it is piped into almost every home, it is also highly accessible. At the other end of the scale are those products or services which are only available in a single location (e.g. tours of Buckingham Palace). Not only are there restrictions on availability (limited opening hours), but accessibility depends upon being able to get to The Mall in London.

Activity

1   Can you think of other services which attain similar standards to those of water supply for availability and accessibility?
2   Are there other examples of unique market offerings which are replicated at no other location?
3   Using your experience as a shopper, which fast moving consumer goods (FMCGs) seem to have the most effective distribution systems?

DISCUSSION

1   Mains electricity, gas, broadcast TV, radio and telephones run water fairly close in universality of distribution.
2   Other tourist destinations, such as Niagara Falls, have yet to be replicated around the world.
3   Newspapers are a good example of FMCGs with complex distribution systems, to the extent that copies are delivered daily to homes throughout the country.

The principal concerns for marketing people in establishing the ground rules for a distribution network should be:

*   **timing** – will the product be available when the market expects it?

* **location** – will it be in the places where consumers expect to find it?
* **reliability** – will the distribution system deliver what is required of it or will stockists be telling consumers, 'Sorry, we're still waiting for another delivery!'?

Why distribution is important

Efficient distribution should be an important organisation objective. Having made a decision to purchase, the consumer will then want the product as soon as possible, and a good distribution system will seek to 'take the waiting out of wanting'.

It is not enough that a distribution system should be adequate; exceptional distribution will provide an organisation with a significant market advantage. In fact, Lee Iaacoca, President of General Motors has gone as far as to claim:

'The company with the finest distribution system often wins the battle for market share, and can substantially block a rival from penetrating a market.'

As you will remember from Chapter 6, the strong grocery brands are those that command prime positions on the supermarket shelves. The weaker brands can survive only at the expense of reduced profit margins. Because there is an obvious relationship between sales volumes of FMCGs and their availability, it is important to ensure that mass market products are available as widely as possible in order to drive up sales still further. However, indiscriminate flooding of distribution channels is not the most efficient way of increasing market share. Getting distribution right is every bit as important as positioning the product correctly, or devising appropriate advertising. This requires shrewd strategy and effective tactics.

Ensuring efficient distribution

In addition to securing the correct strategic solutions to distribution, it is also important to ensure that the process is efficient. Examples of late, damaged, incorrect or wastefully small deliveries, of vast stockpiles of unsold products, and of raw materials or finished goods simply going missing are manifestations of a lack of management concern with the process. It was serious delivery problems with Adidas' successful range of sports footwear, that gave Reebok and Nike their chance to increase their share of the European market in the late 1980s.

As a result of these problems, many organisations now implement *physical distribution management (PDM)* systems. PDM is concerned with the design and operation of efficient systems for the inward movement of raw materials to the point of manufacture, and for the outward movement of finished goods to the consumer.

The influence of PDM can be seen in the increasing importance of *just-in-time (JIT)* systems. Such systems involve the delivery of raw materials or components to factories, or of finished goods to chain retailers or wholesalers 'just in time' to be used in manufacture, or put on display for sale. The system removes the need for extensive storage areas either at the factory or behind the scenes in a retail store. JIT is often claimed to have replaced 'just-in-case' storage systems, where large quantities of raw materials or finished goods were held in reserve – just in case they were suddenly needed. JIT does not necessarily remove the need for storage, however. Very frequently, the operator of a JIT system for supplies resolves its own inventory problems, by simply transferring the stockpile to the supplier.

The pressure to improve distributive practices arises from the fact that finished goods in store or in transit are not yet sold, so they show no return on investment. The longer they are stored or the more slowly they are transported, the longer that return is delayed. In addition, storage space is itself a cost. The less efficient an organisation's distribution system, the more vulnerable it is to price competition.

Effective management of the distribution system is crucial to the profitability of organisations. Leakage (i.e. unaccountable loss) is a major worry for retailers, for example. A report published in 1994 by the British Retail Consortium claimed that profits in the industry would be 23 per cent higher were it not for crime. Shop-lifting accounted for about 1.5 million of a total of 2.1 million crimes in the industry in 1992/93, at a total cost of £516 million. However, leakage caused by staff pilfering was believed to have cost £554 million.

Shops are eight times more likely to be burgled on average than a private house, with grocery shops most at risk. Robbery – which does not involve forced entry – was most likely at off-licences. Ram-raiding usually costs more in repairs to premises than in loss of stock. The retail industry takes these problems seriously

An integrated approach to distribution

Activity

Think for a moment about the various departments in an organisation likely to be concerned with PDM – marketing, sales, production, warehouse, transport, and finance. How might their requirements differ in such a way as to create conflict?

DISCUSSION

While marketing and sales are likely to favour flexibility in the system in order to be as responsive as possible to consumers, the production and transport departments are more likely to want to impose delays in order to batch orders together for the sake of greater convenience. The warehouse may want to build up over-large buffer stocks to avoid being caught short during an unexpected rush. Finance will put pressure on each department to show maximum efficiency. Unfortunately, what is most efficient for production or transport may not be in line with the organisation's marketing strategy.

In order to rationalise these conflicts, the planning of distribution needs to be integrated with that of production, purchasing and sales forecasting. If done properly, distribution can thus become the finely-honed strategic marketing tool envisaged by Lee Iaacoca, ensuring reliable delivery at optimum cost.

Distribution and the product life cycle model

As with other aspects of the marketing mix, product and service distribution objectives will differ from phase to phase within the product life cycle (PLC) – see Chapter 5 if you have forgotten what these are. The key characteristics of distribution management are shown in Figure 8.1.

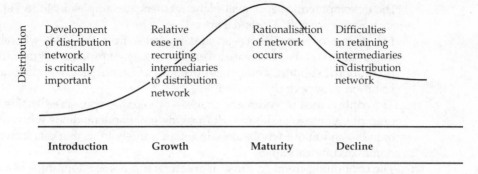

Figure 8.1 – The influence of the product life cycle model on distribution

For the *introduction* phase for a manufacturer's brand, it is vital to secure an effective distribution network by the time that the product is launched. Where the brand is joining an organisation's existing portfolio of branded products this should not pose many problems, as the existing channels are likely to be suitable for the new product. However, wholesalers and retailers will expect incentives to stock a new brand in the form of discounted prices and merchandising support.

Growth is likely to see greater willingness on the part of stockists to take the brand. Demand will at this stage be growing, and intermediaries will want to be able to satisfy this. At *maturity*, however, both the retailer and manufacturer of a brand may review their attitudes. Retailers may want to rationalise the number of competing brands in a product group to concentrate only on the best sellers, while manufacturers may want to concentrate distribution through only the most cost-effective outlets, thus eliminating those which take only small orders. Finally, during the *decline* phase, manufacturers face pressure from retailers to offer ever bigger discounts just to keep the brand on the shelves. It is particularly important to keep these channels open if a relaunch of the brand is imminent, rather than having to re-activate them in the future.

The growing complexity of distribution networks

Do you buy your milk from a petrol station? Your newspaper from a supermarket? Get cash from a dispenser at a motorway services complex? Order your prescription glasses from a discount optician? How many of the clothes in your wardrobe are out of a catalogue?

Each of these questions reflects a recent and continuing change in buying habits in Britain. Doorstep milk and newspaper deliveries are in decline. The tyranny of restricted bank opening hours and days has been replaced by round-the-clock cash dispensers – not necessarily tied to bank premises. Spectacles were once only available from professional opticians' practices – now they are sold by niche chain stores.

The current trends in distribution management include:

* The cross-over of retailer characteristics – retailers are changing the range of goods carried and methods of selling; for example Marks & Spencer's move into home furnishings, grocery supermarkets adding pharmacies, Littlewoods stores entry into catalogue shopping through 'Index', and the growth of 'top-up' retailing at petrol stations.

* The development of specialist niche retailers – examples include Tie Rack, Sock Shop, Toys 'R' Us, and Paper Tree.
* The growth of franchising – an idea imported from the USA, whereby an independent retailer can lease an entire package of products, shop-fittings and promotional support, and benefit from the existence of a national brand; now common in service distribution.
* The continuance of voluntary chains – wholesaler-sponsored chains, for example. Vantage and Numark, provide independent shops with some 'own brands', and allow wholesalers to retain a toe-hold in markets increasingly dominated by multiples.
* The continuing trend to direct marketing and home shopping – volumes of goods sold through direct methods continue to grow, and the creation of satellite TV shopping channels (e.g. QVC) will accelerate this trend.
* Just-in-time deliveries – retailer and industrial customers are now insisting on JIT delivery systems in order to reduce inventories (see page 147).

Selling direct and via intermediaries

One of the major issues facing a manufacturer is whether to sell directly to the end-users or consumers of its product, to do so by means of one or more intermediaries, or to do both.

Activity

Draw up two columns in your note-book, then list all the direct sales methods you can think of on the left, and give examples of intermediaries in the distribution process on the right.

DISCUSSION

Under direct sales methods you might have listed mail order, tele-marketing, party selling, and door-to-door sales; the list of intermediaries should include wholesalers, distributors and a variety of types of retailer.

The relative strengths and weaknesses of direct and intermediary routes for managers can be summarised as follows:

Direct methods	Intermediaries
– enable organisations to build strong relationships with consumers .	– buy more per order than individual consumers
– put the distribution network under the control of the manufacturer	– the economies of scale operate to mutual benefit (i.e. manufacturers produce in bulk; intermediaries buy in bulk)
– increase margins on sales by cutting out the mark-ups of intermediaries	– are physically closer to consumers, and can provide market information
– provide opportunities to complement and reinforce sales made through other methods	– increase opportunities to make sales by bringing complementary products together to the benefit of the consumer

– allow organisations to reach parts of markets not accessible through other methods.

– can offer after-sales service in locations convenient to consumers, rather than returning products to a factory

– fewer relationships to maintain than in dealing directly with thousands of individual consumers.

Channels and networks

Distribution involves the use of one or more channels to facilitate transactions between supplier and consumers. A *channel* is the route along which pass one or more of the following:
* the product or service itself,
* the title to the goods (i.e. ownership),
* payment,
* promotional materials, and
* consumer feedback.

In some instances, manufacturers or owners of a franchised service, will seek to control as much of the channel as possible by, among other things, using their own in-house delivery service and owning or franchising outlets. Breweries, which not only produce beers, but also own many public houses and off-licences, are good examples of this. The Walls Ice Cream company used its own bicycle-powered mobile outlets to increase the availability and accessibility of its products, as the 1930s advert for the 'stop-me-and-buy-one' service (Figure 8.3 overleaf) illustrates.

In the case of mail order, however, the channels used may be entirely outside the control of the supplier, with orders being received over the telephone network, and goods being dispatched by post or commercial carrier.

When channels are grouped together in some way to form a pattern, the result is called a *network*. The more extensive the network, the greater the opportunities for consumers to make purchases, and the greater the challenge of managing the distribution process with maximum efficiency. The various routes from manufacturer to end-user are set out in Figure 8.2.

In the same way that there are different types of distribution channels, so there are varieties of intermediaries within those channels. Types of retailer vary from vast stores on edge-of-town retail parks, to market stalls. Recent phenomena that

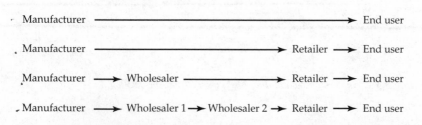

Figure 8.2 – Distribution channels

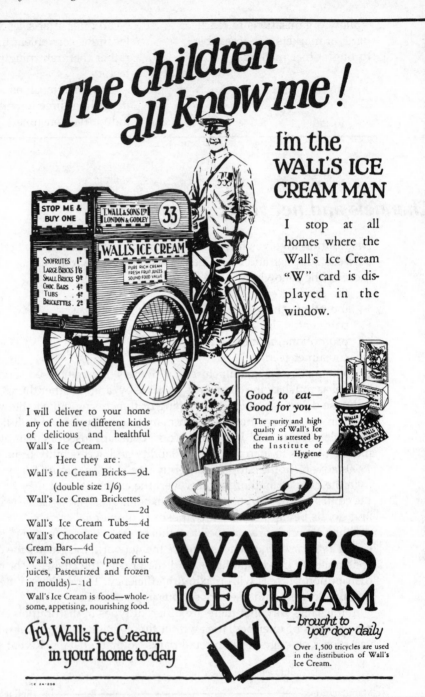

Source: Fifty years of Unilever

Figure 8.3 – Walls 'stop-me-and-buy-one' service from the 1930s

seem likely to establish themselves in the UK by the end of the twentieth century include pan-European shopping chains (e.g. Aldi), TV shopping channels, and warehouse clubs, where for an annual membership fee, consumers buy in bulk from a limited range of goods at greatly discounted prices.

Figure 8.4 contains the major categories of retail and wholesale intermediaries. The categories are not mutually exclusive. For example, Comet is an example of an electrical retailer which is simultaneously a speciality store, multiple, and discount outlet.

Examples of major wholesalers are W H Smith (to newsagents), and the Co-operative Wholesale Society based in Manchester, which is the principal supplier to Britain's 74 retail co-operative societies. The largest cash-and-carry group is Booker (incorporating Linfood), which had 165 depots with an average floor space of 40,000 square feet (in 1992). Secondary wholesalers are usually small-scale operations, breaking bulk purchases into much smaller batches for independent retailers.

Types of retailer

* Variety store
* Speciality store
* Multiple outlet
* Independent trader
* Co-operative
* Franchisee
* Superstore (i.e. 25,000+ square feet)
* Warehouse club
* Discount store
* Mail order
* In-store catalogue shop
* TV shopping channel
* Automated vending

Types of wholesaler

* Primary
* Secondary
* Cash-and-carry
* Co-operative

Figure 8.4 – Types of intermediary

Activity

Draw up a list of examples in each of the retail categories listed above which are active in your own area. Using any market data that you have access to (e.g. AGB Superpanel reports), give some indication of the share of the UK market for each category within that particular market sector (e.g. electrical goods).

The focus of the network

The focus of each network will differ, depending on the nature of the product or service and its positioning. That distribution can affect the positioning of a product is illustrated by clothing brands. Their standing will often be judged by the company they keep. The same garments will command higher prices in chic boutiques than in a mid-market volume outlet. Indeed, if an exclusive label is stocked in such shops, it will be taken as a signal that the brand is moving down market, and may alienate better-off consumers.

The options for the focus of distribution networks can be represented diagrammatically (see Figure 8.5 overleaf).

Intensive	Selective	Exclusive
Many channels in the network; suitable for FMCGs	Used where there needs to be a special relationship between the product and the outlet; such as high-quality gift ware (e.g. expensive perfumes)	Sole rights are granted to a distributor within an area; common with products needing big pre-investment to carry, or after-sales service (e.g. new car sales)

Figure 8.5 – Network focus

Activity

Which of the possible focuses for a distribution network would you expect to be used in the case of the following products orservices?

a franchised carpet-cleaning
b mid-market watches
c bridal gowns
d daily newspapers
e fast-food franchise.

DISCUSSION

Intensive distribution is necessary for the newspapers (d) in order to achieve maximum circulation. Selective distribution is probably best for the watches and bridal gowns (b) and (c), because the manufacturer would be concerned that the company kept by the products, and the prices at which they sell, should reflect the positioning strategy chosen for them. In the case of the two franchises (a) and (e), the extent of the investment necessary would normally justify exclusive rights being granted to the franchisee within that locality.

Intensive distribution is not always the best way of achieving volume sales however. For instance, the network may be expensive to maintain, particularly if outlets are ordering in small quantities.

Key account management

For many manufacturers, the most important objective of their distribution system is to get products into the major retail outlets, as these often account for the majority of sales. In the packaged groceries sector, the multiples account for over 70 per cent of sales volume (1990 figure). Such outlets are called *key accounts*, and in order to keep products on the shelves of these important stores, it is often necessary for manufacturers to:

* appoint one manager for each key account customer,
* offer volume discounts,
* offer promotional deals,
* provide 'own label' products to sell alongside their own,
* design exclusive 'own label' products for the client's special needs for target segments.

Relationships between producers and intermediaries in such cases can best be described as a power balance. Sometimes a producer will be stronger than a retail chain, but only if it has a prestige brand, sold in very high volumes, and is in a position to seriously threaten withdrawal of distributor status. Sometimes, problems with key account intermediaries have led manufacturers to diversify their distribution strategies to 'go direct' to the consumer.

Selecting the distribution mix

Earlier, you learned that it is important to stay ahead of the competition by having the most appropriate distribution strategy. Such a strategy requires manufacturers to achieve a suitable balance between alternative distribution methods. For example, concentrating sales through large multiples may achieve big volumes, but at the cost of reduced profit margins, and the need to compete with own branded goods. Independent retailers, on the other hand, will give better profit margins and will not run their own products in competition.

Similarly, variety stores will offer the opportunity to secure impulse purchases, and place complementary goods alongside each other. However, speciality stores provide better advice and after-sales service. Selling through outlets closed to other manufacturer's products gives an organisation a solus position in such stores, and ensures that all sales will be for its own goods; this strategy is used by Hallmark cards. It is, however, unpopular with other retailers, who may refuse to stock that organisation's range as a consequence.

Finally, there is a balance to be struck between direct selling, and the use of distributors, a point already covered.

Staying friends with the dealers

It is also sensible for manufacturers to maintain good relationships with their stockists, on whose co-operation and enthusiasm for the products, the success of a manufacturer's business so much depends. The key elements of a successful relationship require the manufacturer to:

* provide intermediaries with good profit margins on the lines being stocked;
* inform the intermediaries about new promotions, product changes and price increases;
* listen to their comments about the products, consumers and competition;
* support intermediaries in a number of other ways, including:
    – the chance to purchase on a sale-or-return basis,
    – credit facilities and volume discounts,
    – co-operative advertising (where manufacturer and distributor share the cost),
    – merchandising (e.g. display racks, point of sale literature etc.),
    – product and sales technique training courses,
    – electronic re-ordering,
    – loyalty and performance rewards (e.g. free weekends in Paris for outstanding sales figures).

Push-and-pull tactics

A favourite way of increasing the throughput of products to intermediaries is by the use of so-called *push-and-pull* tactics. This involves 'pushing' products into the trade by offering incentives to stock (e.g. special discounts, sale-or-return, merchandising support, loyalty bonuses, dealer competitions, etc.) while at the same time 'pulling' the product through intermediaries by stimulating end-user demand.

Push tactics can thus be seen to be a sales-led approach, while *pull tactics* are advertising led. Each can operate quite independently of the other, if necessary, but arguably work best in combination.

A good example of the push-and-pull method could be found in the old days of the record business. Thousands of copies of a single would effectively be 'dumped' on retailers on a sale-or-return basis. This had two benefits. First, the records were available and accessible to consumers. Secondly, as some charts of top-selling records were compiled from wholesale, as opposed to retail, figures the record would then appear in the charts, thereby implying popularity. At the same time, records would be offered to DJs together with information about performers, and acts booked onto TV pop shows in order to provide a pull for sales.

Activity

Which elements of push-and-pull tactics – push, pull, or both – would you expect the organisations to use in each of the following circumstances?
a   the launch of a new part-work publication
b   a sales promotion on a packaged grocery line
c   a confectionery count line in an area of the UK where distribution is poor
d   where key account customers are pressuring your brand to accept lower prices, or less favourable shelf locations
e   where a rival manufacturer is offering dealer incentives to increase shelf space to its products.

DISCUSSION

In a, b and e above, push-and-pull tactics are likely to be most effective. A part-work has a very short time in which to establish itself, and must secure early stocking and demand if its is to survive. Sales promotions are also short-term in nature, and require both market awareness and dealer co-operation if they are to succeed. The strong dealer incentives being offered by a competitor might require a counter attraction for stockists, but would also need to ensure that demand from consumers held up, as a twin-track approach to keep dealers loyal.

On the other hand, an area where distribution is weak (c) requires mainly push tactics in order to get more dealers to stock the line, while pressure from retailers to accept lower prices or less good shelf locations (d) is best countered by a rise in demand for the line.

Assignment 8

Porthcarno Porcelain

Scenario
You work as a marketing assistant for Porthcarno Porcelain, a small company based in Cornwall which makes delicate figurines in porcelain. The company's

distribution policy is to secure a number of selective distributors in retail stores throughout the country, in order to complement the refined image of the company's products, and to reinforce the idea that consumers are people with discerning taste.

Three possible retailers have been identified in Galatown, a sizeable town in the Scottish Borders. Your job is to draw up a list of criteria – using this you will make a final selection. The factors you will have to bear in mind in making your choice are:

* site of the shop in relation to pedestrian flow;
* present business profile:
    – sales level
    – current stock (is it complementary?)
    – consumers (who are they?);
* attitude of owner/staff, enthusiasm for the line;
* willingness to purchase stock;
* ability to display stock in a suitable position in a bespoke display;
* credit rating;
* evidence of proper business planning;
* potential for development.

The three candidates are:

* **Store A** – this small unit in the town's new shopping mall is run by the owner, and sells gifts. These include hand-made chocolates, cards and a limited range of crafts and gifts. In order to accommodate the figures, the owner plans to discontinue some of the craft items, on which margins are low. Turnover last year was only £80,000 but this is twice the figure of the previous year. The owner is very enthusiastic to take your goods, and hopes to move to larger premises if present growth continues.

* **Store B** – this is a family-run jewellery business located in a side turning off the main shopping street, which currently turns over £400,000 per annum. The store has been established for 18 years, although the original owners, who were husband and wife, have now handed over the main responsibility for the business to their young daughter who has recently come home from University after taking an engineering degree. The couple are now in semi-retirement. Their daughter is anxious to expand the range of goods sold and sees an opportunity to add good quality glassware and porcelain 'collectables' to the jewellery, clocks and watches already dealt in by the business. A number of other fine art companies have decided to use the shop as their distributor, and the couple believe their daughter's idea could significantly develop the potential of the business.

* **Store C** – this is the town's small department store. It is highly conservative, but enjoys an affluent clientele among the county-set. The turnover of the shop was £1,800,000 last year, although this figure is gradually declining. However, the manager of the china and glass department points out that this is mainly due to the loss of sales of electrical goods and furnishings to the discount warehouses that have opened in the old woollen mills in the town. If this store is chosen, there is no doubt that the figurines would be in very fine company, displayed alongside Dartington, Waterford and Stewart Crystal glass, and Wedgewood, Royal Dalton and Coalport china. Established 125 years ago, the store now belongs to a small chain of such department stores in the north of England and central and southern Scotland.

YOUR TASK

Draw up your proposals for the process by means of which the Galatown distributor will be selected, and present this in the form of a memo to the marketing manager of Porthcarno Porcelain.

CHAPTER 9

Communication for marketing

Getting the message across

What is marketing communication?

Marketing communication includes advertising, sales promotion, direct marketing, public relations (PR), point-of-sale (POS), and salesforce activity. The mistaken, but widely held, view that marketing is nothing more than the deployment of these methods of communication is one that you should now be able to refute when you hear it being advocated. Nonetheless, it is of crucial importance to communicate the availability of products and services and to stimulate interest in them, as was made clear from the definition of marketing given in Chapter 1. This chapter will help you to understand more clearly the methods of doing this.

The components of the communication mix

Figure 9.1 shows that there are several disciplines available to communicate marketing messages. It is extremely unusual for only one of these disciplines to be used for any particular marketing campaign. So it is possible to refer to the use of particular communicative activities and media, in combination, as the *communications mix*, and the ways in which these are used will be the focus here.

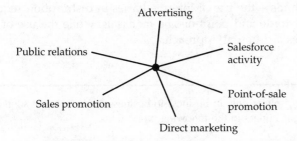

Figure 9.1 – The communications mix

Integrated campaigning

Few marketing campaigns will rely wholly upon a single method. When a new FMCG product is launched, all the marketing communications disciplines will be deployed. Advertising will be used to create awareness of the new product. Sales promotion, perhaps in the form of money-off coupons, will prompt trial of the product. The salesforce, meanwhile, will concentrate on getting retailers to stock the product, offering attractive initial discounts or a special display rack to hold the goods. Public relations staff will organise a launch event, and feed stories about the development and introduction of the new product to the trade and consumer press, and broadcast media. Each method will be used not only to achieve its own specific goals, but to complement the total impact of the integrated campaign.

The selection of communication methods

The process of planning marketing communication campaigns requires that decisions are made about which of the above methods to use, to what extent and in what combinations. The factors influencing their selection will include:

* **campaign objective(s)** – the selection of communication methods will be influenced by what the campaign is intended to achieve. If the goal is strictly short-term, for example 'spoiling' a competitor's advertising campaign, it may be appropriate to make heavy use of sales promotion tactics;
* **target market** – the size of the target market, and the extent to which its occupants are known to the organisation will influence the extent to which general advertising, direct marketing or personal selling methods are used;
* **degree of involvement in the purchasing decision** – high-involving purchasing decisions (see Chapter 4) will require longer and more detailed marketing communication campaigns and be less responsive to sales promotions;
* **market environment** – products with a poor reputation, or towards which there are unfavourable attitudes (e.g. public utilities) will need to work harder to counter those attitudes, while those towards which the markets look favourably (e.g. Marks and Spencer) will require far less promotional support; similarly the strength of the competition will influence the amount of communicative activity necessary; legal constraints close off some avenues (e.g. tobacco advertising is banned from television);
* **distribution methods** – the use of intermediaries in distribution requires advertising to the trade and point-of-sale materials, while the use of direct marketing requires a different approach.

Activity

An engineering company, selling only in business-to-business markets, might spend its marketing communications budget in the following proportions:

	%
Advertising	20
Sales promotion	5
Point-of-sales materials	0
Sales activity	55
Direct marketing	15
Public relations	5

The lack of point-of-sales expenditure reflects the fact that this company is not in consumer markets, and the large cost of sales activity reflects the importance of personal selling to this company.

Try to discover how a company with which you have contact allocates its communications budget. Why are the proportions allocated in this way?

The applications and advantages of each of these promotional methods will now be considered in more detail.

Advertising

It is often useful to define your terms when you begin to study a subject. One definition of *advertising* is as follows:

Advertising is a means of communication, paid for by the originator, which seeks to influence the behaviour and/or attitudes of the target audience.

The role of advertising in capitalist economies

In 1991, total UK advertising spending was £7,577 million, equivalent to 2.06 per cent of consumers' expenditure and 1.52 per cent of the country's gross national product (including exports).

What functions does advertising undertake for producers and suppliers? Do they really need to spend all this money? In order to answer these questions, it is necessary to remember the extraordinary complexity of markets in our society. Rising consumer affluence has been balanced by a rapid growth in spending opportunities. More and different products and services are clamouring for attention. Many of them are – initially at least – unfamiliar to the consumer. Is it any wonder that advertising – which communicates the availability of products and services to markets – has grown in response to this need?

The early growth of advertising can be explained by the needs of mass producers of goods to reach mass markets remote from the point of production. Without such markets, mass production could not be justified, and advertising thus served to stimulate demand in the economy to avoid surpluses of manufactured goods. Early advertising therefore relied heavily upon simple announcement to stimulate demand. More recently, mass markets became subject to a processes of fragmentation, known as *demassification* (see Chapter 2).

In the face of this increasing fragmentation, advertising itself has had to change. This has been seen in the waning importance of *broadband media* (those with mass audiences) such as mass-sale newspapers and television Channel 3, and in the growth of *narrowband media* (those with small audiences) such as highly specialist magazines and some satellite television stations. It also explains the growth of direct mail which enables advertising messages to be targeted directly at consumers known to be interested. This can be contrasted with the rather wasteful use of broadband advertising media which include among their audiences many people who have no interest in the advertised product.

So are there any ways in which consumers benefit from advertising? Arguably, it provides information about opportunities for spending and enables informed choices to be made about purchases – at least in circumstances where advertising is undertaken ethically. From the point of view of entertainment media, the presence of advertising undoubtedly increases the variety available, and reduces the apparent price to consumers.

Objections to advertising

Despite the benefits of advertising, it has many critics – not just those from consumer lobbies.

Activity

The main objections levelled at advertising are listed below. How would you answer them? Can you think of others to add to the list?
* Advertising is a form of social control, and manipulates people.
* Advertising distracts attention from the unfairness in the capitalist system.
* Advertising persuades people to buy shoddy or less efficient goods, and promises satisfactions it can't deliver!
* Advertising exploits women!
* Advertising is offensive.
* Advertising ruins the media.
* Advertising is a waste of money.
* Advertising encourages wasteful and inefficient use of the world's resources, by encouraging people to buy things they do not really need.

DISCUSSION

The objection that advertising manipulates people is a serious attack that has been made by many leading writers – notably Vance Packard in his book *The Hidden Persuaders*. Given that the industry deploys batteries of experts in social motivation, creativity and technical production, it is not difficult to see how consumers might be overwhelmed by advertising messages. In particular, Marxists writers have argued that the cumulative effect of advertising helps to sustain both a consumer society and the more insidious trappings of the capitalist system.

It is here that the charge of exercising social control can be pressed most strongly. Advertising emphasises peoples' roles as consumers, and suggests that this is where they can exercise the greatest control over their destiny – by making purchasing decisions. Such control is largely illusory for most consumers lack both the time and money to take most of the spending decisions offered to them by advertising. Such a lack is a function of the consumer's other role as a producer of wealth. It is as producers that people earn the money to buy those things that they see advertised, but advertising is criticised for diverting public attention from the processes by which wealth is distributed in the first place.

In terms of the effects of advertising on individuals, it can be argued that human beings are not robots, programmed to respond in wholly predictable ways. Consumers are able to exercise their own free will, and are frequently impervious to particular messages from the advertising industry. Your own experience ought to confirm this. How many products have you seen advertised in the last seven days? And how many have you bought? Probably the second figure will be only a fraction of the first. Nonetheless, to argue that advertising has no effect on its audience is equally disingenuous: if it were true, no organisation would advertise its products.

The claim that advertising persuades people to buy shoddy or less efficient goods is based on the assumption that advertising creates an inertia among consumers who might otherwise switch to buying more effective products. Whilst this may be true in the short-term, goods which do not live up to expectations are unlikely to be purchased a second time, and products which do not keep abreast of their competition will also ultimately fail.

The argument that advertising exploits women has been pressed with considerable success by feminist critics in the recent past. Although sexual imagery has not disappeared from advertising, it is now more likely to be used to suggest sensuality, and not simply and crudely to attract male attention or to present women as sex objects. Similarly, women are being shown obtaining satisfaction beyond the confines of home and family, and are depicted in positions of power or influence, again in response to criticism from the women's movement. The argument that such earlier, narrow depictions of the role of women had helped to sustain discrimination against women in society is unanswerable. Nonetheless, advertising did not create such distinctions and attitudes; it merely reflects those found in wider society.

Other criticisms relate to matters of taste. Such complaints can sometimes be resolved through the system of advertising control that exists in the UK, which although voluntary, is strongly supported throughout the industry (see Chapter 10) Unfortunately, the image of the self-regulatory system has been tarnished on occasion, such as in the early part of the 1990s, when advertising for Benetton fashionwear caused considerable distaste. Many people were outraged not just at the ineffectual response of the Advertising Standards Authority, but also by the accompanying high levels of publicity for the company, which it could not otherwise have hoped to achieve.

Advertising in the communications mix

It is because advertising is an effective means of stimulating the awareness of mass markets very quickly that it forms such a major part of the communications mix, particularly for organisations supplying consumer markets.

However, it is important not to overlook advertising's limitations, which include:

* relatively high levels of wastage (i.e. coverage of audiences unlikely to be interested in the products or services being advertised);
* difficulties in evaluating the effectiveness of advertising (so many other factors can influence sales levels or consumer attitudes);
* the inability of even exceptionally good advertising to sell 'dud' products; and
* the ability of audiences to enjoy popular advertising messages purely as entertainment, without much changing their attitude or behaviour.

The advertising trinity

There are three parties to the advertising business:

* the clients (i.e. the advertisers)
* the agencies (i.e. those who plan, create and produce the advertising), and
* the media (i.e. the places in which the advertising appears).

Part one: the clients

Who are the clients and how do they organise their advertising function? Although there are something like 32,000 brands which are currently advertised in the UK, only 9,500 are estimated to spend in excess of £50,000 per annum on advertising.

The 'Top Ten' British advertisers (e.g. Lever Brothers, Proctor & Gamble, Kellogs, etc.) are organisations who regard advertising is an investment. Many of them feature in the league tables of big spenders year after year, indicating that they view advertising as a fixed cost, and not something to be undertaken only when it is affordable.

Expenditure varies not only from organisation to organisation, but also from product type to product type. In some instances, the cost of advertising may account for almost 50p in every £1 that a consumer spends on a product, while in other cases it may be less than 1p.

Activity

What is it that makes some organisations spend millions of pounds on advertising, and others relatively little? Discuss this question with others in your group.

DISCUSSION

There are several factors which can contribute to high levels of spending on advertising. These are:

* the strength of the competition which exists within and between markets; where competition is limited, the necessity for advertising will be less;
* high elasticity of demand and price sensitivity will prompt the need for advertising during periods of price inflation or economic downturn in order to sustain demand levels;
* the importance of branding within the market; where brand identities are strong, advertising is a necessary investment in order to maintain the equity of brands;
* the dominant media choice for advertising; for example, products which make heavy use of television will need to spend more than those using press, for example, because television is a more expensive medium; similarly, products sold heavily through direct mail will have seemingly low advertising spend, because their promotional spending is categorised differently.

Clients' advertising objectives

Advertising is sometimes seen as being an end in itself, and often as a cure for problematic sales figures. The use of advertising in such circumstances is unlikely to be particularly successful, particularly if the problem is not caused by lack of awareness about a product or service on the part of the target market. Advertising should only be chosen as part of the communications mix, if its use accords with the overall marketing strategy for the brand (see Chapter 12). So, for example, an organisation which wishes to increase its penetration of existing markets may decide that direct mail to existing customers or prospects is a better promotional strategy than the use of general consumer advertising. The main objectives for advertising campaigns within organisations' marketing strategies include:

* to develop a brand image,
* to develop a corporate image,
* generic image building (recent examples of such campaigns include those for meat, and sugar, two food products which have suffered from changes in eating habits),

* to defend market share (i.e. against competitors' advertising),
* to encourage trial (particularly important for new and re-launched products),
* to publicise a sales promotion (on-pack and leaflet support for, say, a competition, may not on their own generate sufficient interest),
* to prompt direct responses (such advertising is frequently used to encourage people to identify themselves as prospects, but selling off-the-page is also common),
* to counter hostile criticism (e.g. negative press or television coverage may be muted or even drowned out by heavy advertising spending),
* to change public attitude or behaviour (such outcomes are sought in so-called public service campaigns, such as those to encourage road safety),
* to create awareness (for durable goods, this is important as purchases may only be made infrequently, so it is important to ensure that a brand name is 'top of mind' when the time arrives to make the purchase),
* to test a medium, offer, or particular creative treatment (by the use of split runs in press, or regional exposure on television, particular advertisements can be assessed for their effectiveness prior to a national or full campaign),
* to reassure customers of the wisdom of a purchase (particularly those for durable goods),
* to identify the target market to consumers (by showing what sort of people are the intended consumers of the product, two objectives can be achieved; first, how a product complements particular lifestyles, and second to discourage those for whom it might be unsuitable, perhaps because it is too expensive).

Responsibilities of an advertising manager

Within client organisations there will almost certainly be a department responsible for advertising. The duties and responsibilities of an advertising manager are listed in Figure 9.2 (overleaf).

Choosing an advertising agency

The vast majority of organisations use agencies to handle some or all of their marketing communication activity. That includes not just advertising, but also PR, direct marketing, exhibition attendance, and so on. Given that such agencies will be crucial to the success of the organisation's strategies, it is important to select agencies with as much care as when choosing new employees.

Agency selection check-list

The following is a check-list of questions for a client to consider when selecting a new agency:

1 **Decide what sort of an agency is required**
    - Should the agency have a particular strength, for example, marketing strategy, creativity, media planning and buying, production, research, market sector (such as recruitment)?
    - Is the size of the agency important?
    - Does it need to be located close by?
2 **Identify potential agencies**
    - From trade/professional bodies
    - From directories
    - From advertising/marketing press
    - From personal knowledge/recommendation.

* To the board, for:
  - influencing advertising and marketing policy
  - implementing advertising policy and reporting on its success
  - recommending an advertising budget for each financial year
  - recommending agencies to work on campaigns
  - presenting campaign proposals for approval.
* To agencies, for:
  - explaining the client's products, policies, and strategies
  - visiting agencies and entertaining their personnel when on familiarisation visits to the client's premises
  - liaison on campaign development
  - exchange of data
  - checking accuracy and appropriateness of agency proposals
  - ensuring agencies stay on-budget
  - approving creative proposals.
* To own department, for:
  - management of the budget once it has been approved and monitoring value for money
  - monitoring the effectiveness of advertising
  - ensuring the provision of support materials (e.g. point of sale, and trade sales literature)
  - monitoring competitor activity
  - co-ordinating the work of different agencies on the organisation's roster
* To other departments:
  - to the marketing manager (for advertising execution within the marketing strategy)
  - to the sales manager (for integration of push-pull tactics)
  - to brand managers (for promotional activity)
  - to the PR manager (for co-ordinated promotional activity)

Figure 9.2 – The duties and responsibilities of an advertising manager

3 **Check credentials**
  - Who are their existing clients?
  - Do they win awards for their campaigns?
  - What case-histories of earlier campaign successes can they produce?
  - Who works for them (e.g. well-known creative people)?
4 **Consider other factors**
  - Do they seem likeable people to work with?
  - Do they seem committed?
  - Will there be any conflict of interest with an existing client of the agency who is a competitor?
5 **Making the selection**
  - Draw up a shortlist
  - Give the shortlisted companies a brief (i.e. outline of the campaign requirements)
  - Invite them to 'pitch' (i.e. to present proposals) for the business; some agencies now charge a fee for speculative creative work
  - select the one that feels right for the organisation.

Part two: the agencies

When most people think about the business of advertising, it is the supposedly glamorous world of the agencies that they are likely to think of first. Yet, as we have seen, agencies are only one-third of the equation.

Types of UK advertising agency

The largest agencies in the UK are – at present – full service agencies (see below). Size is defined by the value of the agencies' declared billings, and fees (see Table 9.1). Rankings thus depend very much on an agency's integrity. All the major UK agencies are based in London – and mainly in Soho, Mayfair, Bloomsbury and Belgravia. Regional centres include Manchester, Edinburgh, Bristol and Brighton.

Table 9.1 – List of top ten UK agencies with value of billings, 1994

Rank 1994	Rank 1993	Agency	Billings in £m
1	1	Saatchi and Saatchi	295.59
2	4	Abbott Mead Vickers BBDO	246.03
3	3	J. Walter Thompson	243.00
4	2	Ogilvy and Mather	238.91
5	6	BMP DDB Needham	194.06
6	5	D'Arcy Masius Benton and Bowles	188.84
7	14	McCann-Erickson London	165.60
8	7	Bates Dorland	164.95
9	8	Lowe Howard-Spink	157.44
10	11	Grey London	157.33

(Source: Advertising Association)

Estimates of the number of advertising agencies in the UK vary enormously. Accurate figures are difficult to obtain because of the way in which agencies choose to describe themselves. The categories are:

* **full-service agencies** – these include household names such as Saatchi and Saatchi and J Walter Thompson; these are one-stop shops, offering a full range of advertising services, and easy to deal with from the client's point of view, but the agency may not be equally good at everything;
* **creative agencies**, the so-called 'hot-shops' – these specialise in creating commercials only;
* **media independents** – their function is to plan and buy advertising time or space in the media on behalf of clients
* **other specialists:**
  – by function (e.g. agencies specialising in the launch of new products)
  – by method (e.g. direct marketing)
  – by medium (e.g. poster campaigns)
  – by market (e.g. financial services advertising).

Activity

Try to get hold of either the Institute of Practitioners of Advertising Agency Register, the BRAD Agency handbook, or the handbook published by *Marketing Week*. Alternatively, look up advertising agencies in a local business directory such as *Yellow Pages*. Which agencies operate in your own locality? Ask for a copy of their brochures. Which categories above are represented? Do any of them handle national accounts?

Full-service agency structure

Bearing in mind the dictum that there is no typical agency, Figure 9.3 is a possible full-service agency's departmental structure:

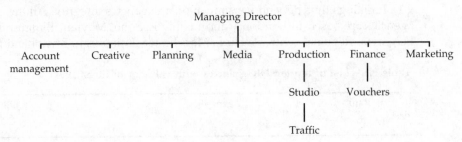

Figure 9.3 – Full-service agency departmental structure

Agency departmental functions

* **Account management** – is responsible for client liaison and internal oversight and integration of agency activity on the account (in small agencies, it is also responsible for new business development which is the job of Marketing in larger agencies). This is a crucial, but often undervalued, role in agencies.
* **Creative** – is the ideas-unit, producing creative strategy and execution (in the shape of words, pictures, sounds, etc.)
* **Planning** – is the department responsible for applying research data to clients' future campaigns to ensure greater effectiveness for the advertising.
* **Media** – is responsible for producing a schedule of candidate media designed to reach a campaign target audience, within the client's budget, and then buys time (television, radio and cinema) and space (press, poster) to that schedule.
* **Production** – sometimes also called creative services, has the task of converting the ideas of the creative department into formats suitable for media (e.g. production of finished artwork for a press campaign).
* **Studio** – this is where the agency's own artists produce artwork for campaigns, often using new technology; however, much work is also farmed out by Production to freelancers or independent production companies.
* **Traffic** – this is the progress-chasing arm of the agency, which ensures that everything happens when it should and thus has a key role in quality control. Traffic circulates material, for example initial briefs for comment, and prints proofs for approval. This section also maintains the job bag which is created for each advertisement. All documentation goes in here, from initial creative brief to supplier invoices. The 'bag' is later passed to Accounts to prepare the client invoice.
* **Finance** – the role of this department is to provide financial management and strategic advice to the agency, bill its clients, pay media and sub-contractors. It must manage cash flow – a particular problem for agencies, who are liable to the media for their bookings, but may face delayed or even non-payment by their clients.

* **Vouchers** – is part of the finance department. Its function is to check 'voucher' copies of publications in which ads have run against media invoices to ensure that the agency is getting what the client paid for.

Working on campaigns – the role of account teams

The description of departmental functions given above might suggest that departments operate in isolation. In fact, the reverse of this is true, and most agencies operate matrix structures to integrate inter-departmental activity. These structures are known as *account teams* (a particular client's business is usually known as *an account*), and might look like the structure shown in Figure 9.4.

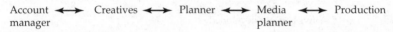

Account manager ←→ Creatives ←→ Planner ←→ Media planner ←→ Production

Figure 9.4 – The matrix structure of an agency account team

Each specialist discipline is represented on the account team set up to handle each campaign being worked on by the agency, in order to integrate activity and keep everyone in touch about developments on that particular client's account.

The account team will be headed by the account manager (sometimes called an account executive or account handler). This individual will be responsible for co-ordinating the agency's work on the account, and for all liaison between the agency and its client. In particular, he or she will prepare the briefs from which the specialists in the team will work, and will lead for the agency at all formal meetings between it and the client.

Two creative people will be assigned to work on the account. One of them will be the art director, and the other will be the copywriter. The art director's rather grand title reflects his or her background in graphic design. The copywriter will have particular skill at composing the slogans, straplines, body-copy or dialogue for advertisements. In practice, the work of the creative partners will overlap considerably.

In the 1980s creativity was king, and prima donna temperaments were tolerated as being an inevitable counterpart to great creative talent. In the 1990s, hard-nosed economic factors have reduced the mystique, but not the value, of a good creative pairing working on an account.

The planner will bring to the team the benefits of market research data, analysis of earlier advertising effectiveness, and advice about the creative approaches which are being considered. Planning as a discipline has had a controversial existence in advertising agencies, largely because its benefits have been oversold to clients in the past. The planner's title is misleading, as he or she is not solely responsible for planning a campaign, but is the one who uses evidence from research to ensure that the embryonic campaign will appeal to the target audience.

The representative from production will advise the account team of the logistical and financial implications of their campaign proposals, and his or her presence at the early stage of campaign development should help to avoid bottlenecks and consequential delays in meeting media deadlines, which may include approvals by media regulatory bodies.

From briefing to appearance in print

The progress of a press advertising campaign from initial briefing by the client, to final appearance in print, is shown in Figure 9.5 (overleaf).

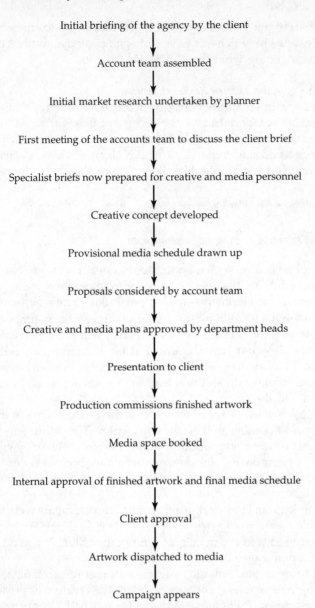

Initial briefing of the agency by the client

↓

Account team assembled

↓

Initial market research undertaken by planner

↓

First meeting of the accounts team to discuss the client brief

↓

Specialist briefs now prepared for creative and media personnel

↓

Creative concept developed

↓

Provisional media schedule drawn up

↓

Proposals considered by account team

↓

Creative and media plans approved by department heads

↓

Presentation to client

↓

Production commissions finished artwork

↓

Media space booked

↓

Internal approval of finished artwork and final media schedule

↓

Client approval

↓

Artwork dispatched to media

↓

Campaign appears

Figure 9.5 – Stages in press advertising campaign development

Part three – the media

The third part of the advertising business is the media in which the advertising appears. There is a remarkable range of media available, including parking meters, the backs of bus tickets and even the sky above us! However, from the point of view of this chapter, we will consider only the major media – press, television, poster, radio and cinema.

How advertising money is spent
UK advertisers spend their money on media in the proportions shown in Table 9.2.

Table 9.2 – Proportions of UK advertising expenditure (1994)

	%
Total expenditure	100
Press (includes:	
national newspapers	
regional newspapers	
consumer magazines	
business titles	
directories, and	
production costs)	55.1
Television	28.3
Direct mail	10.3
Outdoor and transport	3.4
Radio	2.4
Cinema	0.5

(Source: Advertising Association)

Activity

Do the figures shown in Table 9.2 surprise you? Did you expect television to be a larger proportion? Why is spending on advertising on radio and cinema so small? Discuss these points with others in your group.

DISCUSSION

The press figure given above includes, not only newspaper and magazine advertising, but directories (such as *Yellow Pages, Thompson, The Municipal Yearbook,* etc.). The figure also includes classified advertising – for employment, property and motor vehicles – which is such an important source of revenue to regional and local newspapers, and in total accounts for about one-quarter of press advertising expenditure. Display advertising on the other hand is significantly more important in national newspapers which are used much more by advertisers for mass-market campaigns.

If television attracted a smaller proportion of spending than you had anticipated, remember that television advertising is limited to a maximum of seven minutes per hour for terrestrial channels, and 12 for satellite stations, whereas press is a much more flexible medium. Extra pages can always be added to accommodate additional advertising. If you have ever had a job delivering Sunday newspapers, you will be well aware of this phenomenon. However, television is the dominant medium for FMCG and consumer durables advertising, and this is why most people believe it to be the dominant advertising medium.

The relatively low spends for other media have long been a source of concern to their owners. Poster advertising is limited in terms of the complexity of messages it can handle, and it is nearly always used as a secondary medium, topping up campaigns which are primarily using other media, notably television. Radio in the UK has so far failed to achieve the advertising share that the medium enjoys in the USA. The popularity of public service broadcasting and the difficulties of buying national campaigns on local radio stations have explained these disappointing results. However, radio's share of advertising spending is expected to grow by 2000, reflecting declining audiences for BBC radio, the emergence of national commercial radio stations, and improved sales arrangements by local stations.

Competing media – the advertiser's choice

Advertisers and agencies select media in terms of:

* audience profile and compatibility with campaign target – audience data is available in terms of standard demographic segments; these can be matched with the advertiser's target market to suggest the best opportunities;
* audience size – the larger the audience, the more rapidly will the target segment be reached; circulation and audience figures are generally available from independent sources (e.g. RAJAR for Radio, ABC for newspapers/ magazines);
* avoiding wastage – although some media offer large audiences, they may contain a high proportion of people not in the target market; advertising to those people constitutes waste;
* number of opportunities to see or hear the advertisement – an advertisement in a hobby magazine or a single poster may be read and re-read several times, while television, radio, cinema, and press offer the opportunity to repeat and vary advertisements;
* technical and creative capabilities – some media have more obvious impact than others, and their creative potential differs: for example, products that need to be shown will not be advertised on radio; some media can be bought at shorter notice than others;
* relationship of advertising to the media context – television advertisements can be booked into spots either side of, or within, programmes of interest to the target market segment (e.g. alcohol advertising during live sports coverage); press advertisements can be placed in the relevant section of a newspaper (e.g. financial services); poster sites can be bought in shopping malls, adjacent to petrol stations, etc.;
* status of the media (with audience and advertisers) – both viewers and advertisers are liable to see advertisements in terms of the status of the media in which they appear; thus, advertising in prestige media (e.g. *Country Life* magazine, or prime-time television) will reflect well on a products' pedigree or market strength;
* value for money (VFM) criteria – VFM is very subjective; it can be calculated simply on the cost of reaching 1000 audience members, but such a figure takes no account of qualitative factors (e.g. relevance to audience, attention paid to the advertising; timing in relation to buying decision; creative value of the medium etc.).

Media audience data

The selection of suitable media for advertising campaigns, and the usefulness of cost-per-thousand calculations are dependent upon the availability of accurate information about the size and make-up of the audiences for media. Information provided by media owners themselves would be suspect; less scrupulous owners have attempted to 'talk up' the size of their audience. In order that clients and agencies can be confident about the veracity of audience data, a number of industry bodies have been set up to provide impartial and objective data about media audiences. The sources of data include:

* Audit Bureau of Circulation (ABC)
* Verified Free Distribution (VFD)
* National Readership Survey (NRS)
* Radio Joint Audience Research (RAJAR)

* Broadcast Audience Research Bureau (BARB)
* Cinema and Video Industry Audience Research (CAVIAR)
* Joint Industry Council for Poster Audience Research (JICPAR).

Advertising media

Here is a thumb-nail sketch of the advantages offered by each advertising medium.

The Press

This category includes:
* national daily papers
* regional dailies
* national Sundays
* weekend colour magazines
* national weeklies
* pan-national weeklies (e.g. the *European*)
* local weeklies (free and paid-for)
* general consumer magazines (e.g. *Radio Times*)
* specialist consumer magazines (e.g. *What Car?*)
* trade, technical and business journals (e.g. *Farming News*)
* directories (e.g. *Yellow Pages*).

The advantages that press media offer to their advertisers include the following features:
* 80 per cent of adults read a daily paper (national or regional);
* 75 per cent of the population sees a free weekly paper, 40 per cent sees a paid-for weekly;
* nearly half of all women read a weekly magazine, and a similar number read a women's monthly;
* there is high audience loyalty towards valued publications;
* it is possible to achieve a close relationship between advertising and editorial material;
* some titles are highly durable (some women's titles claim to be re-read ten or more times);
* readers can dwell on relevant and interesting advertisements;
* press is suitable for complex advertising messages;
* press offers flexibility (e.g. topical issues, spilt runs, display and classified sections);
* advertising content is not restricted by statute (as is the case for cigarettes on television);
* titles used in combination, are suitable for both broad- and narrow-casting.

Activity

With others in your group, select some editions of recent newspapers and magazines. Do not tackle too many, but do aim to achieve some significant variety in the titles. Then answer the following questions:

1   What proportion of the publication is advertising, and how much is editorial? Does that influence the cover price do you think?
2   What are the relative proportions of classified to display advertising?
3   What is being advertised in the publication? Is there any relationship between the content of the advertising and that of the publication (or section within a publication)?

4   How complex are the messages in these advertisements? Is there a link between the complexity of the message and the likelihood that the purchase will be a high involving decision? (See Chapter 4 for an explanation of this term.)

Television (terrestrial, satellite and cable)

At the time of publication, BBC television stations only carried advertising for BBC products, and commercial advertisers had access only to two terrestrial television channels, and to satellite and cable television. The introduction of digital TV systems will enable householders to receive many more TV stations than at present, without subscribing to satellite or cable services. Inevitably, these stations will offer more opportunities to advertisers.

Relative audience share for stations in 1992 was:

All television	100%
BBC 1	32.6%
BBC 2	10.1%
ITV	37.1%
C4	9.6%
Television-AM*	2.4%
Satellite/cable	4.3%
VCR	4.0%

Note: *now GM-TV.
(**Source:** Advertising Association)

In 1992, television took just over 28 per cent of all advertising spend in the UK, a figure very much in line with its share over the past ten years. The lion's share of this spending is with ITV, stations in the south and east of England enjoying a disproportionate share of this revenue.

The advantages offered by television advertising are:
*   the creative potential for the fusion of pictures, symbols, movement, colour, text, music, effects and dialogue ensures advertising has a high impact on viewers;
*   classic campaigns achieve similar status to the programmes (e.g. Gold Blend 'Love over Gold' advertisements);
*   it gives access to vast audiences, and can raise awareness very quickly;
*   it gives opportunities to match advertising messages to likely audiences for programmes.

Total advertising television revenue is expected to grow, although the ITV share is predicted to fall. As the service fragments, it will become more difficult than ever to reach mass audiences, and advertisers (and media) will have to target market segments much more accurately than was true in the past.

Sponsorship

In recent years, programme sponsorship has been permitted on ITV, and is proving increasingly popular with clients.

The advantage of sponsorship is that it provides an opportunity for the product name to be seen in a high-profile and prestige context. The limitation of sponsorship, under present controls, is that it provides less of an opportunity than advertising to develop a complex brand message.

Satellite television

The growth of non-terrestrial television services has dramatically increased the amount of advertising time available on television. This is not just because there are more channels, but because up to 12 minutes per hour of commercials are permitted – almost twice as much as on ITV and Channel 4. Television beamed from satellite has grown rapidly in the UK, reaching one in seven of all homes by 1992, albeit with an audience share for all Sky channels still less than half that for Channel 4 in that year.

Cable television

Cable television had only 0.4 per cent of audience share in 1991. However, 21 major holders had established franchises in 137 geographically discreet areas of the UK.

The potential for cable is twofold. Firstly it can offer local advertisers realistic access to television as a medium, thus posing a severe challenge to local radio. Secondly, cable has the advantage of being a potentially interactive medium, which satellite does not. This could provide advertisers with exciting opportunities for direct response advertising, using a key-pad – like the present remote controls – to order goods as they are shown on the screen.

Independent radio

This medium, responsible only for 1.7 per cent of advertising expenditure in 1992, can now be divided into two distinct types:

* national commercial radio, for example, Classic FM, Virgin 1215;
* local independent radio, for example, KCBC (Kettering) Great Yorkshire Radio.

Although a major advertising medium in the USA, commercial radio has so far been disappointing in terms of its share of total advertising in the UK. The relative unimportance of radio in the UK as compared to the USA can be explained by the generally small transmission areas of local stations in the UK and the consequent difficulty, until national stations emerged, of buying truly national campaigns. There is also a far stronger challenge from public sector broadcasting than in the USA. The arrival of the first real national commercial radio stations in the early 1990s was expected to increase radio's share of national advertising spend.

The advantages that radio can offer to advertisers are:

* that advertising is perceived to be less intrusive on radio than on television, where it very obviously interrupts programmes and prompts visits to the kitchen or bathroom;
* the opportunities for frequent repetition of messages;
* the direct response potential is good, with free telephone numbers stimulating immediate results;
* the creative potential is more limited than for television, but remains good; comedy writers like Mel Smith and Griff Rhys Jones cut their teeth by writing radio advertisements;
* that most stations will create and record radio advertisements for local businesses;
* that national campaigns can be bought on local stations through sales houses.

Cinema

Although cinema as an entertainment medium has enjoyed a vigorous fight back in recent years, 58 per cent of adults still never visit a cinema (1991 figure from the Henley Centre). The audience is mainly young, and predominantly male.

The advantages offered to advertisers by cinema are:

* the unrivalled creative potential for the fusion of pictures, symbols, movement, colour, text, music, effects and dialogue, greater even than that offered by television;
* that television campaigns can be run simultaneously in the cinema with no extra production costs;
* that it gives access to younger audiences;
* the opportunities to match advertising messages to likely audiences for feature films;
* the potential to advertise products banned from television, such as tobacco products;
* that it allows more adult content for advertising than would be permitted on television.

Viewing figures depend crucially on the product – that is, the film being shown. This is also true of television, but while television can build weekly, even daily, viewing habits for top programmes, the cinema cannot.

Posters

Posters are suitable for raising awareness quickly and they are a frequent choice for new product launches. However, they are often used as a secondary medium, and thus when budgets are trimmed, this medium loses more than its share of revenue.

The medium enjoys a base load of advertising from products restricted from using other media – principally tobacco and alcohol. Unfortunately, industry estimates for outdoor revenue exclude the tobacco industry spend.

The 'top ten' product categories advertising outdoor in 1991 are shown in Table 9.3.

Table 9.3 – Outdoor advertising expenditure categories, 1991

Product	£m
Drink	32.3
Motor vehicle	21.1
Financial	12.0
Food	9.4
Publishing and broadcasting	9.2
Travel	9.0
Retail	6.8
Household	6.8
Government	6.3
Confectionery	5.8

(Source: Advertising Association)

Broadly speaking, the volume of spending on outdoor advertising is about twice that on transport sites (airports, bus sides, tube and surface rail stations).

The benefits of poster advertising are that:

* it is a mass medium (the total number of UK sites is estimated to be 106,000+, excluding transport) capable of making a rapid impact;

* the frequency of impact upon passers-by builds a cumulative effect;
* advertising can be located close to the point-of-sale (e.g. petrol advertisements near filling stations, paperback book advertisements in shopping malls, etc.);
* supersites (i.e. 96 sheet size hoardings) create startling impact;
* the advertising content is not limited by statute;
* in-bus and train advertising is seen by a captive audience.

Unfortunately, the poster industry is still generally regarded as a low-cost top-up to national campaigns. The challenge for the future is to sell the medium as a strategic solution to advertising challenges.

Activity

What limitations do posters have as a medium? What sort of campaigns are they most suitable for? Think about this for a few minutes.

DISCUSSION

The major limitations of posters are: the difficulties of communicating any but the most simple of messages; the fact that the audience is unlikely to dwell on, or return to, any particular advertisement; and the fact that, despite recent improvements in audience data, much of the communicative impact of such campaigns is wasted on those who are unlikely to be interested. Where poster advertising scores is in advertising products strictly controlled on television, and as reminder advertising for those embarking on a shopping trip.

Public relations (PR)

An important part of the communications mix is a range of activities collectively called *public relations* (PR for short). The Institute of Public Relations defines the practice as:

> 'the planned and sustained effort to establish and maintain goodwill and mutual understanding between an organisation and its publics.'

The three main types of public referred to in the definition are:
* internal publics, for example, employees and existing investors;
* external publics, for example, customers, legislators and potential shareholders;
* intermediary publics, for example, journalists.

External publics include those who already buy an organisation's products, those who might buy them in future, those who can influence the decisions of those who do buy, and those who could change the legal framework within which the organisation currently operates. This last group would include Members of both the national and European parliaments, and local councillors.

Intermediary publics are those people who are responsible for presenting and interpreting information to external publics. They include those who work in the media and in other information-processing roles in society, such as teachers. Such people will be resentful at any attempt to manipulate them. Relationships with intermediary publics, therefore, need to be developed over the long-term, and with integrity, if they are to be successful.

Activity

How does PR differ from customer care? (See Chapter 5 if you need to refresh your memory on the latter.)

Objectives for public relations

There will normally be three key objectives for PR to achieve in an organisation's end-user markets. These are:

* high levels of awareness of an organisation and its products or services;
* a favourable reputation for an organisation among its various publics;
* high levels of goodwill towards an organisation's products and activities.

The media for public relations

The various communicative media used for PR activity include:

* **press releases** – these are statements of the news, opinions and background information about issues (e.g. new product launch) that an organisation wishes to see in the news media;
* **newsletters and journals** – these are publications produced on behalf of organisations, which contain material favourable and/or complementary to the organisation's activities;
* **corporate gifts** (e.g. calendars, diaries, deskpads, etc.) – these items can be used to promote the organisation's corporate identity, by reinforcing recognition of a logo, organisation name, or campaign slogan;
* **exhibitions** (e.g. Wedgwood Visitor Centre) – while some organisations find it worthwhile to maintain permanent displays which promote a positive image of the organisation (even charging for admission in some cases), the vast majority of exhibitions are temporary and/or mobile (e.g. supporting the launch of products at a trade show);
* **video and audio-visual presentations** – these are particularly used when dealing with dealers, distributors and opinion formers;
* **educational publications** – information presented impartially can prove to be excellent PR for an organisation (e.g. DIY hints at stores, educational information for use in schools);
* **sponsorship** – the growing practice of sponsoring television programmes, will probably be handled by the advertising department; PR will aim for public goodwill by supporting a 'good cause' (e.g. an arts festival or sports event).

Activity

Which of these tactics are used by your own organisation, or by the college at which you are studying? Make a list of the PR activities they include in their communications programme. In your view, are they appropriate to their internal, external and intermediary publics?

Public relations in the communications mix

The mistaken belief that PR constitutes 'free publicity' for an organisation can be discounted by costing some of the media which are listed above. It is no longer necessarily true that when an organisation-created story appears in the press or broadcast media that it will do so free of charge; some publications now expect that an organisation will take advertising space in return for featuring a press release.

The value of PR activity is that it complements, reinforces and develops an organisation's messages to its publics. The more messages to which members of a target audience are exposed, the more likely they are to be aware of the message. The particular advantage of PR is that its manifestations look less like self-promotion than, say, advertising.

PR does have its limitations, however. In situations in which an organisation is alleged to have been guilty of malpractice or environmental damage, even the retains a positive image in the eyes of its publics. For example, McDonalds has experienced difficulty in shrugging off an unfavourable environmental image.

In other cases, the conflicting demands of different external publics are difficult to reconcile. The operators of telephone services may wish to make some of their prospective customers think that certain of their services are outrageously explicit, while seeking to reassure legislators (as guardians of public morals) that these same services are harmless fun. Can both points of view be argued concurrently, with credibility?

Case study

Crisis management

One function of an organisation's PR department is to contribute to the handling of crises that confront the organisation. All organisations face crises periodically and it is sensible to plan how they will be managed.

The crisis that faced the French-based sparkling water company Perrier was potentially disastrous. Officials in the USA detected minute traces of benzene in the product. Benzene is known to cause cancers so the product was immediately withdrawn from sale in the USA. Believing the problem to be localised to its US bottling plant, however, Perrier remained on sale in other countries.

News of the ban in the USA soon spread. Perrier came under intense official and media scrutiny in other countries, notably the UK. The delay in withdrawing the product other than in the USA became the subject of growing criticism. Eventually, when it became clear that the problem was not localised, the parent company arranged a press conference in Paris to announce a worldwide withdrawal of the product. The conference was badly organised and officials of the company appeared badly informed. In short, Perrier was facing a PR crisis.

Fortunately, the UK company, with its crisis management plan, was better prepared. Although frustrated by the parent company's decision not to make any announcement until its own press conference, the UK company arranged for a senior executive to talk individually to journalists, briefing them personally and in detail on the problem. It also arranged to set up a battery of telephones to take calls, and sent couriers to leading customers, warning them of an impending ban. Full page newspaper advertisements announced the decision and detailed arrangements for returning bottles and obtaining refunds.

Even then, the worst was not over. The source of the benzene was eventually traced to the company's carbonating plant, where the gas was added to the water to ensure consistency. This damaged the public's image of a product that had been advertised as 'naturally carbonated' leading the public to imagine it bubbling from the ground, already naturally fizzing. As a result of the contradiction between the company's production methods and its claims, the leading UK retailer of Perrier, Sainsbury's supermarket, refused to restock the item.

The relative success of Perrier in riding out this crisis – at least in the UK where it is still brand leader – is attributed to the success of its damage limitation efforts provided for in its crisis management plan. However, the company was also probably helped by a lack of surplus capacity on the part of the bottled water suppliers who could not capitalise quickly on Perrier's weakness. The important lesson for all organisations in international markets is that a problem in one national market can no longer be treated in isolation, and that refusal to act promptly when faced with a potential risk to human health will not readily be forgiven by consumers.

Activity

Assume that your college is going to change the pattern of its marketing courses from next autumn, and that you are acting as a PR consultant. Make notes for a presentation you might give to a senior manager of the college, explaining how you would expect to be involved in communicating details of the change to the appropriate publics.

DISCUSSION

Some ideas are set out in Table 9.4. Check your ideas against these.

Table 9.4 – Ideas on communicating change to an organisation's publics

Category	Public	Information-need	Media choice
Internal	Admissions/advisory staff	Changes to admissions procedures and course availability	Briefing for staff Internal newsletter
	Existing students	New opportunities	Notices External newsletter
Inter-mediary	Careers service	Changes to courses New opportunities	News release External newsletter
	Professional bodies (e.g. IPR)	(As above)	Display stand at local meeting
	Published and broadcast media	Matters of interest to audience	News release
External	Local employers	New opportunities	External newsletter and direct mail
	Prospective students	(As above)	External newsletter

Sales promotion

The task of sales promotion is to achieve direct improvements in the sales of products. It does this by offering additional value to consumers as an incentive to purchase. Those incentives might be a money-off coupon, additional quantities offered at no extra price, or a competition. The definition used by the Institute of Sales Promotion is:

> *'those marketing techniques which are used, usually on a temporary basis, to make goods or services more attractive to the consumer by offering some additional benefit, whether in cash or in kind.'*

That benefit does not have to be directly received by the consumer – a substantial number of sales promotions benefit charities instead.

Activity

Look through your larder or fridge at home. Can you find any examples of current sales promotions on the packets and bottles? Are you aware of their having influenced your decision to purchase? Do any of them benefit charities rather than the consumer?

Sales promotion in the communications mix

A sales promotion is an event in itself, and requires it to be promoted, either by advertising, direct mail, at the point-of-sale, as an on-pack offer, or any combination of these. By offering a concession or inducement to increase motivation, the consumer's attention is gained for the product. The promotion also bestows urgency, inviting the consumer to act at once or risk losing the benefit. Any decision to use one of the battery of sales promotion tactics will therefore have implications for the rest of the communications strategy. It is also often the case that a sales promotion will be planned strategically to enhance the image of a brand. For example, an instant tea brand might offer a free tea-towel bearing the brand image in return for a stipulated number of special offer wrappers. The gift is both appropriate and a permanent advertisement when in use.

Scope of sales promotion methods

Owing to the difficulties of tracking all the sales promotions being offered by organisations in the UK, it is difficult to estimate the amount spent on it each year. However, in 1987, the Advertising Association and the Institute of Sales Promotion estimated the spend to be about £2,500 million, with £1,000 million of that being non-price related promotions. That total was between one-third and one-half of the amount spent on advertising, and indicates the importance of these activities.

Types of sales promotion include:
* special offers, either to the trade or to consumers,
* trial offer (i.e. to prompt trial of a product),
* competitions,
* personality promotions (e.g. the Honey Monster, Ronald McDonald).

Perhaps the best known form of sales promotion is the coupon, offering money off the next purchase of a brand. More than 8 billion coupons were distributed in the

UK in 1991, but only 5.56 per cent were actually redeemed. Redemption rates are highest for on-pack, in-store and door-to-door distribution methods. Newspapers and magazines are the least effective media.

The advantages and disadvantages of sales promotion

The advantages are as follows:
* a sales promotion can be used to gain attention to product advertising;
* it will normally encourage increased buying – at least in the short term;
* it can be used to obtain additional shelf-space for promoted products in retail outlets during the period of the sales promotion;
* it encourages switching from competitor brands;
* complimentary products can be promoted jointly (e.g. package holidays and suntan oil);
* new technology allows coupons to be printed at point of sale to reward loyal shoppers or attack rival brands.

The disadvantages are as follows:
* malredemption – the redemption of coupons by retailers, even when the consumer has not purchased the promoted product; in effect, this is fraud;
* heavy price-cutting or other promotional activity can damage a brand's long-term image by making it seem dependent upon these activities to maintain sales;
* a short-term sales peak may be followed by a trough as consumers use up stock over-purchased during the offer period;
* a manufacturer may be faced with the return of unsold stock from retailers at the end of the promotion;
* if a promotion is not effective, the extra production may sit too long on shelves and be in a poor condition when eventually purchased, leading to consumer dissatisfaction;
* special offers are now very common, and it is getting harder to excite consumers with them.

Activity

Assume that a friend of yours who runs her own pottery has asked you to suggest how sales promotions could be used to promote her business. What advice would you give?

Use the information in the section above, and collaborate with others in your group on this activity.

Point-of-sale (POS) promotion

Sales support materials at the point at which consumers make their actual purchasing decision can help to persuade a consumer to prefer one brand to another. Even if a rival organisation's advertising has stimulated consumer interest in the product type, good POS material for a different brand may be enough to provoke a switch at point of purchase. POS materials are sometimes also called *merchandising*. Such POS (or merchandising) materials include:
* show cards
* shelf stickers

* display racks and cabinets (see Figure 9.6)
* sales literature and dispensers
* special lighting
* demonstration products
* dummy packs and products, actual- and over-size
* shop window displays
* demonstration video playback (widely used to support the sale of specialist kitchen utensils).

They may be used in conjunction with opportunities to sample a product and other sales promotion tactics.

Figure 9.6 – A point-of-sale display for Kiwi shoe care products, produced and serviced by NDI Display Ltd

Direct marketing

Of all the manifestations of contemporary marketing, none features more large in popular demonology than direct marketing. Sadly, the unscrupulous and indiscriminate use of direct selling techniques by some practitioners – particularly in the use of confidential information culled from databases, intrusive forms of telemarketing, and badly targeted mailshots – have earned the industry a reputation which it is still struggling to shrug off.

Direct marketing is a method of both promotion and selling – and can therefore claim to be part of an organisation's distribution system. The key characteristic is that the distributor – whether manufacturer or retailer – deals directly with the consumer at home, either by post, telephone or electronic data exchange. It should therefore be seen to be an alternative to, and complementary with, those methods described above which involve either:

* the consumer visiting the seller (e.g. a shopping trip), or
* the seller visiting the consumer (e.g. a domestic milk delivery).

Definition of direct marketing

Direct marketing has been defined by the Institute of Direct Marketing as:

> *an interactive system of communication between distributor and consumer, which uses one or more media to effect a transaction or other measurable response.*

Although it is tempting to see direct marketing purely as a means of selling, other measurable responses are also valid, as you will see later.

The major categories of direct marketing are:
* direct mail
* mail order
* telephone marketing
* direct response advertising, and
* developing media (television shopping channels, computer networks),

each of which is dealt with in more detail later. Confusingly, some marketing textbooks also list such methods as party selling (as used by Tupperware), door-to-door sales and factory shops as direct marketing methods because they involve no intermediaries, other than the salesperson or agent, who are working on behalf of the distributor. However, the real defining characteristic of direct marketing is the absence of face-to-face contact between buyer and seller, and the use of intermediary media – mail, telephone and advertising – for promotion and order-taking.

The advantages and disadvantages of direct marketing

Advocates of direct marketing can point to some strong arguments in its favour. These include:
* greater accuracy in targeting consumers;
* being a more powerful communication medium, because it is personalised, relevant and solus (i.e. not competing simultaneously with other advertising messages);
* timing can be controlled to maximise impact;
* all outcomes are precisely measurable;
* provides more opportunities for feedback from consumers thus improving subsequent marketing activity;
* competitors are less aware of activity (than in established or broadcast media, or intermediary channels).

However, there are disadvantages. These are:
* public cynicism about 'junk mail',
* the view of consumers that telemarketing in particular is highly intrusive,
* higher initial costs than for traditional advertising methods.

All the evidence shows that the advocates of direct marketing are winning the argument in organisation boardrooms. There are a number of good reasons for this. First, direct marketing offers a way of dealing with the demassification of markets, a problem identified in Chapter 3. Secondly, it helps organisations with the problem of media fragmentation, which is paralleling demassification, by providing more cost-effective ways of reaching prospects. Thirdly it is, as we have seen already, an additional channel which many organisations use to complement existing ones. Finally, the increasing capabilities and decreasing cost of computer hardware and software to establish direct links with consumers, provide organisations with compelling logic for embracing the direct approach.

The uses of direct marketing

The definition of direct marketing did not specify a sale as the necessary outcome of direct marketing activity, but simply a 'measurable response'. The responses that direct marketing can help to achieve include:

* direct sales to consumers (e.g. by telephone or mail order);
* other marketing objectives (e.g. increased awareness, brand repositioning, attention to traditional advertising, etc.);
* appointments for salespeople – the high cost of salespeople's time has led organisations to use direct marketing techniques to secure leads which salespeople can then attempt to convert into deals; this can apply equally to consumer and business-to-business markets, to double glazing as much as to automotive components;
* fund-raising – charities and political parties are big users; a parish church in an affluent commuter dormitory village recently raised all the cash it needed for roof repairs in one short direct marketing campaign;
* consumer loyalty and feedback – although not all communications may seek to secure a sales response, they can be used to create a bond between the consumer and the organisation; for example, follow-up telephone calls after purchase to check that consumers are completely satisfied; newsletters to members of clubs run by manufacturers of collectables (e.g. cottage-modeller Lilliput Lane has 60,000 in its owners' club), and market research questionnaires, should all feature in communication programmes.

Activity

A leisure centre offering bowling and laser battle-gaming is about to open near your college. How would you expect it to use direct marketing to develop its business?
Note down your ideas in your note-book.

DISCUSSION

Presumably the leisure centre has already analysed the local neighbourhood in terms of ACORN or similar geo-demographic categories (see Chapter 3). This will have identified the postcode areas with high concentrations of families with older children and young adults – likely targets for a direct mailshot or leaflet drop for an introductory offer, particularly for membership of the centre.

Mailshots to local places of employment could be used to encourage corporate customers for so-called team-building, or out-of-work social activities.

Once people use the centre, the capturing of names and addresses of users makes possible targeted mailings based on known interest and propensity to purchase. Those people who become members can then be the subject of loyalty mailshots to secure long-term interest in the centre and its activities.

Direct mail

This is a method of selling in which the offer, or offer and order, are facilitated by post. It is big business in the UK. In 1990, direct mail generated £7 billion worth of business and accounted for about 11 per cent of total advertising expenditure. It is claimed that charities collect more than £100 million each year in this way.

Figures produced by the Royal Mail (also for 1990) claimed that:

* 80 per cent of direct mail is initially opened;
* 61 per cent of direct mail is opened and read;
* 19 per cent of direct mail is discarded, with only a cursory glance at headlines
* an average UK household receives six items of direct mail each month;
* the UK is ninth in the European league on the basis of mailings per household (Switzerland is top).

Much criticism is levelled at this method, which is popularly described as 'junk mail'. The trade prefers 'unsolicited advertising material, not wanted by the recipients', on the basis that such direct mail is badly targeted, and therefore, is a waste of time and effort. However, the use of the term 'junk mail' by people depends upon the nature of the mailing; if it contains an offer of interest to the consumer, then it may, in fact, be very welcome.

Mail order

Mail order also uses the postal system. Some of the major users of mail order are the home-shopping catalogues, such as Littlewoods, Great Universal Stores and Grattan. Charities also use mailed-out catalogues to generate revenue from sales often of merchandise reflecting the charity's aims. Oxfam, for example, sells many Third World products this way. The best-selling mail order items of the 1990s, according to catalogue owners Scotts of Stow (quoted in *Marketing Week*) are:

* 'sensitive' purchases for personal use (e.g. health products, marital aids, outsized clothing, surveillance equipment);
* high-involving purchases requiring explanation and advice which shop assistants may be unable to provide;
* novelty goods and gifts (e.g. Italian Water Sandals or Pink Pig Phones).

However, mail order is now a questionable term for this medium, as many orders are actually taken by telephone with consumers quoting their credit card number for payment.

Telemarketing

The use of the telephone in direct marketing has grown dramatically in recent years and seems certain to grow further. There are two forms of telephone marketing (telemarketing for short): in-bound and out-bound.

In-bound telemarketing

In-bound telemarketing is essentially an order-taking process, with calls initiated by customers. *Out-bound telemarketing* is initiated by the organisation itself, and may occur for a variety of reasons – not necessarily for immediate sales.

In-bound telemarketing is popular with consumers, who like the convenience offers. Consumers can buy from home without completing challenging order forms, and know that the ordering process is quicker than by post. The widespread use of credit cards, computerised stock-control and customer-record systems, and the introduction of freephone numbers (beginning 0800) have made possible its rapid growth. Television telethons, in which millions of pounds are pledged over the telephone for charitable work within a few hours of viewing, indicate the volumes of business that can be handled over the telephone. The growth of television shopping channels, which put the contents of the catalogues onto the small screen, coupled with touch-pad ordering systems, offer scope for enormous further growth.

Out-bound telemarketing

Outbound telemarketing is more controversial. These are calls initiated by businesses – not consumers. Great care is needed if they are not to prove counter-productive. All telephone calls represent an interruption to someone else; people who are genuinely waiting for the telephone to ring are not hoping it will be the Crystotherm Double Glazing Company! So cold-calling is to be avoided, except in circumstances in which the organisation has an exceptionally carefully selected list of prospects, and a highly relevant offer to put to them.

Consequently, out-bound telemarketing is mainly used for:

* contacting regular customers for repeat business,
* responding to an enquiry,
* upgrading an order already received,
* offering a new product to an existing customer,
* courtesy calls to re-activate former customers.

For calls of this type, there is an important need for some form of scripting to help the caller in dealing with respondents. Fortunately, reactions to particular offers made during out-bound telemarketing are reasonably predictable, and this makes it possible to draw up a list of responses to a prospect's objections, delaying tactics and procrastination. Using a script prepared in advance makes it possible for relatively untrained and inexperienced people to make a success of telemarketing, because they follow a logical sequence of arguments through to the point where they hope to persuade their prospect to act. Even when this desired objective is not attained, telesales people are urged to end conversations in a polite and friendly fashion, in order that the prospect is not lost to the organisation forever.

Direct response advertising

The other media used for direct marketing are those which also carry general consumer or business-to-business advertising. However, press, television, and radio, are used far more than posters, and cinema. This is because direct response advertising requires audiences to be able respond easily, so a hoarding seen on the way to work, or a commercial screened at the pictures will have been forgotten by the time home is reached.

The difference between direct response and general consumer advertising lies in the measurability of the response. Whereas with most advertising it is necessary to infer the response rate, direct response advertising allows very precise measurement of its achievements.

The usual methods of obtaining response are to include coupons in the copy of a press advertisement, or to give a freephone reply number. Although some advertising does attempt immediate sales in this way (known as selling 'off-the-page'), rather more of it is designed to get prospects to announce themselves, so that they can then receive directly mailed details of a particular offer. Purchase may not be expected to occur until the second or third mailing if the products concerned require high-involving purchase decision-making.

Activity

Find your own examples of direct response advertising in Sunday newspapers. Why types of product are advertised there? What inducements are offered to respond? How do advertisers make a positive response from readers more likely to occur?

DISCUSSION

You have probably found advertising for products or services which are:
* novelty goods
* sensitive purchases
* high-involving decisions (e.g. financial services, holiday resorts).

Special offers or discounts are used to prompt reply, the freephone numbers and payment by credit card are offered to make response easier for the consumer.

Developing media

Other direct response media include television shopping channels and computer networks. Neither of these is advertising in the narrow sense of the term. The content of shopping channels is a continuous sales pitch for consumer goods, and is really the logical development of the mail order catalogue, except that now the home-shopper can see the products in use. The first such channel in the UK was QVC (Quality, Value and Convenience), which began transmission on the Astra satellite in 1993. Although panned by the critics, its backers expect it to make significant inroads into high street shopping.

Computer shopping also has a bright future, but in the early 1990s was limited to bulletin board systems on subscription to the Computer Information Exchange (CIX) or Compuserve networks. These are accessible only to those people with a modem, and mostly offer sales of computer equipment, albeit with some travel bookings and traditional mail order, too. Bulletin boards are interactive, so shoppers can leave messages, endorsing or condemning the deals on offer. Rip-off merchants, beware!

Comparisons of media cost and effectiveness

As we have already seen, different media offer differing characteristics of audience reach, creative potential and response rates. Research carried out by The Institute of Direct Marketing has produced the comparisons shown in Table 9.5.

Activity

Look at Table 9.5. What do you notice about the relationship between the cost per thousand (CPT) figure and audience size, and the CPT figure and message complexity? Is this significant?

DISCUSSION

There is an inverted relationship between audience size and cost per thousand. Television can be a spectacularly expensive medium if advertisers want prime-time spots across all the regional stations, but when the vast audiences delivered by television are taken into account, the CPT figure puts the cost of such advertising into perspective. This begs the question, however, of whether those thousands of audience members are the ones that the advertiser wishes to reach.

Table 9.5 – Comparison of media for direct marketing purposes

| | | Comparison of media | | |
Category	Media in Category	Audience Sizes	Approx Cost per thousand	Complexity of selling message possible
Broadcast	TV Teletext Radio	Mass Local	Low 50p-£1.00	Limited
Published	Press Magazines Inserts	National Groups Identified Groups	Increasing £50 £100 £150	Increasing More space Available
Controlled	Door-to-Door Mail Telephone	Individuals within neigbourhood Individuals Highly personal	£250 £500 £5,000	Maximum information content Decreased info but interactive

(Source: Direct Marketing Foundation)

Direct marketing costs much more than general consumer media to reach one thousand audience members. However, it is important not to judge direct marketing on the basis of a crude CPT comparison with other media. Remember that direct approaches to individual consumers enable messages to be targeted with remarkable accuracy, ensuring that the promotion goes only to those people most likely to be interested in the content of the message. This alone should be enough to call into question the usefulness of CPT comparisons in evaluating direct marketing.

Direct media also deliver advertising messages and selling opportunities to potential consumers 'in the comfort of their own homes'. Responses are easy; mostly the consumer simply makes a telephone call. When direct channels are used, the messages have minimal competition for the consumer's attention from other advertising, the timing can be very precisely controlled, and competitors will be less aware of the campaign. Arguably, however, the most critical analysis of media performance is the amount of response it generates. In general consumer advertising, it is often difficult to ascribe campaign results with absolute certainty to the advertising, because other factors may have been at work in any measured change, whether that is improved sales or increased awareness of a product on the part of the target market. With direct marketing, however, competing media can be more precisely assessed for their effectiveness by measuring the exact level of response that they stimulate (see Table 9.6 overleaf). Here the measure is not the cost of reaching one thousand members of the audience, but the cost of getting just one of them to respond in the desired manner (e.g. by asking for details, or making a purchase).

It must be realised that these costs are illustrative of one particular campaign only, and are dependent upon its creative characteristics too, so they should not be seen to be universally applicable statistics for the comparison of media effectiveness. You may also notice that the final option is for the use of direct mail

Table 9.6 – Comparisons of response rate by media in a multi-media campaign

Media	Volume	Cost per '000	Total Cost	Likely Resp %	No of Responses	Cost per Lead	Rank
Press Advertising	300,000	£50	£7,000	0.025%	75	£94	4
Inserts	25,000	£250	£6,250	0.25%	63	£100	5
Telephone Marketing (outbound)	5,000	£6,500	£32,500	10%	500	£65	3
Direct Mail	15,000	£500	£7,500	1%	150	£50	2
Direct Mail Telephone Follow–up	5,000	£7,000	£35,000	15%	750	£47	1

(Source: Direct Marketing Foundation)

with out-bound telephone follow-up. This seems to be the most effective method with a cost per lead of £47, but it also requires total expenditure of £35,000 to reach just 5000 people.

The importance of a database

'The most wonderful mailing on earth will die if it goes out to the wrong names. The worst mailing on earth can sometimes succeed if it goes to the right list.'

This quotation from Drayton Bird emphasises the importance of having an up-to-date and relevant list of names for direct mail or telemarketing – names which may perhaps be gathered from direct response advertising, from an organisation's own records, or from segmented lists of suspects, hired from list agencies. The names, with addresses, telephone and fax numbers, are the core of any organisation's database. However, a database ought to be much more than just a list of contacts. A *direct marketing database* can be defined as:

'an integrated series of informative records, capable of rapid interrogation, retrieval, updating and synthesis, which can be used to develop mutually beneficial long-term relationships with customers and add to their numbers'.

Those records would contain details of the consumer's previous response history (how often, how recently, how much is spent and on what), together with standard market research categorisations and any self-disclosed information. Figure 9.7 lists the data that will typically be held about domestic customers. Such records will be similar to those kept by salespeople about their client and prospect organisations.

The development of personal computer technology has meant that such databases no longer need to be held on expensive mainframe machines, from which information retrieval might be slow and expensive. The application of

* Personal identification number (PIN)
* Customer's name, address and telephone number
* Sex
* Date of birth and current chronological age
* How acquired (e.g. from list rental)
* Occupation or income (if known)
* Psychographic, life cycle and demographic categories
* Previous offers made
* Response history
* Complaints received

Figure 9.7 – Typical customer database information categories

modern computer technology at last makes it possible to apply very precisely the vast quantity of research data available to ensure that offers are sent to precisely those people most likely to respond. Not only are computerised databases cheap and quick to use but the development of neural networks means that computers can be programmed to make their own decisions about which messages should be communicated to which prospects, without human intervention. In short, computerised databases should ensure that the right message is sent to the right people at the right time and in the right way – with the right result.

Targeting for direct marketing

There are two options in targeting a mailshot or telemarketing campaign:
* **Geographic targeting** based on geo-demographic data to select concentrations of likely prospects. This is superficially cheaper than individual targeting (see below), but resources are wasted sending material to some people who are unlikely to buy, while good prospects in areas outside those targeted are missed.
* **Individual targeting** requires more data in order that likely prospects can be selected on a scoring system. The criteria chosen for scoring will vary depending upon the nature of the product or service, but known interest in the product type and previous purchasing behaviour by mail order or telesales will feature in the formula.

Activity

Using the information above, summarise the pros and cons of using geographic and individual targeting for fund raising for a national animal rescue charity.

Salesforce activity

One of the major players in communication with customers can be the sales man or woman. In retailing, personal selling is confined to the purchase of durable or speciality goods – new cars and perfume, for example – where advice and assistance is needed by customers in making their purchases. In most other outlets, consumers are left to their own devices.

The importance of personal selling

Personal selling retains its critical importance in business-to-business marketing, and in getting manufacturers' products into retail outlets in the first place. There are a number of reasons for the survival of personal selling in these markets:

* manufacturers are anxious to secure appropriate outlets for their products (depending on their network focus, see page 154), and to develop good relationships with retailers; the salesforce is vital in achieving this;
* manufacturers also need to develop relationships with buyers in business-to-business markets; the combination of a knowledgeable, trustworthy salesperson backed by good quality, delivery and price is unbeatable;
* negotiations over pricing, delivery and specification are much more likely in business-to-business marketing where customers may have special requirements;
* many of the products, materials or services sold in these markets need to be handled by customers or demonstrated; there are no equivalents of the retail store where consumers can do this, so the salesperson's visit provides this opportunity.

Field sales operations

There are two types of sales staff: those who travel to represent an organisation – *field sales staff* – and those who take orders at the organisation's premises by post, telephone or in person, raise invoices and order new stock. Most organisations have both. A minority of the field sales staff still see themselves principally as order-takers, and rely on a senior manager to represent the organisation in dealings with any new potential client. This is a fairly passive attitude, and dangerous in markets characterised by extreme volatility and shifting loyalties.

Field sales staff may be directly employed by the organisation that they represent, or they may be agents, operating on behalf of a number of complementary organisations. Sales agents are suitable for organisations who have not developed the need for a full salesforce, or who want to 'top up' their sales activities – for example when launching a new product, or in an overseas market.

Agents are only paid for what they achieve, and because they are likely to handle a number of clients, will have useful contacts with potential customers, and can be a source of market advice. The drawback with using agents lies in possible conflicts of interest with other clients, and in that they will not owe allegiance wholly to the organisation, unlike a member of an in-house sales team.

Activity

Lammermoor Fashions in Edinburgh has formerly been a contract garment maker, cutting, making and trimming clothes to designs specified by chain retailers. Now, the (fictitious) company plans to launch its own collection of women's fashions, for sale through independent shops and department stores throughout the UK. Having in the past concentrated exclusively on contract garment making, Lammermoor has no salesforce. How should it now handle the selling of the collection to retailers – by employing its own salesperson(s) or using agents?

DISCUSSION

As this is a new venture for Lammermoor, the safest route would seem to be the use of agents. That way, if the collection fails to make an impact, the company's selling costs at least will be negligible. In addition, they will be able to draw on the experience of the people whom they recruit to act as agents, in breaking in to a market with which they are unfamiliar. Trying to cover the whole country with an embryonic salesforce would also be a daunting prospect.

The role of sales

What does the sales function involve? To begin with there is the task of creative selling – that is communicating the benefits of a product to potential consumers. However, there is also a wider role as organisation representatives; the salesperson is often the only personal contact between an organisation and its clients or prospects. He or she has therefore the potential to develop considerable goodwill – perhaps by providing merchandising support to a retailer, recommending best-selling lines, or by offering technical advice to clients on how to install or use their new piece of equipment. The sales department in an emergency may sometimes have responsibility for panic deliveries.

Role of the sales manager

Crucial to effective sales is the role of the sales manager. He or she will be responsible to the Marketing Manager for sales performance, supervise the field sales team and the sales office, and liaise with other departments to ensure that sales are pulling in the same direction as everyone else. For example, forthcoming advertising campaigns need to be notified to the sales team in order that it can give special emphasis to this when making calls and presentations. Production schedules will affect the length of time customers will have to wait for their orders, and salespeople need to know about these in order not to promise unachievable delivery dates. Equally, marketing needs to know what sales are being told by customers; in particular about the organisation's own and its competitors' products and promotions.

The sales manager will have a number of specific tasks to perform in managing the salesforce. These are:

* **To determine sales force size** – a number of factors will shape the actual size of the field sales force:
  - financial constraints,
  - the number of customers, actual and potential,
  - the geographical area to be covered,
  - time taken to make calls (five calls a day is a good average),
  - the frequency of calls; this will be influenced by the value of the business obtained during visits;
  - the need for face-to-face contact (i.e. is telemarketing an alternative?).
* **To allocate work** – the organisation of a salesforce can be based on any combination of the following elements:
  - geographic area (this is common, particularly where the organisation's products sell nationwide),
  - products or product groups (in such cases salespeople specialise in a single brand, or group of brands, either because they are dealing with complex technical products, or because the market is so volatile that the salesperson is a market-specialist, for example, in detergents),
  - customers (this occurs when a salesperson deals only with one or a limited number of clients because of their importance in terms of sales volume; known as *key account management*).

        * **To support the salesforce** – It is not just the salesperson's time, travel and expenses that make salesforce activity expensive. Think of all the support materials that are needed, for example:
  - sales brochures and price lists
  - samples
  - give-aways
  - demonstration aids
  - merchandising
  - order pads and other stationery items
  - lap-top computers
  - mobile telephones
  - company cars.

        * **To motivate the salesforce** – It is important to motivate salespeople in order to raise performance still higher, and to encourage identification with the organisation (sales staff are popularly believed to be rootless). This can be done by:
  - good supervision (i.e. being interested in, encouraging and supportive of salespeople),
  - responding to salesforce feedback – often an early indicator of a change in the market,
  - target setting: arbitrary targets are usually of short-term benefit, but mutually agreed ones considerably enhance the effect of targets,
  - gradual promotion: to increase self-esteem,
  - financial reward: 'salary only' is less effective than 'salary plus commission'; 'commission only' may keep people on their toes, but can lead to rapid staff turnover.

        * **To recruit, develop and appraise sales staff** – This covers:
  - the selection of new staff
  - regular briefings and staff training sessions
  - performance appraisal: quantitatively (e.g. sales volume, number of calls) and qualitatively (e.g. supervisor and self-evaluation of sales skills, customer feedback).

Role of sales representatives

Any member of the organisation's salesforce has a wide range of tasks, which extend well beyond representing the organisation and 'showing the line'.

Activity

Must a salesperson be born to sell, or can he or she be trained to do it? Is having the 'gift of the gab' the most important feature of a salesman or woman? Or is there more to it than that?

DISCUSSION

To begin with, I think most people would agree that a good sales person must be a good communicator. That does not simply mean having a disarming and persuasive manner when it comes to pitching for new business, negotiating on price and delivery, and closing the deal. It also means being open to feedback from customers, taking their complaints seriously, listening to their requirements, and reporting back to the organisation. A salesperson can be a valuable source of news to a customer about his or her competitors and, with luck, the customer will return the favour.

Communication skills cannot exist in a vacuum, however. The effective salesperson is well briefed with thorough product and market knowledge, information about the client and about their own markets. Most writers on selling agree that good organisation is the key to sales effectiveness. That means sales staff need to keep good records, logging a customer's past purchases, further opportunities for sales hinted at by customers, and plans for expansion, as well as personal information such as customers' preferred names, hobbies, interests, and the best days and times to call. Finally, sales staff need to prospect for potential clients by following up leads provided by the organisation, or on their own initiative.

Activity

Assume that Astro Software – a small software house specialising in computer packages particularly for small businesses – is to appoint its first sales executive, and that your group is to advise the company on the appointment.

Draw up in outline a specification for the job, together with suggestions about the kind of person that Astro should seek to appoint.

Assignment 9

Zydeco Ltd – 'gums' the word

Scenario

Assume that you work in the marketing department of Zydeco Ltd, a company based in Wigan, which manufactures sweets mainly for sale as own-brand counter lines in chain stores.

The company has recently been developing its own branded chewing gum, which it plans to test market in the North West of England for six months prior to a national launch.

The product will be marketed as a low-sugar gum, aimed at helping people to avoid the temptation of eating between meals. The main target market segment will be B, C1 and C2 women aged 15–34 who are health-, weight- and figure-conscious.

YOUR TASKS

1 At next week's meeting of the Product Working Party you must present broad outline proposals showing how the communication elements of the campaign for the six month test in the North West might be integrated. You should cover communication with both the trade and consumers.

Your proposals for the use of particular elements of the communications mix – advertising, sales promotion, direct marketing, public relations, salesforce activity – should indicate what each element will be expected to achieve, its suitability for the task, and how it would inter-relate with other elements in the collective task.

You need not produce creative ideas, except where you wish to illustrate the materials that you would expect the campaign to include.

2 As yet, no agencies have been appointed to work on the campaign, and you are expected to recommend whether Zydeco should use one agency for the whole campaign, or employ specialists for each discipline. You should recommend the steps Zydeco should take to appoint such agencies.

3 As Zydeco's existing sales department is mainly concerned with dealing with own-brand purchasing departments at chain retailers, you must also suggest how the company can reach CTN (confectionery, tobacco and news), leisure and catering outlets in the North West.

CHAPTER 10

Ethical and legal controls for marketing

Buyer beware!

Parting consumers from their loose change

Do you remember that right at the beginning of this book, you encountered the idea that some aspects of marketing were rather seedy? That it was, in the words of Anthony Pye Jeary, 'done by spivs'?

Such views have a long pedigree. In an early study of marketing, the esteemed US writer, Theodore Levitt, referred to marketing, only half jokingly, as 'the devious art of separating the unwary customer from his loose change'. Such opinions are based upon an element of truth. It would be either dishonest or naive to assert that businesspeople always seek to make profits only from the satisfaction of legitimate wants or needs, in an open and fair manner. History has been littered with charlatans and rogues, who have done quite the opposite.

It is only comparatively recently that the guiding principle in developed economies has changed from *caveat emptor* – let the buyer beware – to *caveat vendidor* – let the seller beware – the consequences of devious trading.

Businesses also suffer at the hands of unscrupulous rivals. There is a saying – 'All is fair in love and war' – and there is plenty of evidence that some people think it applies to business, too. Recent years have seen allegations of industrial espionage, ranging from dustbin emptying, 'bugging' rivals' premises with electronic surveillance equipment, 'hacking' into competitors' computers, and bribing competitors' employees, to planting a spy in another business. Such conduct emphasises the value that is placed on advance information, particularly in pricing, branding, new product and takeover planning.

Intimidation is not unknown either, whether it is applied to another organisation, to suppliers or even to consumers. Bribery has also been used, particularly in securing lucrative contracts from big corporations and governments. In Italy, and in Russia since the collapse of Communism, kickbacks and backhanders to 'fixers' had become an inescapable part of doing business in those countries.

Breaking the rules

What motivates businesses to transgress moral and even legal codes in doing business?

* **Highly competitive markets** – organisations which operate in fiercely competitive markets and lack genuine competitive advantages over rivals, may be tempted to cross the boundary of ethical conduct.

* **Industry standards** – where unethical conduct becomes the norm in a market, businesses may be forced to lower their ethical standards in order to survive.
* **High expectations** – where organisations or employees find that higher performance levels are constantly demanded of them, reducing ethical standards is one way in which this might be achieved. The practice of using 'bottom line', or outcome criteria, rather than asking questions about how results have been achieved, encourages deviant conduct by managers.
* **Expediency** – in circumstances in which organisations can avoid confronting the outcomes of their lack of ethics, it is easier to behave improperly; for example, where there is little repeat business, or where there is little chance of detection.

Unfortunately, the scoundrels who sacrifice long-term rewards for a short-term gain, have often damaged not only their own interests, but those of all businesses in general. Their own economic sector has often been particularly affected, both by the damage caused to the public's confidence, and the imposition of tighter legal controls.

Ethics in business

Ethics may be defined as self-imposed behavioural standards, based upon generally understood concepts of right and wrong embedded in contemporary social mores. Ethics in business are as important as they are in our private lives. Without trust between buyers and sellers, commerce would be impossible.

Increasingly, organisations are defining the ethical standards that they set themselves. A *Financial Times* article (dated 17 September 1993), estimated that 'one-third of large UK companies and four-fifths of their US counterparts now have codes of ethics'. Sometimes, they are adopted only after a scandal, when allegations of improper conduct reported in the media has had a damaging effect upon:

* staff morale,
* relationships with the public in general, and consumers in particular, and
* shareholders' confidence in top management.

Activity

Whether as individual consumers, citizens of a democratic society, or managers of thriving businesses, we all benefit from integrity in commercial transactions. However, our motives for seeking such integrity will differ, depending upon our standpoint. For example, the consumer wants honesty in advertising messages in order to avoid being duped. Advertisers, meanwhile, ought to be equally keen to ensure such standards, in order to maintain consumer confidence in the integrity of advertising messages in general.

List the reasons why:

a   consumers,
b   society, and
c   businesses,

all benefit when high standards of business ethics are achieved.

DISCUSSION

Buyers benefit from high standards of business ethics in circumstances in which

* products are safe to use;

* products are fit for the purpose for which they are sold, and will last for an acceptable length of time;
* products meet the claims made for them in advertising or on the pack;
* prices are not raised unfairly, simply to exploit short-term shortages;
* transactions are open and above-board, without hidden obligations or surprise extra costs.

Society benefits from high standards of business ethics, in circumstances in which:

* goods and services do not cause either pollution, the depletion of non-renewable resources in their production, unnecessary suffering to animals, or workpeople to be exploited;
* goods and services are not environmentally harmful in their use or disposal;
* goods and services are at least neutral, or positively beneficial in their social effect (this explains why there are controls on the sale of drugs, hand guns, and violent or depraved videos);
* advertising does not disparage people on the grounds of disability, race, gender, or age;
* sellers do not make use of consumers' personal data obtained or stored without consent.

Businesses benefit from high standards of business ethics in circumstances in which:

* fair competition can occur, unhampered by cartels, monopolies, or market distortions caused by devious rivals;
* rivals are prevented from copying product ideas which have been the subject of expensive research;
* consumers trust the claims that are made on behalf of goods and services being offered;
* there are high levels of public, employee and shareholder confidence in an organisation;
* there is minimal need for interference in their operations by governments.

How can high ethical standards be achieved?

The attainment and maintenance of good ethical standards, however desirable, cannot be guaranteed to occur spontaneously. What controls can be exercised over markets to encourage the development of high standards? Each of the following groups can exercise some influence:

* **Consumers** – either individually, or collectively, can put pressure on businesses to change their behaviour by avoiding purchases of goods or services which do not meet ethical standards. It is unlikely that a small number of individual consumers will make much difference, but the situation can be very different if consumers' behaviour is orchestrated through the mass media.
* **Businesses** – either individually, or acting in agreement, can influence ethical standards in a particular sector. For example, an individual organisation may create its own customer charter, or organisations may act through their trade associations to establish codes of conduct, relying upon media exposure to pressurise non-complying members to come into line.
* **Employees** – acting either individually, or collectively through their trade unions, can influence the ethical standards of the businesses in which they

work. However, there may be pressure, either from peers, or from the organisation, not to 'rock the boat'. In extreme cases, some employees have resorted to 'whistleblowing' – that is revealing unethical practice to a regulatory body or to the media. Such action requires great courage, as many who have done this have suffered dismissal.

* **Government** – acting on behalf of society, consumers and businesses, can and has intervened to correct abuses where market forces, and the efforts of consumers and businesses, have failed to achieve the desired outcome. This intervention may be indirect, for example, by exhorting organisations to clean up their act (and threatening legislation if they fail to do so), or it may be direct, through passing laws to restrict improper conduct, (e.g. The Property Mis-Descriptions Act to control abuses by estate agents in describing the houses and flats they sell). However, some legislation can be genuinely liberalising (e.g. the opening up of domestic air routes in Europe to competition, as a result of an EC directive).

Activity

Assume that you work for an engineering company. You are aware that the liquid waste from one of its processes, which is mildly toxic, is being illegally disposed of in a stream which runs through the industrial estate. The company is in a weak trading position, and this process is important to the its cash flow. Would you be a 'whistleblower'? Discus this with others in your group.

Self-regulation in marketing

In most circumstances in which alleged abuses might damage public or business confidence, industries usually prefer to control those abuses by self-regulation, rather than having to live under a regulatory system policed by a public authority, and backed up legal controls. However, self-regulatory systems are not always effective (e.g. the behaviour of the tabloid press in the UK).

Activity

The reasons for industry's enthusiasm for self-regulation are not difficult to discern. What do you think they are? Jot down your answers before comparing them with the suggestions below.

DISCUSSION

Most industries prefer self-regulation because they feel that keeps the process 'in the family', with the industry able to gain public confidence by being seen to put its own house in order. There is also a fear in most industries that if they lose their regulatory function to the government, the regime that politicians would impose would be a great deal tougher than any that is likely to be dreamed up within the industry.

The other advantages that are claimed for self-regulation include:
* it is done by the trade (i.e. poachers turned game-keepers) and that this increases the likelihood that dubious practices will be identified and tackled;
* it is easier to change codes of practice than it is to amend Acts of Parliament, so that new abuses can be tackled quickly, without waiting for legislation to catch up;

* the process is both a cheaper and more accessible process than turning to the courts (civil or criminal) for remedies;
* self-regulatory codes of practice require observance of the spirit, not just the letter of the regulations, and require less exacting standards of proof, making it less likely that abuses will slip through the net;
* it engenders a spirit of consensus; through discussion of ethical standards and the need for co-operation in penalising those who transgress, agreement is more likely to be reached on what the ethical standard should be;
* it preserves basic freedoms, by reducing the need for the state to enact statutes which, once introduced, might then be extended to further restrict freedom of expression or trade.

Activity

Are there any disadvantages to reliance upon self-regulation as a means of controlling unethical conduct? Note down your ideas and compare them with the following suggestions.

DISCUSSION

The problem with self-regulation is that it may have limited effect. Not only is it difficult for self-regulators to impose punishments upon the guilty (who may be influential businesses within the industry), it may also be difficult to secure any compensation for those who have suffered as a result of the abuse. Such schemes are voluntary, and therefore organisations may refuse to be bound by any decision of the self-regulatory body. Although the existence of voluntary codes does not preclude anyone from seeking redress through the courts, that process may be delayed while a settlement is sought initially through a self-regulatory system.

In addition, abuses which work in the interests of those who make up the self-regulatory bodies may not be subject to effective control in this way. When the judge and jury consists of others who are prone to behave in a similar way, they may be more lenient. This allegation has been made against the self-regulatory system for maintaining standards of propriety in the press.

However, there are more philosophical questions, particularly surrounding controls over the advertising industry. Those who argue for self-regulation of advertising on the grounds that statutory controls restrict freedom of speech, need to remember that advertising is undertaken in our society largely by major corporations with sophisticated marketing communications strategies and a vested interest in promoting their goods and services with the minimum of external control. Some of these products and services are the subject of considerable public disquiet, for example, tobacco and alcohol. Is self-regulation ever likely to be taken to the point at which one of these products might fail as a consequence?

Advertising has also helped to create very powerful organisations, ownership of which is concentrated in a small sector of the population. Its existence has had a profound influence upon the very structure of the media, upon other forms of communication – including political dialogue – and has even influenced the process of socialisation. So central is advertising to developed economies that social policy must inevitably deal with questions about the role of advertising to an extent that self-regulators are unlikely to contemplate.

Control of markets by non-statutory bodies

As we have seen, control of markets is achieved indirectly through pressure by consumers, individually or in groups, or through the exposure of improper business conduct to public scrutiny through the mass media. More direct control of business ethics may be achieved by adherence to individual organisation codes of ethics, or to those established by the industry. It is examples of these latter controls – over advertising, sales promotion and direct marketing, and marketing research – which are the subject of the next part of this chapter.

Control of advertising

During the nineteenth and early twentieth centuries, advertisers operated in a spirit of *caveat emptor*, but so flagrant were some advertisers' claims that pressure grew for controls, particularly after the formation in 1898, of the Society for the Control of Abuses in Public Advertising (SCAPA). The growth first of printed, then broadcast, and more recently of electronic media, has undoubtedly created a greater potential for abuse, particularly of those people in society (e.g. children), who are arguably most vulnerable to exaggerated claims.

The advertising industry as whole has long recognised the need for some form of control; without it, the value of advertising may be reduced by public scepticism and cynicism. However, as the noted writer on advertising Frank Jefkins has pointed out, present day controls are based not on the idea that advertising as an activity is intrinsically evil, but on a recognition that it might be used for improper ends.

The Advertising Standards Authority (ASA)

One of the major controls is the Advertising Standards Authority (ASA). This was established voluntarily by the industry in 1962 as a body to regulate press, cinema and poster advertising. It was a response to threatening noises from the Labour Party, then in opposition, which had identified a growing public concern with the effectiveness of the existing Committee of Advertising Practice. This was a trade body and, as such, was believed to look after the industry's own interests rather better than it did those of the general public.

The prime function of the ASA is to administer the British Code of Advertising Practice (BCAP), which regulates all advertising material other than television and radio commercials which are the subject of other media controls (see later). The main principles of the Code are that advertising should be:

*   fair, legal, decent and honest,
*   prepared with a sense of responsibility to the consumer and to society, and
*   in line with the principles of fair competition.

To achieve these objectives, the Code makes many specific stipulations.

Although the ASA is independent of the advertising industry, it is funded by it, through a compulsory levy of 0.1 per cent on all display advertising collected by the Advertising Standards Board of Finance. Nomination rights to the ASA are held by the President of the Board of Trade.

Using the same offices as the ASA, the Committee of Advertising Practice assists with the drawing up of the BCAP. This committee comprises people working in the advertising industry, and it provides help to agencies who seek guidance on the interpretation of the BCAP. It has a number of specialist sub-committees who oversee specific areas of responsibility (e.g. health/medicine), or other codes (e.g. British Code of Sales Promotion Practice).

The ASA considers complaints received from the public or trade, or abuses that it has identified. Its decisions are reported in a bulletin. The ASA must ensure that the Code is fairly applied.

Courses of action available to the ASA

What happens if the ASA decides that the Code has been breached? It may take any of the following courses of action:

* request amendment or withdrawal of an offending advert;
* request the media not to publish an offending advert;
* publish unfavourable comment about an advertiser's breach of the code, which is likely to be reported in the mass media;
* request that apologies and/or redress be made to those who have suffered adversely as a result of the Code being breached.

To those outside the industry, the ASA may seem to be a rather toothless watchdog. However, it is a requirement of media sales contracts that advertisers must agree to abide by BCAP, and no advertising should be accepted without such an undertaking. In the event that an advertiser does not abide by the decision of the ASA, it is open to the Director General of Fair Trading to take action under the Misleading Advertising Regulations. This happened in 1992 in the case of unsubstantiated claims in the advertising for Femme Hair Removal (see Figure 10.1 overleaf).

Controls over broadcast media advertising

Television advertising is controlled by the Independent Television Commission (ITC), which has its own Code of Practice. Unlike the British Code of Advertising Practice, this has statutory force, in that the ITC can insist that the Code is adhered to, and can even ban offending television commercials. Prior approval is necessary for all commercials before screening, and this requirement applies equally to the terrestrial, satellite and cable channels. However, where a signal originates overseas, it is clearly much more difficult for the ITC to regulate the contents of television advertising. For this reason, the EU is attempting to draw up common regulatory systems.

The Radio Authority (RA) also operates a Code of Practice for commercial radio advertising. In this case, the responsibility for ensuring that the advertising complies with the Code lies with the contractors responsible for independent radio stations.

Other codes of practice are operated by trade bodies, for example, the Cinema Advertising Association, and British Transport Advertising, in addition to the BCAP controls. The trade bodies which represent the press (the Newspaper Publishers Association, the Newspaper Society and the Periodical Publishers Association) have codes of practice which apply particularly to direct response advertising. These codes are intended to protect readers who respond to advertisements carried by the publications concerned, to ensure that the

Anthony Green & Co:
a case study

Over several months, the Authority had been investigating claims relating to a range of health and beauty products marketed by Anthony Green & Co through advertisements produced by their agency Lavery Rowe. These products included a number of depilatory creams, sold under a variety of brand names.

When requested to do so, Anthony Green & Co could not prove their claims that the products could slow hair growth or achieve long periods of non-growth as described in their mail order advertisements. The Authority asked the advertisers to amend their copy and offered advice as to how they could produce acceptable advertisements. But the company continued to contravene the Code.

So, having given the company every opportunity to resolve the matter voluntarily, the ASA proceeded to the next stage under the Control of Misleading Advertisements Regulations 1988. It referred the contraventions to the Office of Fair Trading.

The OFT took up the complaints against Anthony Green & Co and Lavery Rowe under the Regulations · the first time it had ever enjoined an agency to such action. Both agreed to give formal undertakings to stop making their unsubstantiated claims.

Director General of Fair Trading Sir Bryan Carsberg welcomed the companies' willingness to give undertakings without a need for court action to obtain injunctions, but observed that "...it would have been better if they had responded more positively to the ASA's initial objections to the advertisements". He also warned other advertisers that he would not hesitate to take court action over misleading advertisements.

ASA Chairman Sir Timothy Raison added that "this instance will serve as a useful warning to advertisers and their agencies that they must observe the Codes' requirements for honesty and truthfulness".

In the wake of this successful action, publishers are being issued with guidelines to press the need for pre-publication advice for health and beauty mail order advertisements. The Authority is now establishing stronger links with Anthony Green & Co and others in the field to help them achieve acceptable advertising copy for their products.

Femme

HAIR REMOVER

The PERMANENT
solution
to
hair removal

*Removes all unsightly, embarrassing facial and body hair in one painless 5 minute treatment – **STOPS** regrowth for up to 3 months!*

Figure 10.1 – Controlling misleading advertising

(Source: 1992 ASA annual report)

reputations of these publications are not tarnished by association with unscrupulous advertisers. Their provisions are additional to those of the BCAP.

Control of direct mail and telemarketing

In order to protect the direct marketing industry from government regulation provoked by consumer reaction to 'junk mail' and intrusive telephone selling, ethical standards have been drawn up by the Institute of Direct Marketing of the UK, and reputable businesses have signed up to observe these standards.

The standards cover factors such as the honesty of the claims made, identification of the seller, operation of prize draws, mailing or telephone list rental practices and telemarketing.

Additional protection from 'junk mail' is available through the Mailing Preference Service. This is a system whereby householders can opt out of the receipt of unsolicited sales material. Registration with the service should ensure that the contact's name is deleted from mailing lists. The weakness with these arrangements is that they rely upon the direct marketers complying; not all of them will.

Activity

At first sight, the Mailing Preference Service seems to be of greatest benefit to a disgruntled consumer. However, it is arguably of equal value to organisations using direct mail techniques. Why is this?

DISCUSSION

It is in the interests of direct mail users to honour the conditions of the Mailing Preference Service because any mail shots which reach people who have asked to be expunged from mailing lists will only be a waste of resources.

Control of sales promotion

Sales promotions are also the subject of a twin-track approach, featuring elements of both self-regulation and legal controls. The British Code of Sales Promotion Practice (BCSPP) offers protection to consumers over and above that provided by the British Code of Advertising Practice. Its major additional requirements govern:
* the suitability of promotions for the likely recipients (e.g. where children may take part in the offer);
* the necessity to ensure adequate supplies of products offered in a promotion, and to offer comparable alternatives in situations where demand exceeds supply:
* entitlement to participate in sales promotions; and

*   the necessity to treat products offered as part of a promotion as if they were purchases by a consumer, and to offer replacements or refunds for defective items.

Many sales promotions offer prizes. These are also the subject of legislation, principally the Lotteries and Amusement Act 1976, and the Gaming Acts, in addition to the BCSPP. The four types of prize promotion – competitions, draws, lotteries and games – are quite distinct, and it is important not to confuse these promotions, or an organisation may fall foul of the law.

So, if a prize promotion is described as 'a competition' it should require the exercise of a significant degree of mental or physical skill or judgement. A company may require participants to pay, or make a purchase, in order to enter. However, if a prize promotion is described as 'a draw' the prizes are either distributed on the basis of predetermined random chances (as with many newspaper loyalty promotions), or by the chance selection of winning numbers. In this case, neither a significant degree of skill is required of participants, nor may an organisation require them to pay, or make a purchase, in order to enter.

If a prize promotion is described as 'a game' it should take the form of a simulation of an actual game played by people (e.g. Bingo, Monopoly, Trivial Pursuits, etc.). Again, no significant degree of skill may be required of participants, and an organisation cannot require them to pay, or make a purchase, in order to enter. In addition, restrictions under the Gaming Acts may apply. No prize promotion should be described as 'a lottery'; this term is reserved for non-commercial or charitable draws, in which prizes are distributed by random chances. Participants may be required to make payment in order to enter, as in the UK's National Lottery. A lottery is controlled by the Lotteries and Amusements Act 1976.

Activity

The manager of a local carpet warehouse is planning a prize promotion. He has sketched out some alternative proposals (see Figure 10.2).

1   Which of them could go ahead, and which would fall foul of the rules?
2   Could those which are unacceptable, be changed to make them acceptable?

DISCUSSION

Promotion One – as this is a lottery, it would be legal only if it were promoted by a charity or other voluntary group; it cannot go ahead in this form.

Promotion Two – as a prize draw, it is not possible to restrict entry to those making a purchase; anyone walking through the door must be allowed to enter; it cannot go ahead in this form.

Promotion Three – as this is a competition, requiring a significant element of skill or knowledge, it is possible to make purchase a pre-condition of entry; it may go ahead in this form.

Promotion Four – as games are treated much as prize draws, all the conditions appear to be fulfilled, and it can go ahead in this form. However, some retailers have found that such games merely stimulate traffic through the store, and not necessarily a lot of extra business.

Promotion One

Instant-win tickets available for just 25p at Mister Tufty's Carpet Warehouse. Call in to see Mister Tufty's exciting range of luxury carpeting – and you could win up to £100 – instantly!

Promotion Two

Free Prize Draw with every carpet you buy from Mister Tufty's Carpet Warehouse during April. Up to £250,000 worth of wonderful prizes to be won – but only if you buy a carpet from Mister Tufty's exciting range of luxury floor coverings!

Promotion Three

Take part in Mister Tufty's 'Magic Carpet' contest. Just identify six glamorous holiday destinations from their photographs and you could win an all-expenses paid weekend for two in Siberia. Entry is free to anyone who buys a new carpet from Mister Tufty's Carpet Warehouse during April.

Promotion Four

Anyone can play Mister Tufty's Prize Bingo. There's more than £200,000 to be won at Mister Tufty's Carpet Warehouse during April. Just pick up your Prize Bingo card from Mister Tufty today. You could be a Mister Tufty prize-winner. One card per person per visit. No purchase necessary.

Figure 10.2 – Mister Tufty promotion ideas

Case study

How Hoover's managers were carpeted for a sales promotion fiasco

In the annals of sales promotion disasters, surely none can equal the Hoover 'free flights' saga. In the early 1990s, the company offered a free return flight for two, to the USA or other holiday destinations, for anyone who spent more than £100 on its electrical appliances.

This unprecedentedly generous offer was to cost Hoover more than $30 million, and inflicted enormous damage to its reputation in the process. What went wrong?

The promotion began as an attempt by Hoover to stimulate sales during recession. Sales promotions which offered cheap overseas air travel had become popular with consumers. In particular, the 'air miles' system of offering credits towards air tickets had been a big hit with organisations and consumers. Within five years of the launch, it was estimated that 15 per cent of UK households were collecting 'air miles'.

Airlines and tour operators were also keen on these promotions because they were able to sell what would otherwise have been empty seats to the promotion companies.

Hoover's offer, of completely free travel, was remarkably generous. Most travel promotions restricted themselves to offering discounts, requiring the consumer to contribute towards the cost. This acted as a safety mechanism in restricting the take-up of the offer. At first, however, the early signs for Hoover were good. Retailers were soon reporting complete sell-outs of Hoover products, and the Cambuslang factory in Scotland was put onto seven day working to cope with demand. However, as the classified columns in newspapers began to fill with small ads for new and completely unused Hoover appliances, mostly vacuum cleaners, that people had bought simply to get the free flight offer, it became clear that the market was being flooded and that demand would soon turn sharply downwards.

Then the thousands of applications for free flights started to arrive, rapidly exceeding the estimated number of returns by over 100 per cent. The take-up rate for overseas travel promotions is generally believed to be around 10 per cent but Hoover's promotion far exceeded this. The explanation was partly the remarkable generosity of the offer, and partly a combination of consumer gullibility and lack of forthrightness by the company over the small print of the offer, which made the free flights 'subject to availability'. People who thought that they could travel when they liked between certain dates discovered that Hoover could specify the date, time and destination of their journey.

Consumer dissatisfaction was triggered by the discovery of these restrictions on travel. By the time people came up against them, they were emotionally committed to taking the flights. Further discontent was prompted by the lengthy delays which consumers faced in the processing of their applications. Rapidly, a feeling grew that Hoover was trying to renege on its commitments. The affair was the subject of unfavourable exposure in the press, and an investigation by the BBC TV consumer programme 'Watchdog'. Hundreds of complaints were made to Trading Standards Officers and the Consumers' Association, and questions were raised in the House of Commons.

This tide of mounting criticism eventually forced Maytag, Hoover's US parent company, to take action to arrest the declining reputation of the electronics firm. A task force was appointed, three top Hoover managers were sacked, and a sum of $30 million – equivalent to 28 cents a share – was earmarked to meet all the unfulfilled expectations for air travel. How much the company will have to pay in the future for lost goodwill is impossible to calculate.

Marketing experts who have examined Hoover's conduct of this sales promotion have identified several mistakes made by the company. These include:

* **being too ambitious** – using the sales promotion to induce purchases that consumers otherwise had no intention of making; most promotions merely aim to persuade those already in the market to choose one brand as opposed to others;
* **being too generous** – most free offers are of trivial, low value items, but Hoover was offering £400 worth of travel in return for expenditure of only £100;
* **lack of clarity** – not making it sufficiently clear right from the start the conditions which attached to the offer;
* **inaccurate forecasting** – failing to estimate accurately the take-up rate for this offer, and relying on the conditions attached to it to restrict participation; and
* **being uninsured** – not taking out insurance against higher than expected take-up.

Activity

Using Hoover annual reports, or Keynote, Mintel or other market research sources from 1994 onwards, try to find out whether this affair has done any long-term damage to Hoover.

Control of market research through legal and voluntary means

In Chapter Two you read about public disquiet about market research – principally about it being used as a front for selling or fund-raising – and fears about the disclosure of confidential information to third parties. The regulatory framework which attempts to deal with this disquiet is composed of a two-pronged attack using Acts of Parliament complemented by codes of conduct in an attempt to stamp out unethical conduct.

Data Protection Act 1984

The Data Protection Act 1984 establishes eight principles:

1   That information contained in personal data shall be obtained and processed fairly and lawfully.
2   That personal data shall be held only for specified and lawful purposes.
3   That personal data shall not be used, or disclosed in any way that is incompatible with those purposes.
4   That personal data held for those purposes shall be adequate, relevant and not excessive for those purposes.
5   That personal data shall be accurate and kept up-to-date.
6   That personal data shall not be kept longer than is necessary for those purposes.
7   That an individual shall be entitled, without undue delay or expense, to be informed that personal data relating to that individual is held by the data user, to have access to such data, and, where appropriate, to have the data corrected or erased.
8   That appropriate security measures shall be taken against unauthorised access to, or alteration to, disclosure, destruction, or accidental loss of, personal data.

However, because market research ought properly only be undertaken for research and analysis purposes, and not for the purpose of keeping individual records about respondents, it is possible for market researchers to gain exemption from principle 7 of the Act when they register with the Data Protection Registry; they must register under the Act.

Market research Code of Conduct

This Code has been drawn up by the Market Research Society and the Industrial Marketing Research Society. These bodies represent those individuals and groups involved in marketing and social research. Their aim is to ensure the maintenance of professional standards, and to communicate to the public and to business an appreciation of the value of research activity.

The Code attempts to prevent abuses of market research which would damage the activity in the eyes of the business community and of the general public. Its clauses prohibit abuses which include:

*   betraying the confidences of informants, whether business or individuals;
*   attempts to influence the opinions or attitudes of respondents to surveys;
*   using market research as a front for gathering politically or economically sensitive information, or as a front for fund-raising or sales activity.

Legal controls on marketing

There are broadly two kinds of legal control exercised by the courts over marketing activities – by common law and by statute. *Common law* is a vast body of law created by precedent (i.e. by previous decisions of the courts), while *statute law* is enacted by Parliament.

Over the years, attempts have been made to challenge advertising by invoking the law of contract, most of which is based upon common law. The courts have held that advertisements have fallen into three categories:

* mere puffs
* invitations to treat
* simple contracts.

Many of these attempts to invoke contract law founder on the fact that advertisements seldom make claims which are specific enough to constitute a contract. Advertising which simply announces the availability of products and makes no pledge about performance will ordinarily be considered an *invitation to treat*. The same principle applies to goods on display at a marked price in a shop. The shopkeeper is under no obligation to sell the item, or to sell it at the marked price. The price tag on the displayed item is merely an invitation to treat.

Where an advertiser makes a deliberately exaggerated claim, which the public are not expected to take literally, such an advert would be considered a 'mere puff'. For example, if a household appliance were sold for 'a million and one uses in the home' that could be considered to be a legitimate use of hyperbole. Only if a very specific claim is made will an advertisement be considered to constitute a contract – for example, if a shop claims that it will refund the difference in price to consumers who find the same product available more cheaply elsewhere.

Much interpretation of common law in its application to advertising dates back to the celebrated case of Carlill versus The Carbolic Smokeball Company in 1893. This company had claimed it would pay $100 to anyone who contracted influenza after using their product in the specified manner for the specified period. When the Carbolic Smokeball Company refused to pay a dissatisfied user, they were successfully sued on the grounds that their offer had been accepted by the customer in carrying out the conditions of use. In other words, this contract had been honoured by the customer, but not by the company.

All of these examples are of civil, rather than criminal actions. Civil law is also invoked where contracts between organisations and their agencies or suppliers are broken, or where defamation of an organisation's products or services occurs. These are defined as *slander* if published and *libel* if broadcast.

Passing-off actions, which also involve civil law, can be taken by an organisation whose unregistered brand is being copied (see page 112).

Important statutes affecting marketing

Fair Trading Act 1973

This Act achieved two objectives. It reformed the law governing restrictive practices (see below), and extended consumer protection by creating the Office of Fair Trading (OFT). OFT has a proactive role to investigate and eliminate instances of conduct detrimental or unfair to consumers.

The post of Director General of Fair Trading was also created by this Act. The Director General, in conjunction with the Monopolies and Mergers Commission, has a duty to investigate actual or possible monopolies, defined as a situation in which 25 per cent of a total market supply is controlled by one individual, or corporate entity, or is covered by an agreement between producers.

Restrictive Practices Acts

Since the 1950s, increasingly tough legislation to control restrictive practices has been enacted in Britain. Restrictive practices are those which restrict the free operation of a market. Until 1956, it was common for prices to be tightly regulated in many industries by trade associations. This meant that organisations would not be competing on price, but on quality and delivery. When an organisation broke the agreement on pricing, it might find its supplies were cut off by the pressure its competitors put on its suppliers. Later, other restrictive agreements, such as those which made it difficult for new advertising agencies to gain recognition from media owners, were brought within the legislation.

Any agreement between two or more people which is of a restrictive (i.e. anti-competitive) nature, must now be registered with the Director General of Fair Trading, unless it:

* exists exclusively between two people,
* is authorised by other statutes,
* is considered to be important for the UK economy, or
* refers to the use of patents, registered designs, know-how or trade marks.

The agreements affected by this legislation might cover:

* prices to be recommended (i.e. by a trade association) or charged,
* terms or conditions upon which goods are supplied,
* quantities or descriptions of goods,
* processes of manufacture,
* person to whom, for or from whom, or areas or places in which, goods are to be supplied.

Any restrictive practice agreement must be registered, even if it is not intended to be legally enforceable. In order for an agreement not to be declared invalid by the Restrictive Practices Court, it must be shown to be in the public interest, it must not materially restrict competition, or be otherwise 'reasonably necessary' to protect businesses from other restraints upon trade.

Trade Descriptions Act 1968
The purpose of this legislation is to curb the making of false or misleading statements about products and services, their quality and price; to define trade terms in widespread use; and to require the display of other information about products.

Sale of Goods Acts
Goods offered for sale must be fit for the purpose intended; that is, they must be of *merchantable quality*. Where this is not the case, a purchaser is entitled to a refund or replacement.

Trade Marks Acts 1938 and 1994
The present UK rules governing what can and cannot be registered as a trade mark, and the penalties for copying, were established by these Acts. A *trade mark* is 'any symbol which a person uses in the course of trade in order that his goods may be readily distinguished by the purchasing public from similar goods and traders'.

Copyright, Designs and Patents Act 1988
Just as trade marks are protected from copying, so to are new inventions, designs and artistic and creative works, including advertising. This Act brought UK legislation into line with that of the EU. Without protection from copying, it is

argued that there is little or no incentive to improve existing products or processes, or create new art works.

The practice of 'passing off' a product or service as if it is the product or service of another person or organisation is covered by civil law. It covers the use of trade names, marks and product design or appearance used in such a way as to mislead the consumer into believing that the product is that of another organisation. However, such actions are not always successful. McVities had to redesign the box containing their popular Jaffa Cakes, after failing to win an action for passing off against Burton Biscuits, who were marketing Jaffa Cakes in a near-identical pack.

Unfair Contract Terms Act 1977

The use of exemption clauses in contracts covering the supply of consumer goods was dealt with by this legislation. It restricts the use of get-out clauses, particularly in so far as they relate to negligence on the part of the supplier, and liability for loss on the part of the consumer arising from purchase. The legislation applies equally to hiring as to outright purchase. The liability of the supplier can only be restricted to what is 'reasonable' under the circumstances. So, for example, the erection of a notice in a public car park, claiming that the operator of the car park will accept no responsibility for any loss or injury to patrons, however caused, could not be held as constituting an exemption clause if a customer did, in fact, suffer injury. Only if the operator had exercised all reasonable care in the operation of the car park would there be a defence.

Consumer Credit Act 1974

This permits a consumer a five day 'cooling-off' period after signing a contract, and is intended to protect people from high-pressure sales techniques. During the five-day period, the consumer may cancel a contract without incurring any financial liability.

Unsolicited Goods and Services Acts 1971 and 1975

This legislation seeks to protect the consumer from inertia selling, a notorious practice whereby organisations sent goods to consumers without their being ordered, thereby putting the onus on the customer to return the goods if they were unwanted. Failure made the consumer liable for payment. Now, if unsolicited goods are sent, and if within 30 days of notifying the supplier they have not been collected, they become the property of the recipient.

Consumer Protection Act 1987

The European Commission's Directive on product liability was implemented in the UK by this Act of Parliament.

Misleading Advertising Regulations 1988

Similarly, these Regulations also implement an EC Directive, in this case by empowering the Director General of Fair Trading to take action in cases where the British Code of Advertising Practice has been breached, and the Advertising Standards Authority has been ineffectual in its attempts to deal with the situation (see the earlier case study on Femme Hair Removal).

Advertisements (Hire Purchase) Act 1967
An advert is required by this Act to specify whether payment by higher purchase (i.e. in instalments) will incur a higher price than by paying the full amount in one go.

Wireless Telegraphy Act 1984
This Act outlawed 'pirate' radio stations, but specified no punishments for advertisers who communicate the availability of products or services on these stations.

Data Protection Act 1984
This Act regulates the use of databases for marketing purposes. Its eight principles were covered earlier in this chapter.

Assignment 10

Scenario
Assume that you work in the offices of the Advertising Standards Authority, and are responsible for considering reported breaches of the British Code of Advertising Practice. The press adverts shown in Figures 10.3, 10.4 and 10.5 have been referred to you for an initial assessment.

'More and more young people are choosing the fuller-flavour of Ironbrand traditional cask-conditioned ales.'

IRONBRAND. You hear more and more youthful drinkers in Scotland asking for this relatively young beer by name these days.

But that's not surprising. You see, **IRONBRAND** has been brewed to a totally new extra-strength specification by Sue McEwan and Rex Cameron, two recent graduates, who joined our research team at Ironmonger's only three years ago.

So far, it's only been available at a select few bars and clubs in the capital. But already, our market research tells us*, **IRONBRAND**, has developed a reputation as a friendly and sociable drink, selected by outgoing and confident people.

Now its your chance to show your good sense and discerning taste. **IRONBRAND** is now available in all Ironmonger's pubs, and bars, and at good clubs and off-sales. When you're a novice, it's important not to make a fool of yourself by ordering a naff beer.

That's why ordering a pint of IRONBRAND makes such good sense.

After all, no-one's going to call an **IRONBRAND** drinker a nerd, are they?

IRONBRAND – from Ironmonger's Traditional Brewery, Leith.

*Source: Internal Research Project

Figure 10.3 – Advert one

Hey, kids! Does your mum deserve an extra-special treat?'

You may think your Mum is the best Mum in the world – and why not? She probably is. Cooking all your meals. Washing your clothes. Looking after you when you're sick. Buying you sweets and toys.

Isn't it time you did something for her?

Well, now you can. Something she probably doesn't have time to do herself, but that she often dreams about. You can send her, absolutely free, our catalogue of over 1000 lovely dresses for her to choose from.

Just imagine your Mum dressed like a princess. What would you friends say when she opened the door to them? Your Mum could be the loveliest lady in your street, and it wouldn't cost you a penny.

Just print your Mum's name and address on the coupon below and we'll send your very special Mum our latest catalogue absolutely free. There are over 300 glossy pages with lovely colour pictures for her to look at. And, for introducing your Mum to us, we'll send YOU a balloon with your name on it – if you print your name on the coupon, too.

Cut out the coupon and put it in a red pillar box – it won't need a stamp. And don't tell Mum – unless you want to ruin her loverly surprise, that is!

Mum's Own Wardrobe – the clothing catalogue for Britain's best

Mums!

Figure 10.4 – Advert two

While you're reading this magazine, a violent and sadistic criminal may already be breaking into your home.

Nowadays, nobody's safe. Least of all at home. Last year, more than 5,000 people were attacked in their own homes (these are official figures). Seventeen of them died horribly, 5 more than the year before. Dozens were mutilated. There were also record numbers of burglaries, and record insurance claims. No wonder insurance premiums are going through the roof!

But, now you can do something. Bastion Security provides a comprehensive range of security services from fitting locks on your windows to mounting an armed guard on your home, from as little as £9.99.

Dial Bastion's 24 hour FREEPHONE number now and we'll talk.

But do it NOW. Tomorrow may be too late.
Bastion Security – FREEPHONE 9876.

With Bastion Security, an Englishman's home can be his castle.

Figure 10.5 – Advert three

For the purposes of this assignment, you will need to obtain a copy of the British Code of Advertising Practice (BCAP). Your public library may have one. Otherwise, you can order one free of charge, by telephoning the Advertising Standards Authority on 0171 580 5555, and politely requesting that a copy be sent to you.

Work with others in your group in smaller groups of four to six people. Assume that you are all members of the Advertising Standards Authority considering these advertisements.

YOUR TASKS

1   Study each advertisement and list all the points which seem to you to be breaches of the code.
2   What recommendations would you make? Role play the meeting.

CHAPTER 11

International marketing

Going global

The globalisation of the marketplace

Organisations that only ten years ago might have identified their main competitor as a major domestic rival are now just as likely to refer to an organisation in Europe, the USA or the Far East. Some organisations outgrew their home market years ago, and now make most of their money outside their original national boundaries. To that extent, corporations like Coca Cola, Nissan and Michelin have become almost stateless, owing no allegiance to any particular country: their markets are *global*.

We are accustomed enough to the pressures that cause businesses to grow in this way – a desire for larger markets, increased turnover and bigger profits among them. But these changes could not have occurred without at least acquiescence from consumers.

Activity

Make a list of brands (products, services or corporate) which are strong performers in pan-national or global markets.

Compare your answers with those of another student, or with those below.

DISCUSSION

A whole host of names springs to mind. Did you list Lego (toys) from Denmark, Reebok (shoes) from the USA, Benetton (clothing) from Italy, Nestle (Chocolate) from Switzerland, Toyota (cars) from Japan, Perrier (natural bottled water) from France, IKEA (furnishings retailer) from Sweden, or Cannon (copiers) from Japan?

International marketing: more than just exports

International marketing does not differ fundamentally from domestic marketing; the same principles are involved. It differs only in that overseas markets, being both further away and containing consumers from other cultures, pose a higher degree of risk than those of known markets. Successful entry into an overseas market thus requires even greater care and attention to planning.

Ironically, many organisations enter overseas markets because they have surplus production that they want to dispose of. If, however, a business cannot sell its products at home, it is unlikely to be able to do so internationally. There is the world of difference between simple exporting, and a proper approach to international marketing.

Activity

Having read this far through this book, you should now be able to explain the difference between exporting and international marketing. Jot down your answer in your note-book.

DISCUSSION

Although most attempts to sell overseas involve exporting, a venture into export markets which is not based upon the defining principles of marketing – the identification, stimulation and satisfaction of consumer needs – is guilty of a sales orientation. Such an organisation simply wants to sell more of what it already makes, and may even decide to withdraw from exporting if domestic demand picks up. Overseas customers will not tolerate that. So, if overseas marketing is to be done strategically, it will require an organisation to understand what customers in export markets require, whether they can supply suitable products at an attractive price, and still make a profit in doing so.

Not all international marketing solutions involve export. Alternative methods of supplying overseas markets include setting up production capacity in the country concerned, entering into a joint venture with an indigenous organisation, or granting a licence or franchise for that market to an organisation already located abroad. In the case of the service sector, international marketing may involve persuading customers to come to the UK to buy. This is what happens in the tourist industry, of course.

The importance of exports to UK Ltd

In the late twentieth century, Britain's dependence upon overseas trade is considerable, with enormous quantities of both imports and exports flowing across national boundaries. Unfortunately, as Figure 11.1 reveals, the trend in recent years has been for imports to exceed exports.

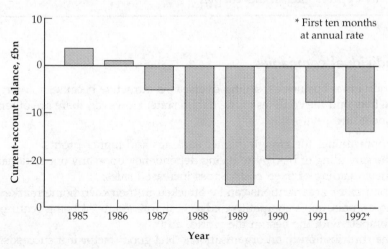

Figure 11.1 – Balance of trade on Britain's current account

(Source: The Economist)

Britain, like any developed country, recognises the value of exports, because they enable growth to occur in an economy without creating internal inflationary pressure, from which this country suffered markedly in the 1970s and 1980s. In addition, the internal domestic economy of Britain has been weak throughout these two decades, so the country is particularly dependent on overseas markets to counteract recession. In terms of a nation's standing in the international community, exports are important, too. A trade surplus is widely regarded as a sign of a healthy economy, and the international value of the pound has suffered because of the country's substantial trade deficits with the rest of the world.

Activity

Using *Economic Trends* (HMSO) or back issues of the *Financial Times* or the *Economist*, find out the current balance of trade between Britain and the rest of the world. How do these figures compare with the recent past?

DISCUSSION

Current expectations are for a long-term worsening on Britain's trade imbalance with the rest of the world, largely because the depletion of North Sea oil reserves will force Britain to import oil for many years.

Owing to the importance of a favourable overseas trade balance to the health of the economy, government agencies provide advice and encouragement to exporters. (Some of these sources of advice are listed later in this chapter.) Part of the government's strategy is to publish news of British companies' export successes in the Department of Trade and Industry (DTI) magazine *Overseas Trade*. These reports provide a shop window for the achievements of the organisations concerned; they also serve as role models for other businesses whose export attempts have so far been more tentative.

A recent issue of the magazine included accounts of how different British companies were helping with the conservation of the Pyramids and the Sphinx in Egypt, improving duck breeding and egg-laying cycles in Indonesia, and providing computer equipment and software to the major bus operator in the Zimbabwean capital, Harare. A case study illustrating overseas success by a UK company appears later in this chapter.

Benefits to individual companies

For individual businesses, selling overseas is attractive because it enlarges their market beyond the confines of the nation state. However, there are other benefits, too, including:

* opportunities for growth, higher earnings and higher profits;
* the spreading of risk, by reducing dependency upon any one national market;
* the spreading of fixed costs across increased sales;
* competitor organisations can be attacked in their own home markets;
* an organisation's competitive edge is sharpened, by it being required to compete with the best in the world; and
* the contribution to an organisation's 'feel good' factor if it succeeds.

Once an organisation has achieved a significant share in its home market, adding even 1 per cent to its sales against established domestic competition can be very hard work. The possibility of sales into other countries where the market conditions appear to be similar is therefore understandably tempting. Organisations which do this successfully, can achieve significant growth in sales and profits.

Furthermore, such a strategy makes an organisation less dependent upon any single market and better equipped to ride out negative sales trends peculiar to one market. However, organisations which try to add exports to compensate for declining home sales may simply be ignoring a fundamental problem with the mix of their products which will be as much a problem to them in export markets as it is in their domestic one.

The ability to be able to spread fixed costs across additional markets is a major factor in the success of global brands, against which purely national products find it increasingly difficult to compete. This is particularly true of those products with high development costs; the automotive and pharmaceutical industries are examples of this. Organisations in both have to support vast research programmes in order to stay ahead of their rivals; such costs have to be recovered through the purchase price. The wider the market for their products, the greater the opportunity to spread the cost of research.

Successful incursion into export markets is a powerful boost to an organisation's self-esteem, with all the excitement that comes from the feeling that a business is really going somewhere. Indeed, there are real dangers that the leaders in domestic UK markets may lose their dominance if they do not have an international marketing strategy, because overseas rivals, with lower unit costs, will undermine their position either through superior product development, lower prices, or both. In either case, their superior competitive position will be attributable to strength in world markets, which organisations who remain locked in domestic markets, can never have.

Factors upon which international trade depends

Of course, it has not always been possible to consider every other part of the world as a potential market for UK goods. There are four groups of factors which need to be satisfied before international trade can take place. These can be discussed using the acronym PEST which we encountered in Chapter 2.

Political factors

* Stable political relations between states are a pre-condition; during war or isolation by trade sanctions, buying and selling becomes difficult.
* Legal and tax systems may discriminate against non-national businesses in some countries.
* Lawlessness and piracy will be endemic in parts of the globe.
* Buying systems and regulations in other states may make trade difficult or even impossible, where there is a ban or limit on certain types of imports.
* The freedoms enjoyed by citizens vary enormously; restrictions upon personal choice will clearly affect buying behaviour.

Economic factors

* Level of economic development in other countries will affect their ability to purchase; for example, people living in subsistence economies will not have any disposable income.
* The relative strength of national economies – some countries have such weak economies that they are unable to afford to pay for imports, except perhaps by barter.
* Existence of compatible banking and payment systems is essential to reassure exporters about the likelihood of receiving payment from overseas customers.

Social factors

* The beliefs and values of people in overseas markets will affect export potential, in terms of:
  – attitudes to overseas goods,
  – influence of consumerism,
  – business etiquette.

Technological factors

* Existence of compatible technology is essential (e.g. similar systems of electricity supply, size of batteries, video cassettes, CDs, etc.).
* However, technology transfer around the world is now so rapid, that even companies with a leading-edge technology will soon find it being copied elsewhere around the world, legally or illegally.

Trade barriers

For a variety of reasons, the view that international trade is mutually valuable is not always accepted by governments.

Activity

Why should this be so? In your note-book, list those reasons for which governments have tried to limit imports, and occasionally exports.

DISCUSSION

You will probably have noted some or all of the following:

* social impact on domestic population – concern about the damaging effects of certain products, notably drugs, and seditious or immoral literature, have led to restrictions;
* adverse balance of payments – when a country has a trade deficit, the value of its currency will go down, and its financial reserves may be depleted;
* loss of employment in vulnerable industries – the fear of political unpopularity due to high unemployment has encouraged governments to limit imports which undercut the price of domestic products;

* embryonic industries protected against unfair competition – attempts by foreign competitors to strangle rivals at birth by fierce price competition may lead a domestic government to try to protect fledgling businesses;
* preservation of domestic industries with strategic importance, for example, power generation, agriculture and fisheries, armaments;
* prevention of exports of sensitive material, for example, works of art, high technology products, scarce raw materials and armaments.

Methods of trade regulation

A variety of methods for regulating trade to the advantage of national interests has evolved. These include:

* formal bans on imports and/or exports;
* import quotas – while not banning imports completely, these are bureaucratic limits to the volume of goods that can enter a country during any one year;
* tariff barriers – i.e. the use of excise duties to price imported goods out of the market;
* subsidies to domestic industries – these are paid to companies which would otherwise have difficulties in competing either in their domestic market, or overseas;
* non-formal barriers – complex regulations are used to discourage importers, rather than ban them completely;
* cultural factors – 'buy national' campaigns or anti-foreigner hysteria may be exploited by domestic politicians to discourage the purchase of imports.

In an attempt to reduce interference with free market mechanisms by individual states acting in their national interest, a number of agreements have been reached between governments. There are a variety of 'free trade' treaties which commit the signatories to the promotion of liberal trade practices and the avoidance of those practices listed above designed to promote the interests of national organisations to the detriment of those from overseas. These agreements include, on a world-wide level, the General Agreement on Tariffs and Trade (GATT), and at a 'regional' level, the Association of South East Asian Nations (ASEAN), CARICON (a Caribbean trading agreement), and the European Union (EU), among others.

The EU is, of course, more than just a group of countries who wish to trade with each other. It also has political objectives, such as the creation of a single currency as a long-term goal. However, the completion in 1993 of the Single European Market was an attempt to remove the many informal barriers which had continued to distort trading between member states long after the removal of formal barriers. The objectives specified for the Single Market by the then European Community were, in outline:

* the removal of physical barriers to the movement of goods and people across Europe;
* the removal of technical barriers covering quality, technical standards and purchasing by public bodies; and
* the removal of fiscal barriers, for example by the standardisation of excise duties (e.g. VAT) across Europe.

The formation of the Single Market has had a gradual effect upon UK organisations. Many of them woke up slowly to the fact that Europe was genuinely one market, giving them the opportunity to sell as easily to Brussels or

Barcelona as they might already do to Birmingham. One of the factors that stimulated such an awareness was the discovery, that organisations from Brussels and Barcelona had for some time been targeting their products at consumers in Birmingham and elsewhere in the UK.

Activity

Using the figures for UK imports and exports that you obtained for the activity on page 218, calculate the relative importance of the USA, the old Commonwealth and the rest of the European Union as markets for UK Ltd.

What trends do you notice?

DISCUSSION

The trend has been very much for UK companies to do more business with Europe, such that the EU accounted for 54 per cent of UK exports by 1993. Over ten years, exports to the EU had grown by 143 per cent, while those to the USA had risen only by 57 per cent. During that period, Germany overtook the USA as the UK's single most important export market. Despite this growth, however, the UK still has a smaller share of its overseas trade with other member states than the average for member states.

Investigating overseas markets

The most obvious way of segmenting overseas markets is on the basis of nation states (i.e. by geographic segmentation).

In examining any national market for consumer marketing, it would be necessary to consider the following market characteristics:

* population structure (i.e. distribution, age structure),
* national income and distribution,
* educational standards (particularly literacy),
* culture and religion,
* social systems (i.e. class structure and importance),
* consumer media available and advertising standards,
* availability of consumer market research data (e.g. do categories reflect those used in the UK?),
* distribution systems (i.e. structure of retail sector).

Business-to-business overseas marketing also requires investigation of national market characteristics. The factors to be considered in this case include:

* industries and their importance,
* nature, scale and ownership of business organisations,
* availability of industrial market research data.

Many features of the investigation of a potential overseas national market will be common to both groups. These are:

* climate and weather patterns (e.g. rapid decay of food products; rapid corrosion of metal products);
* import controls, taxation and attitude to repatriated profits;
* the legal system (e.g. similarities to the UK and attitude to overseas organisations);

* level of economic development;
* state of the country's infrastructure (e.g. roads, telephones, mail);
* language(s) spoken;
* attitude towards change;
* business etiquette (e.g. reciprocity of favours and status of representatives are important in many Arab countries);
* number and strength of competitors; and
* the suitability and life-expectancy of their products.

The purpose of this initial investigation is to establish those markets which are most likely to reward more detailed investigation. Once that decision has been made, more detailed research can be undertaken, perhaps by commissioning an agency within the target market itself.

Such research should enable an organisation to achieve what should be the objectives of any organisation entering overseas markets. Namely to:

* understand the needs of overseas buyers,
* design market offerings which will provide maximum satisfaction,
* establish long-term presence in an overseas market, and
* maximise an organisation's return on its investment.

Overseas market research data

Regrettably, many organisation make only a perfunctory attempt to understand the export markets that they try to enter. Quite frequently, they have wilfully ploughed on into markets that seemed to be unsuitable after investigation, usually because they felt that too much time had been invested to pull back. This is regrettable, because overseas market research data is becoming easier to obtain as public and private sector providers respond to the growing need of organisations for data about opportunities outside their own domestic markets. The sources of available data are as follows:

* **supra-government**: EU; United Nations (UN); Organisation for Economic Co-operation and Development (OECD); World Bank;
* **governmental**: DTI Export Market Reports; British Overseas Trade Information Service (BOTIS);
* **Commercial sources**: publications from the Economist Intelligence Unit (EIU); Kompass directories (available for many developed countries); market research agencies in the UK and in target markets; advertising agencies (with overseas links).

(Many of the sources of UK market research data dealt with in Chapter 2 are paralleled in developed overseas markets.)

Overseas trade assistance

In order to encourage organisations to venture into overseas markets (and thereby improve the UK's balance of payments), much help is available to UK organisations wishing to expand into overseas markets. The Department of Trade and Industry, often with co-operation from the Foreign Office, made the following services available during 1993:

* Export Market Research and Advice – for a fee, the DTI will provide a market

intelligence (MI) report on the appropriate segment of one overseas national market. These reports are collated by trade attaches at the embassies and consulates in the country concerned. They provide an excellent initial assessment, and can be used to plan further intelligence-gathering.

* Outward Trade Missions – these are organised visits to overseas countries, providing briefings on export potential, and introductions to overseas buyers
* Inward Trade Missions – for those unwilling or unable to afford a trip abroad, the DTI provides a service whereby buyers from overseas companies are brought to the UK. UK companies can then take the opportunity to sell to them during their visits.
* Sales Information and Publicity Support – under the Export Representative Service, local consulates will act as shop windows for UK goods abroad.
* Revenue Guarantee Schemes – these provide reassurance to exporters that they will not lose out by supplying largely unknown customers in distant countries from whom it might be difficult to recover goods in the event of non-payment.

Note that this list is a representative sample only; changes in government policy may have caused revisions to it.

Activity

Other inexpensive sources of information for prospective exporters include the clearing banks nearly all of whom provide free 'How to Export' booklets as a service to their corporate clients Ask in a local branch for these. Your local Chamber of Commerce will also make advisory publications available to exporters. Alternatively, you can contact the National Association o Chambers of Commerce. Other booklets are available from your DTI regional office.

Using these suggestions, build up a list of information sources. You will need it for the assignment at the end of this chapter. To help start you off, copy this table into your note-boo and add to it as you go along.

Organisation	Address	Tel
Association of British Chambers of Commerce	9 Tufton Street LONDON SW1P 3QB	
British Exporters Association	16 Dartmouth Street LONDON SW1H 9BL	0171 222 5419
Export Credit Guarantee Department (ECGD)	Export House 50 Ludgate Hill LONDON EC4M 7AY	0171 382 7777
British International Freight Association	Redfern House Browells Lane Feltham MIDDLESEX TW14 7EP	0181 844 2266
DTI Regional Office		
Local Chamber of Commerce		

Managing the overseas marketing mix

As with all marketing, penetration of export markets depends upon achieving the right mix of the factors:

* **Product** – Are the features (and benefits) appropriate to the new market?
* **Positioning** – How are the occupants of the target overseas market categorised? Is the market segment at which it is aimed similar to those of other national markets? If re-positioning is necessary, how will this affect other elements of the mix?
* **Price** – What is the aim of the market strategy – a premium price, or penetration? Will existing suppliers respond to entry with price-cutting? Can the cash flow cope with typical overseas payment terms of up to 180 days credit?
* **Place** – How and where does the market currently buy? Will the organisation sell direct or use intermediaries? Is a dedicated distribution network necessary, or will existing distribution systems be used? How critical are delivery deadlines in this market?
* **Promotion** – What mix of promotional tactics seems suitable for the new market? How will different cultural values affect the style and content of promotional messages?
* **People** – How important is personal selling in this market? Is it more important to have people from the target market undertaking sales, or those familiar with the organisation's products and ways of working? What are the training and development implications for existing staff of moving into a new market?

Products for non-UK markets

Realistically, for most organisations venturing outside their home market for the first time, their initial question will be 'Is our existing product range suitable for this country?' This question will have to be addressed for each target country.

Some products may be expected to achieve a recognised product standard before being permitted to be sold. Possession of the equivalent British Standard is no guarantee that a product will be accepted without testing by another country. The requirement that products should meet a variety of standards in different countries has been a powerful informal disincentive to overseas trade. As a result, the harmonisation of such standards is a major objective for the Single European Market.

The convergence of consumer lifestyles across continents makes it easier to market a single product across larger numbers of countries. You listed examples of global products earlier. This does not mean that all national markets can be treated as being identical. For example, while some people in the UK appear to be quite happy to exist on a diet of ready meals which move from freezer to microwave to plate in one seamless process, the majority of French consumers still value their culinary skills.

Theoretically, the marketing of products in business-to-business markets should be easier for would-be exporters. Cultural factors which might make a consumer wary of buying an import are arguably less important to commercial buyers who are more interested in quality, price and reliable delivery than country of origin. Indeed, many manufacturers are now committed to policies of global sourcing; that is, of wanting to buy from the best in the world, wherever those suppliers may be located.

Choosing an international product strategy

Almost every organisation that ventures beyond its home market will be doing so on the basis that it has at least a moderately successful product with which to do so. Sooner or later, it will be necessary to resolve the problem of whether to sell standardised goods throughout all the different national markets, or whether to customise products for some or all of these countries.

Advertising and promotion

Once again, the convergence of national markets does not mean that there are not important differences between states in terms of public attitudes to advertising, legal controls, and the nature and availability of advertising media.

The most effective advertising will be that which recognises those national characteristics. Just as in the UK, campaign planning requires knowledge of:

* who is in the target market;
* motivations and attitudes of target market occupants;
* what media they see, read and hear;
* local advertising conventions;
* the market's attitude towards advertising;
* colloquial language use (in order to avoid bad translation of English campaign slogans).

Many organisations in business-to-business markets use overseas trade fairs. These are seen as being a highly cost-effective way of bringing together sellers, distributors and buyers.

International direct mail is another way of reaching potential overseas customers. There is still probably more interest in a letter or fax that has come from abroad, than for the domestic equivalent. The gradual homogenisation of postal services, particularly in Europe, the availability of an international pre-paid reply service, but most of all, the opportunity to address a customer in his or her own language, are all factors which are stimulating growth.

Sales and distribution

Overseas selling requires answers to some tricky questions. Should an organisation have a specialist overseas sales team? Should it maintain its own 'person on the spot'? Should he or she be an ex-patriot or a native of that country? Should an agent be used? Each organisation must decide what is most appropriate for its business.

Maintaining a salesforce overseas makes control difficult – particularly if it needs frequent updates on technical matters. It is much more costly than operating a salesforce in the home market. For those who are working abroad, there are few opportunities for promotion – a possible disincentive. On the other hand, an overseas agent may be cheaper, but may not be promoting the line as enthusiastically – indeed, may be damning it with faint praise.

The full list of choices facing would-be exporters for organising their sales activity in export markets is as follows.

Within the UK

* Crown Agents are a legacy of the British Empire; they act for prospective purchasers in overseas markets, principally public bodies in Commonwealth countries.
* Export houses act as a shop window for UK goods, and will be visited by overseas buyers and purchasing agents.

* Foreign buyers – many organisations overseas will periodically send buyers to the UK in an attempt to seek new suppliers; others maintain permanent branch offices in the UK.
* Purchasing agents – similar to the above, but are freelance and may act on behalf of a number of customers.

Overseas representation
* Field sales personnel – the use of in-house sales teams in world markets is extremely expensive, but in return an organisation is able to build long-term relationships with customers, and receive market intelligence very rapidly.
* Agents – recruiting a local person with good market knowledge is the alternative option. Agents may sell on behalf of more than one organisation, but that need not be a disadvantage, so long as the products are complementary. Close monitoring of an agent's performance against expectations will enable organisations to spot representatives who are not acting in the organisation's best interests.
* Distributors – there is often confusion as to the exact difference between an agent and a distributor; the latter is someone who buys in stocks with his or her own capital, whereas an agent merely takes orders (and sometimes accepts payment) on the organisation's behalf.
* Licence holders, franchisees, or joint ventures – as an alternative to territorial invasion, it is possible to utilise the skills and market experience of another organisation in the target market by licensing or franchising it to produce the product on behalf of the UK organisation. Another alternative is the joint venture, under which a new product is launched to the new market jointly by the exporting organisation and a partner organisation in that market.

Manufacturing abroad
Ultimately, an organisation may wish to set up its own manufacturing subsidiary in an overseas market. There are considerable advantages in doing so. These may include:
* **avoidance of import restrictions** – Japanese motor vehicle manufacturers have circumvented EU import quotas by establishing bridgehead factories in the UK from which to supply the rest of Europe;
* **achieving cost benefits** – global corporations have relocated from countries with high labour costs and strong unionisation to those where cheaper and unorganised labour are to be found; laxer governmental regulations may apply, or grants be made available to encourage relocation; corporations with plants around the world can move production from site to site to reflect changing cost bases;
* **easier response to 'local' markets** – as overseas markets grow in importance, so does the need to be able to respond quickly to changing market conditions, including competitor activity.

Activity

Work together with a partner on this. Assume that you both work for a small clothing company that has developed its own branded range of up-market, weather-resistant anoraks and ski suits. So far, they are selling fairly well in specialist sportswear shops in the UK, but your company wants to enter other markets, particularly in Europe.

Role play a meeting between the marketing director and the managing director of the company, at which you should decide on the best method of spearheading your sales bid for European markets.

Export logistics

When an order is sent out within the UK, it will probably be accompanied by nothing more complicated than a delivery note. Export orders, however, may require more extensive documentation, depending upon the country of destination. Exports within the EU, for instance, require less documentation than those for the Far East.

The full list of items accompanying an export order might be:

* an invoice, showing the value of the goods for customs purposes, to enable the value of UK exports outside the EU to be calculated;
* shipping instructions, containing directions for those handling and delivering the order;
* special documents, such as an export license, where the goods are covered by special regulations (e.g. armaments); and
* miscellaneous documentation, (e.g. insurance cover note, details of weight/volume, customs documents relating to the origin regulations of importing countries, etc.).

Attempts to reduce the paperwork burden for exporters are being led within the UK by the Simpler Trade Procedures Board (SITPRO), which aims to cut back the red tape that can enmesh export orders. SITPRO has developed systems for preparing documents accurately, quickly and cheaply without the need for the repetition of identical entries. It is also pioneering the use of electronic data interchange (EDI), a paperless system for handling international orders. The system, which can be used by any organisation with a personal computer and a modem, is claimed to be quicker, cheaper and more secure than paper, and to provide a more responsive service for the customer.

Another way of overcoming unfamiliarity with export documentation is to use the services of a freight forwarding company. These companies can arrange a full logistical service for exporters.

Pricing

It is sometimes argued that the costs of packaging, handling, storage, transport, bad debts and credit control, fulfilling service-warranty obligations, and operating an overseas salesforce makes exporting prohibitively expensive. Equally, these costs may be offset by other economies of scale, particularly in spreading product development costs across much larger sales volumes. Either way, pricing policy needs to reflect competitive market conditions, and many exporters may begin by using penetration policies based upon marginal costing in order to gain a foothold in the market (see Chapter 7).

The prices for export markets may be quoted in one of three ways:

* **delivered, carriage paid (DCP)** – this is an inclusive price (in which the costs of transportation are hidden within the total);
* **free on board (FOB)** – this price includes transportation as far as the producer's national boundary, beyond that point the customer is responsible for the goods;

* **ex-works** – this price excludes all delivery charges; these may be added as an optional extra charge, or the customer may be left to make its own arrangements.

One of the uncertainties about fixing prices for exported goods is the variation of exchange rates between the currencies involved.

Other financial risks involved in exporting include the strain on the cash flow imposed by being forced to allow customers to buy on 'open account', where this may involve a delay of up to 180 days before payment is received. Ideally, an exporter might want payment in advance for goods, but that is unrealistic except in circumstances where demand for the exporter's product is at a premium. It is much more difficult to assess the credit-worthiness of customers in overseas markets, and the difficulties of recovering non-payments become infinitely more complex in the myriad different legal systems of overseas countries. For this reason, many organisations now insure their overseas credit risks.

Readiness for exporting

The PICKUP Europe Regional Centre in Birmingham produced a paper on the characteristics associated with manufacturing organisations that are contemplating exporting for the first time. These characteristics include:
* spare capacity and/or high stocks of finished goods;
* an associated decline in home market share;
* product- or sales-orientation phases of development;
* possibly some indirect experience of exporting (e.g. of supplying a customer who subsequently exports components in finished products);
* enthusiasm for foreign travel;
* ad hoc market information;
* links with UK agencies for hand-holding and encouragement.

Although this list is not definitive, it does indicate that many organisations enter overseas markets for the wrong reasons and with inappropriate preparation.

International marketing: a check-list

So how can organisations contemplating ventures outside their home markets, assess their readiness for the move? The following check-list details the issues which they need to consider.

Company resources
* **Finance:**
  - Is there sufficient working capital to fund overseas activity?
  - Will it cover the anticipated pay-back period?
* **Systems:**
  - Are the present production planning, order-taking, credit-control and debt-collection systems adequate for overseas expansion?
* **Personnel:**
  - Do existing people have the necessary knowledge and skill to deal with overseas customers?

* **Products:**
  - Are the organisation's existing products acceptable to new markets?
  - Do they conform to technical standards?

Market intelligence

* Have target markets been researched to establish their size, potential for growth and principal competitors?
* How similar are the markets to those in the UK?
* Who are the customers? How do they buy?
* Has the market been examined for existence of tariff and non-tariff barriers?
* Are transportation and distribution systems available?

Representation

* Have all the options for overseas representation been examined, (i.e. agent, distributor, franchise/license holder, own salesforce and subsidiary company) and a choice made on the basis of rational criteria (rather than guesswork)?

Transactions

* Have the requirements of any necessary documentation been considered?
* Have decisions been made on how export prices will be quoted?
* Has the problem of currency fluctuation been discussed with the organisation's bankers and appropriate arrangements been made to minimise risks?
* Have steps been taken to secure any export cargoes against damage, theft, and delayed or non-payment?
* How will overseas customers be expected to pay? Is this method likely to be acceptable to customers and cost-effective for the organisation?

Activity

Assess the company described opposite for its export-readiness at the time the article was written. How do you rate its performance?

Assignment 11

Scenario

You have been given a work experience placement with a small company making electronic components. The company would like to become involved in exporting because many of the major electrical consumer durable brands are now made in Europe.

Your task

Outline the steps that you would take to secure initial intelligence about the market for electronic components in Europe, where you would seek the information, and what you would expect to find out.

You should use the section dealing with overseas market research, and your own list of information sources from earlier in this chapter, to help you with this assignment.

What the doctors order

What the doctor ordered in the UK is being ordered by the medical profession in the Netherlands, Luxembourg and Belgium. Soon, if a UK company's aggressive single market penetration plans are successful, it will also be prescribed to doctors in France, Germany and Spain.

A new drug? No, it is a compact manual filing system called Fleximetric. The system, particularly suitable for surgeries where space is at a premium, is just one outlet for Flexiform Business Furniture Ltd of Bradford, West Yorkshire.

David Boon, Head of Marketing at Flexiform, which has a £20 million turnover, says the filing system can save an estimated 60% of floor space, a factor which, together with a well thought out European marketing strategy, is helping to boost the company's profitability. Despite computers, there is a strong legal requirement throughout Europe for actual documentation to be retained. The Flexiforn system can provide for this.

Euro-language

Flexiform may have a good product, but how does it sell to the European market? 'First, speaking a Euro-language is important,' says David Boon, who speaks French and is also studying German. 'Our Export Manager is fluent in German and my marketing assistant is a German language graduate. Everyone speaks English, they say, but it's important to have the ability to switch languages.' In addition Flexiform's export consultant visits Europe regularly, maintaining contacts and establishing new ones.

'You have to remember,' says David Boon, 'that although our system has so much going for it it has to be brought to the attention of our potential EC buyers'.

Strategies

To this end, Flexiform, which also make workstations, including desks and VDU facilities, adopts carefully considered strategies to assure its present and future customers.

European distributors come to Britain for frequent training and product appraisal seminars where views are exchanged and developed. 'For instance,' says Mr Boon, 'the distributors asked how we could get our products into a service lift which was on a different space scale to those in the UK. We solved the problem in knock-down form' .

Standards

Manufacturing standards at Flexiform conform to BS 5750, equivalent to European EN 29000, and all products meet relevant British performance standards. There is a five-year warranty on all products – important in a single market context, where all Europeans are assured of uncomplicated redress should standards fail.

'Customer confidence is really important,' he says. 'Much of our market is based on this in addition to the product.' Flexiform's sales material has been recently translated into German, an important new market for the company. There are also plans to translate into French, Spanish and Italian. David Boon emphasises that sales literature should be colloquially but correctly translated not just by someone with a dictionary. This applies equally to videos and letters.

R&D investment

Heavy investment in research and development is part of Flexiform's plans to expand into the single market. 'Germany, for instance, is very strong on black and white finishes,' he says. 'So we have projected special designs for this in terms of office furniture.' The company co-operates with their European contractors on product inception through every stage.

To promote its office furniture systems, Flexiform exhibited at the Orgatec exhibition in Cologne in October 1992, the largest office equipment show in the world, held biannually, where they were able to learn from their potential customers.

Another important, though lower key, activity is David Boon's personal friendship in the German town of Duren via the Congleton Round Table. 'My connections were extremely helpful,' he says. 'My German friends helped us with translations, product development and colouring. I suggest to others interested in Europe that this level of contact can be a really fruitful source of progress.'

Environmental policy

Flexiform is also very environmentally conscious. The company has specifically listed its environmental policies which include using wood from managed sources only. Apart from being morally desirable, Mr Boon points out, it is a reassuring selling point.

Source: *Single Market News*

Figure 11.2 – What the doctors order

CHAPTER 12

Marketing planning

Looking ahead

The nature of planning

At one extreme, there are those organisations that do not plan at all. They simply stagger from one day to the next, fire-fighting each crisis as it emerges. If they are operating in an uncompetitive market, they may be successful. At another extreme are those that plan everything down to the smallest detail, and adhere rigidly to the plan document, even when it does not appear to be working, perhaps because the plan is based upon inaccurate information or incorrect assumptions.

For other organisations, the annual planning cycle may have degenerated into a bureaucratic exercise, with little use being made of the resulting document.

In an ideal situation, the evolution of an organisation's marketing strategy and tactics, will be a top-down, bottom-up process; that is, one which involves staff at all levels from director to office junior. It will be an integral part of the organisation's operations, and not simply a panic reaction to a crisis. It will be flexible enough to permit immediately workable ideas to be put into practice, without waiting for the final plan to be drawn up. It should not be cast in tablets of stone; if circumstances change during the implementation of the plan, then the plan must change too.

McDonald and Morris in their excellent book, *The Marketing Plan: A Pictorial Guide* suggest four categories of business planning:

* **anarchy** – this state provides complete freedom for individuals; there is no planning system in place, and while it might make an organisation highly responsive, it could equally be pulled in different directions by its management;
* **apathy** – no system exists in these organisations because people do not consider planning has any value; morale in such businesses is poor, and long-term survival unlikely;
* **bureaucratic** – excessively rigid systems operate; there is little or no scope for opportunism by individual managers within the plan framework;
* **complete marketing planning** – there is a formal planning structure and objective-setting occurs, but scope remains for entrepreneurial initiative by individual managers.

MacDonald and Morris clearly favour the fourth category. While such an organisation would have a clear idea about its future destiny as a result of producing a plan, such a plan is not envisaged as a straight-jacket which prevents it from pursuing a new opportunity when it crops up. Rather, a proper planning process provides a framework against which to judge new business opportunities when they arise. For example, the planning issues against which opportunistic

development can be judged, include:
* Is this new product idea compatible with the long-term aims of the organisation?
* Will it complement the present corporate image? Or detract from it?
* Will it meet the organisation's criteria for profitability within an acceptable period?

The value of planning

Undertaking formal planning can be expected to bestow advantages upon those organisations which adopt it, in five important ways:
* it gives an organisation a clear sense of purpose in which all employees can share;
* it reduces uncertainty about future market trends, and about how to respond to them;
* success results from anticipating trends rather than merely following them;
* it provides a disciplined framework for evaluating options for the future; and
* it generates systems with which to control and monitor strategic decision-making.

Many business which have gone through the process of business planning for the first time have commented upon the clearer sense of purpose apparent in their business at the culmination of the exercise, of the greater commitment and enthusiasm on the part of key employees, and the greater levels of confidence in facing future challenges. Ultimately, businesses have reported making significant changes in the way they operate, either by relocating to new premises, modernising production processes, improving their management information systems, targeting new markets, making higher profits, or all of these things!

Strategy and tactics – what is the difference?

Strategy refers to the medium- to longer-term objectives that a business sets for itself, while *tactics* are the specific actions which it takes in the short term in order to bring those objectives about. So, your own strategy may be to improve your career prospects by gaining a marketing qualification. Studying a particular course and, in particular, reading this book, are tactics that you hope will help you to achieve that.

In business terms, an organisation may decide its strategy is to increase its sales in particular markets. Of many organisation plans produced over recent decades, this has been an understandable general objective. On its own, however, this is not enough. The strategy is unfocussed. Where are the extra sales to come from? From competitors' customers? From people who do not yet buy? From existing customers who will be persuaded to buy more? Strategy must not only state objectives; it must suggest how they will be met. The strategy must also be based on a rational case, otherwise the process will be little more than wishful thinking, and the resulting tactics are unlikely to be successful. Strategy selection and planning, therefore, go hand-in-hand. A strategy without a plan is pie-in-the-sky, while a marketing plan without strategy will probably lack a sense of purpose.

The hierarchy of organisational plans

Organisations will differ in their use of planning, and in the nomenclature of plan documents. This often leads people to ask what the difference is between a corporate plan and a marketing plan.

A *corporate plan* is a document which charts the immediate strategic objectives for the whole organisation. It will contain the organisation's mission statement, which sets out the nature of the business and its most important objective. Any such plan should, properly, be influenced very strongly by market conditions. However, it is likely that it will also contain much non-marketing material (e.g. human resource plans, or production plans).

A *marketing plan* is a document which contains the chosen marketing strategy for achieving the quantified objectives set out in the corporate plan. Such a plan may be produced either for the whole organisation, for a product group, or even for a single brand. It will then set out how that strategy is to be implemented. Included in its pages will be details of how the organisation's products or services will be positioned, promoted and distributed.

Business planning cycles

Despite the rapidity with which change affects modern businesses, many organisations plan within a very long-term timescale. For example, the Japanese car company Nissan planned to establish themselves in Western European markets over a 40 year period. In the car industry particularly, the lengthy gestation period for new models means that ten year planning horizons are usual. However, the most widely used period for strategic business plans ranges from three to five years. Such a corporate plan will reflect the longer-term objectives of the business. However, in order to respond to changes in an organisation's environment which have occurred since the original was drawn up, the plan will also be subject to annual review and updating. By doing so, an organisation can avoid the twin dangers of either pursuing out-of-date objectives, and of having a business plan which is so irrelevant that the whole planning process is discredited.

Activity

There is a point for discussion here. If markets are so volatile that it is difficult to make predictions for even three years ahead and plans must be redrawn every year, does that not question the value of drawing up the plans in the first place?

Discuss this point with your lecturer or others in your group, or with colleagues at work. What are your conclusions?

DISCUSSION

You should have concluded that planning remains valuable despite the likelihood that it will not always anticipate future trends with complete accuracy. Apart from the increased sense of purpose that employees will share in an organisation that seems to know where it is going, it is more likely that the organisation will have anticipated the major market changes if it has been through the planning process than if it did not plan. Businesses that anticipate trends rather than merely follow them are often those that emerge as market leaders.

However, it cannot be denied that from time to time, well-planned businesses will misread the signs or plan for changes which do not in fact occur during the plan period. For example, McDonalds signed up as sponsors of British television coverage of the World Cup finals in 1994, only for all the UK national sides to be knocked out at an early stage of the competition! Whilst changing circumstances are bound to upset targets and performance, they will only be seriously damaging if an organisation has not made contingency plans. This will be dealt with later in this chapter.

Marketing plans are less-wide ranging in scope than corporate plans, and it is usual for them to have a currency of only one year. Thus, a new marketing plan will be produced in advance for each new financial year. In addition to this, the marketing department will also be involved in providing data on which the revised three year corporate plan will be based. From this you can see that planning is a crucial area of the department's work, and not simply a 'bolt-on' function to be squeezed in when other commitments permit.

Preparing the marketing plan

In getting a plan ready, there are in essence three questions to be asked:
* Where are we now?
* Where do we want to be?
* How do we get there?

In asking the question 'Where are we now?' an organisation is forced to take stock of its current position, by analysing both its own performance and that of the markets in which it is trading. In posing the question 'Where do we want to be?' it will need to make forecasts about both its own performance and market conditions for the whole of the plan period. It will then need to select goals which not only reflect its 'best guess' about market conditions in the future, but which are likely to be achievable during that time. Finally, the question 'How do we get there?' forces an organisation to draw up an implementation plan for the achievement of such targets.

Another way of putting this is represented by Johnson and Scholes' model of the strategic planning process (see Figure 12.1).

Figure 12.1 – Johnson and Scholes' strategic planning model

(Source: Johnson G and Scholes K, *Exploring Corporate Strategy*, Prentice Hall International, 1984)

Johnson and Scholes' model also includes three basic steps, and they match closely with those given earlier. Their **strategic analysis phase**, involving an assessment of an organisation's values (or philosophy), resources and environment, is an appropriate way for an organisation to answer the question 'Where are we now?' Their **strategic choice phase**, requiring the generation, evaluation and selection of options, is equally effective in formulating a response to the question 'Where do we want to be?' Finally, the **strategic implementation phase** of Johnson and Scholes' model, focusing on resource planning, people, structures and systems, is another way of tackling the issues raised by the question 'How do we get there?'

Activity

The strategic planning model described above is not limited to planning for marketing; its use is generic. So assume that your college group would like to organise an end-of-term celebration. Working on your own, use the model to draw up an outline plan for such an event.

Compare your ideas with others in your group. Did you find the model useful?

Strategic analysis phase

The purpose of analysing an organisation's existing position is to provide an informed basis for its future plans. One of the first factors to be taken into account is an organisation's values; that is, what it exists to do, and the way in which it believes it should operate. For example, charitable and public sector organisations may not have a profit-orientation, and this will considerably affect their operating cultures, pricing policy, and attitudes towards competitors. Some organisations will see themselves operating in clearly defined market segments, and this will make it less likely that they will respond to opportunities outside their existing markets.

Many organisations now enshrine their business philosophies in their strategic plans in the form of a mission statement. Any new plan will need to take an existing corporate mission statement into account. Yet, even where none exists, it is usually quite easy to identify an organisation's actual philosophy by reflecting upon its recent activities.

It is also important to review an organisation's resources in terms of finance for investment, premises, plant and people. Any decision to update existing products or introduce new ones which is contained in the resulting marketing plan, can only go ahead if money is available for investment, and may require additional or different types of premises, new production plant, and retraining for existing employees.

The marketing audit

The major element of the strategic analysis phase of the plan process will be the undertaking of a marketing audit. Such an audit is an assessment of an organisation's present position in the market, an appraisal of its current marketing policies, and making forecasts for its future trading.

Undertaking the audit

Most of the analytical and planning tools which will be used for the marketing audit have already been covered in the earlier chapters of the book; this chapter will now help you to understand how those earlier concepts are applied to the marketing planning process.

Financial performance

The organisation's financial performance – either as a whole, or for individual brand or product lines or groups – needs to be monitored not just in terms of turnover (total revenue), but in terms of profitability and return on investment in order to assess the real worth of any activity to an organisation. Recent financial performance will have implications for future activity and investment. For information on the analytical methods used, reread the section starting on page 139.

Market performance

Information about the total size of a market, its recent trends and a particular organisation's own share, may be obtainable from published market research data. Data about the occupants of markets, particularly consumers (as opposed to industrial customers) may need to be gathered by specially-commissioned market research.

Any organisation will need at least to know its customer profile and what motivates customer's behaviour. Is the composition of the market changing? Is the segment that buys the product growing or shrinking? Are there new ways for the market to achieve the satisfactions that – until now – this product has provided? How far has the market progressed along the product adoption curve? All these questions must be answered by means of market research. (Data sources and research methodologies were the subject of Chapter 2.)

Reviewing market share strategies

Actual market share (that is, the proportion of total sales for that product category achieved by the organisation) should then be compared with the share of the market that the organisation had earlier planned to achieve, and any difference between target and performance accounted for.

There are four strategies for market share which are commonly selected, and these are:

* **to be the market leader** – such an organisation holds, and wishes to retain, the number one spot in its market (e.g. Coca-Cola);
* **to be a market challenger** – such an organisation seeks to displace the current number one organisation in its market (e.g. Pepsi Cola).
* **to be a market follower** – an organisation that chooses this strategy is quite happy to copy the market leader, but without mounting an aggressive challenge – sometimes referred to as a *'me-too' strategy* – for example, other cola manufacturers;
* **to occupy a niche market** – a small- to medium-sized organisation may choose to operate in a market segment of too small a size to interest major organisations, but which is still sufficiently large to provide a good income (e.g. an antique dealer).

Achieving desired market share

Although most organisations fervently desire to grow their share of the market, spectacular gains are hard to achieve, especially in mature markets. An organisation which launches an innovative product and in so doing creates a genuinely new market or segment, may gain an important advantage over those that enter the market later. However, as new organisations enter, the original one will find it harder and harder to maintain its early dominance of the market. As markets mature, growth in share is often achieved when one organisation buys up its rival, and adds those sales to its own.

The three most commonly used weapons in skirmishes for market share are:

* branding elements
* pricing, and
* promotion.

However some organisations adopt multi-brand strategies, which means having more than one brand available in the same market. The brands thus compete with each other as well as those of rival organisations. The combined share from the sales of both brands will give their owner a larger share of the market than would be the case with one brand alone. This was the strategy that lay behind the launch of Tab by Coca-Cola, and it is employed by both Proctor and Gamble, and by Lever Brothers, in their perpetual battle for dominance in the detergent market (see the case study, 'The gladiators for our laundry' in Chapter 6).

Opting to be a market follower is an altogether less stressful strategy. The expensive and risky business of market development has already been undertaken by the leader and challengers. Their attitudes towards such an organisation are likely to be more benign because it is not perceived to be much of a threat. Such a strategy can therefore be highly profitable – more profitable than that of a market leader, if it is constantly having to spend heavily to defend that position. The drawback to being a market follower is that the organisation may have difficulty in getting its brand stocked by intermediaries because it sells in smaller volumes.

Niche marketing looks – superficially – like an even cosier strategy. By setting its sights low, an organisation may believe that it will not become involved with aggressive competition. This requires a market small enough to ensure that a major organisation's costs would be so high, and profits too small, to warrant its interest. Such niches may be defined geographically, by the level of quality being sought by consumers (usually high), or by the element of specialist skill or knowledge being provided. However, more and more niche markets are now being penetrated by major organisations, and are being enlarged by the very presence of those organisations.

In auditing an organisation's market share strategy, it would be necessary to ask whether its objective – market leadership, for example – had been achieved. Any difference between the goal and the result would need to be accounted for, even if the result is better than expected. Understanding any discrepancies will make objective-setting in the new plan more likely to be accurate. It is also important for those organisations which choose to be followers or operate in niche markets to decide whether their markets are changing in such a way as to make such strategies untenable in the future.

Analysing product and brand performance

Next it is necessary to undertake an audit of other aspects of the organisation's products or brands. Once again, this involves the use of marketing tools dealt with in the earlier chapters:

* product life cycles – these should be reviewed to alert the organisation to any necessary changes in the marketing mix for products; as we have seen, the stage of a product's life may considerably influence pricing, positioning and promotion (see Chapter 5);
* competitive advantage – how attractive are the organisation's products or services when compared with those of competing organisations within the same market? The tool suggested for carrying out such an analysis was the Porter matrix (see Chapter 5);
* SWOT analysis – the impressions formed as a result of gathering the data for the marketing audit can then be summarised in a SWOT (strengths, weaknesses, opportunities and threats) analysis for each of the products or services. Strengths and weaknesses are internal to the organisation; opportunities and threats are external.

Activity

Try out a SWOT analysis on an organisation that you know well, for example, your college, your own employer, or a major company in your area. Compare your results with others in the group. To give you an example of what a SWOT might look like, below is a SWOT analysis for Marks & Spencer.

Strengths	Weaknesses
Strong brand name	Own branded clothing is not
Leading UK retailer	considered stylish by some
Anchor sites in town centres	Not strongly represented in
Underwear is ubiquitous	out-of-town retail parks
Good staff selection and	Not innovatory in product
retention	development
Good quality control	Only has mid-range products
Pleasant in-store environment	Currently will not accept
Own credit card and associated	standard credit or debit cards
financial services	
Opportunities	**Threats**
Develop non-traditional M&S	Demise of town centre shopping
brands	Ageing customer profile
Replicate success formula in	Attack from UK competitors
non-UK markets	Growth of EU shop chains
Catalogue/television shopping	Growth of home-shopping
methods	
Establish premium and bargain	
stores under different names	

Remember – in drawing up your own SWOT, the existing characteristics of a business should be categorised as strengths or weaknesses, while external changes should be categorised as threats or opportunities. Sometimes, a factor can be both a strength and a weakness, or a threat and an opportunity. For example, television shopping channels such as QVC are a possible threat to Marks & Spencer. However, Marks & Spencer could itself provide such a service.

Assessing the current product portfolio

Once the existing position of each product has been audited, it is then possible to compare the relative performance of the organisation's products, categorising them as either stars, cash cows, question marks or dogs, by using the Boston Matrix (see Chapter 5). The current assessment can then be compared with the matrix produced 12 months ago, and predictions can also be made about the progress of each product over the next plan period. For example, will a star begin to wane? Will the flow of revenue from a cash cow dry up? Will there be an answer to the question mark? Is there life in an old dog yet?

The use of the Boston matrix for logging the predicted change to a product's market size and share is illustrated in Figure 12.2. The current position for Brands A, B, and C is marked as A1, B1 and C1. The anticipated position after a year is shown as A2, B2 and C2. The direction of movement within the matrix can be shown by an arrow.

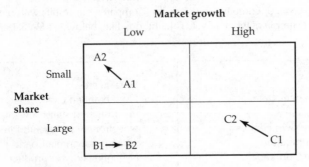

Figure 12.2 – The Boston matrix: its use in planning

Activity

Given the changes predicted for the performance of products A, B and C, do you think the organisation should consider any changes, and if so, what should they be?

DISCUSSION

The predicted position of each product suggests that A, as a dying dog, should be put out of its misery. B, as a cash cow, looks set to prosper as the market grows but it could attract more competition. The decline in the fortunes of star product C should prompt a rethink, and perhaps its eventual replacement.

Identifying market trends

Predicting how markets will behave in the future is a remarkably difficult activity. It is very similar to gambling – studying the form, weighing up the odds, then placing a bet. For every one gambler with a successful system, there are many others who lose time after time.

Forecasting

Forecasting is the process of making predictions about the future. It is not, in itself, the same thing as planning. Knowing from a weather forecast that a storm is imminent will not mean necessarily that people will prepare for it. Furthermore, some things which are forecast can even be prevented. But if forecasting is not the same thing as planning, then it is an inevitable part of it, for all plans will be based on some form of forecast.

The methods used for making forecasts range from the wildly emotional to the impeccably rational. All have their place from time to time, but the carefully deliberative nature of the planning process increases the likelihood that organisations will make most use of rationally-based forecasts. The range of methods available can be placed along the continuum shown in Figure 12.3.

Irrational beliefs	Blind guesses	Informed judgement	Linear statistical projections	Computer models
(e.g. use of lucky rabbit's foot)	(i.e. a hunch)	(e.g. scenario planning)	(e.g. sales trends)	(e.g. for forecasting car fuel consumption)

Figure 12.3 – Forecasting methods

Despite the prevalence of irrational belief and guesswork in forecasting – even for business purposes – they will not be described here, for obvious reasons. Rather, we shall consider the use of informed judgement, statistical projections and computer modelling.

Informed judgement

In practice, all forecast methods, no matter how objective they may appear to be, require the exercise of judgement in some form. This may occur either in the selection of those factors that are considered to be important indicators of future performance, or in applying the results of a statistical projection to particular products or markets.

However, there will be occasions on which it will not be considered appropriate to base forecasts upon statistical or computer predictions – for example, when there is no accurate or valid data upon which to base predictions, or when data exists, but it would not be cost-effective to gather and process it, or when the number of variables is so great that it is not possible to produce a workable model with which to make predictions. In such circumstances, an organisation may use one or more of the following:

* *extrapolative techniques* – these are used when recent trends are projected (extrapolated) into the future using the judgement of the forecaster, rather

than a mathematical formula. They are used when recent statistical evidence is not thought to be valid for the plan period (e.g. in predicting how much longer sales of slow cookers will hold up against microwave cookers);

* *scenario planning* – this term refers to a process in which a number of possible outcomes is described, depending upon the influence and behaviour of a list of factors. These may be suggested by a PEST analysis of the future trading environment, identifying possible political, economic, social and technological changes. Where these changes are only speculative, a number of different scenarios are described, each one dependent upon a change which at this stage has yet to, and may never, occur;

* *impact assessment* – this is used where the changes speculated upon in envisaged future trading scenarios are more certain, but their effects remain difficult to quantify statistically. For example, many organisations drew up impact assessments for the effects that the formation of the Single European Market could have on them, to help them introduce necessary changes well in time.

Statistical projections

All statistical projections are based on the assumption that past performance is a guide to future behaviour. Their main value lies in indicating where trends are likely to lead, assuming that no unexpected changes in market factors occur. Their value is likely to be greatest in the immediate future, during which unforeseen developments are least likely to occur.

The major statistical forecast methods consist of:

* *mathematical trends* – these calculate future trends by projecting existing trends at a consistent rate. For example, if sales have grown on average by 5 per cent in the most recent three year period, it will be assumed that 5 per cent will also be the rate of growth during the plan period;

* *exponential 'smoothing'* – this method will again use a formula derived from averages from earlier periods, except that more recent data will be weighted more heavily. For example, even though sales have grown on average by 5 per cent over the past three years, greater significance will be attached to the most recent year, when growth was only 3 per cent;

* *econometric modelling* – this is an attempt to relate outcomes to the interplay of those factors which affect the trading activity, in order to make predictions more accurate. For example, sales figures of ice-lollies may have traditionally been highly seasonal; if this relationship is then modelled (i.e. a set of theoretical assumptions is drawn up for the inter-relationship of sales and the seasons), it is possible to predict future sales according to months of the year, as shown in Figure 12.4;

* *computer modelling* – the econometric model illustrated above is very simple – it shows only two related factors, sales and seasonality. More complex models are possible. A three-dimensional model would add a third variable, such as price, to show the inter-relationship between all three factors. Once a model progresses beyond three dimensions, it becomes easier to calculate the complex permutations of variables using the memory of a computer; examples of such computer-based forecasting systems are those used to predict weather patterns.

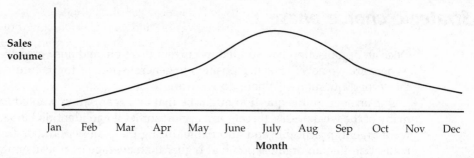

Figure 12.4 – Example of a two-dimensional econometric model of the relationship between sales of ice lollies and months of the year

Many econometric models have become easier to use and apply with the aid of computers. Examples include the misleadingly titled simplex modelling method, and the Monte Carlo technique. For details of these and other methods referred to here, see *Operational Research Techniques* by John Littlechild.

Activity

Identify the statistical forecasting methods you would expect to be most useful in the following circumstances:

a   picking the winner for the Grand National
b   predicting the outcome of a general election
c   assessing the effect of a new competitor in an established market
d   launching a wholly new product into a wholly new market
e   selecting an appropriate price strategy.

DISCUSSION

The answers are as follows:

a   exponential smoothing
b   mathematical projection
c   impact assessment
d   scenario planning
e   econometric/computer modelling.

Time-limiting the strategic analysis phase

As you can see from the amount of space dedicated to it in this chapter, the undertaking of the strategic analysis phase of the planning process can be very time-consuming. So much so, that too little time and effort is then given to the strategy setting and implementation phases of planning. Inevitably, this results in defective strategy selection and only partial implementation. Indeed, the top management consultants, Ernst and Young, estimate that during the 1970s and 1980s, almost 98 per cent of strategic plans were not fully implemented.

Strategic choice phase

Once an organisation has audited its current position, and answered the question 'Where are we now?', it is in a position to generate options for its future to answer the second question – 'Where do we want to be?'

One answer to this question might be that an organisation wanted to tackle as many of the weaknesses, threats and opportunities it had identified in its SWOT as were urgent, practicable and affordable during the plan period. For example, the realisation that an organisation had higher than average overheads might initiate a programme of cost reduction over the coming months. Equally, the growth of a new potential market ought to prompt the modification or development of products to satisfy it, and so on.

Activity

Turn back to the SWOT analysis that you undertook for an organisation or particular product/brand in the activity on page 239. Make a list of all the actions that you think the organisation might now consider, based upon your matrix. Note that, at this stage, you are not being asked to identify which of them should be considered to be more important than the others.

In answering the question 'Where do we want to be?', many organisations will say they want to grow. The range of strategies open to an organisation for expanding its business are helpfully set out in Ansoff's matrix (see Figure 12.5).

Markets

		Existing	New
Products	Existing	Market penetration	Market development
	New	Product development	Diversification

Figure 12.5 – Ansoff's matrix: business development strategies

The strategies identified in Ansoff's matrix can be summarised as follows:

* **market penetration** – this involves selling more of existing products into existing markets, for example, by further strengthening an existing brand identity. It involves the least degree of change or risk on the part of an organisation, but is only likely to be successful if existing products are underperforming and have considerable room to grow within existing markets. Pareto's principle is helpful here – by finding more customers like the 20 per cent who are responsible for 80 per cent of business, it may be possible to achieve impressive sales growth;

* **market development** – this strategy involves selling existing products into new markets; the most clear-cut example of this is to develop export markets. However, a different segment may be identified which will buy for different reasons (e.g. outdoor workwear sold as fashion garments);

    *   **product development** – this strategy involves selling new or modified products to existing markets. For example, Persil washing-up liquid was launched in the expectation that it would appeal strongly to people who used the original fabric-cleaning product for their household wash. However, at a less risky level, breakfast cereal manufacturers have attempted to reposition their products as all-day foods, in order to encourage existing customers to eat them at other times of the day (and so eat more);

    *   **diversification** – this strategy represents the greatest degree of change and risk on the part of an organisation because it involves selling wholly new products to wholly new markets. The development of Bic perfume, however, was not successful because the market confused it with Bic's lighter fuel (the main product). For this reason, a preferred method is to buy an organisation already trading successfully in the desired area of expansion (e.g. purchase of a holiday and leisure business by a retail chain).

Activity

Try to categorise the following organisational growth strategies.

a   NHS Trust hospital which decides to make a specialist form of health care available to patients from health authorities throughout the country in addition to those in its immediate locality;

b   educational publisher which decides to add interactive video titles to complement its existing book list;

c   meat packaging company which decides to offer an attractive bonus scheme to retailers who stock more of its products;

d   civil engineering contractor which decides to enter the plant hire business.

DISCUSSION

The answers are as follows:

a   market development
b   product development
c   penetration
d   diversification.

However, organisations do not always decide that they want to develop their businesses. Instead of one of the business growth strategies identified by Ansoff, it is also possible to select one of the following strategic objectives:

    *   **consolidation** – an organisation may wish merely to maintain its present position, particularly if there has been a recent period of rapid growth or contraction – for example, by achieving higher levels of consumer satisfaction. The danger of such a reaction is that the organisation that decides to stand still may be overtaken by its rivals;

    *   **harvest** – an organisation with a financial problem may decide to sacrifice the long-term position of one or more of its brands for a short-term need for profit and cash-flow. Products identified as stars or cash cows in the Boston matrix are suitable for cuts in development and promotional budgets;

    *   **defence** – in situations where an organisation faces aggressive competition, it may need to concentrate its resources in attacking the competitor, or in dissuading a potential newcomer from entering a market in the first place, in order to defend its own market share;

* **exit** – an organisation may decide to leave a market altogether. In such circumstances, it will want either to sell up completely, or sell a single product from it's portfolio (likely to have been identified as a dog or question mark in the Boston matrix), perhaps to a former rival.

New tactics required from a changing strategy

Making a choice for a future strategy inevitably requires an assessment of the necessary operational changes (i.e. tactics) that will be necessary to achieve the strategy. Some of those operational changes may not be feasible or affordable, and will prompt a re-think of the strategic objectives. Even a decision to exit from a market will require the operation of the business during a managed run-down or until sale to the new owner.

Some of the tactical changes implied by the strategic outcomes already listed in this chapter, include:

* **merger/joint venture** – in circumstances in which an organisation wishes to expand, but lacks the necessary capital, it may wish to consider a merger with a rival to pool resources. Alternatively, a joint venture may be initiated with another organisation, without a formal merger, which allows co-operation over development, and each organisation to exploit the outcomes in its own markets;
* **granting a franchise or license** – organisations which do not want to operate directly in new remote geographical markets can offer franchises or licenses to others within those markets to do so instead;
* **relocation** – businesses which do wish to service new, more remote geographical markets, may need to add new locations, or move existing plant closer to the new markets, if these possess better long-term potential;
* **modernisation of products, or production processes** – product development can be achieved both by research and development on the products themselves, and by up-dating the production process;
* **acquisition of market share through purchase** – this can be an extremely expensive way of gaining market share, but it is also much quicker than growing organically. The knowledge that a major rival is seeking to acquire the target business is likely to force up its price;
* **increased productivity** – this will be necessary if an organisation is to increase its output, and compete effectively on price. For many years, organisations have been sensitive to the productivity of their manufacturing operations, introducing standardised parts and processes, 'right first time' quality schemes, and just-in-time delivery systems. More recently, similar attention is being paid to the management and administrative functions of businesses;
* **changes to the marketing mix** – new product features, revised positioning, changed pricing policies and distribution methods, a shift in promotional strategy, and greater emphasis on customer care are all potential tactical changes which are consequent upon a revised marketing strategy.

Evaluating the implications of strategic change

Only by fully evaluating the implications of the strategic options generated for the planning process does it become possible to select the preferred option of Johnson and Scholes' model. Any strategy will need to be evaluated in terms of at least four considerations:

* How different is this product/service proposal from existing operational capabilities and know-how?
* How different is the proposed market from existing ones?
* How much additional finance will be required?
* How easy will it be to obtain that additional finance?

Once again, a matrix forms a convenient method for evaluating the options, after they have been researched. Figure 12.6 shows a two-dimensional matrix for plotting an option in terms of the extent to which it would require operational and marketing knowledge which differs from that which the organisation already has. The closer the option falls to the top left-hand corner of the matrix, the less the level of risk posed to the organisation. Options which are plotted towards the bottom right-hand corner are doubly difficult for the organisation because they would require quite different operational and market knowledge to that which the organisation already possess. Only in exceptional circumstances would such options be proceeded with.

Operational knowledge and capability

	Existing	New
Markets Existing	X – low-risk option	
New		Z – high-risk option

Figure 12.6 – Operational-risk assessment of strategic plan options

Activity

In the previous activity (on page 245) you categorised four proposals for business growth into the strategies suggested by Ansoff's matrix.

Using the same four proposals (refer back to that activity), categorise them according to operational risk, by copying the matrix in Figure 12.6 into your note-book.

DISCUSSION

You should have marked the matrix as shown in Figure 12.7.

Operational knowledge and capability

	Existing	New
Markets Existing	c	b
New	a	d

Figure 12.7 – Answer to activity

A similar process can also be used to assess the level of financial risk, by marrying an assessment of the need for additional capital investment, with the likely level of return in the short-term. A low-cost option may look attractive at first sight; however, it may also offer only a poor rate of return. A high-cost option may be acceptable if it offers better rates of return on the investment.

		Level of capital investment required	
		Low	High
Short-term rate of return on investment	Low	Piggy-bank finance	Tax write-off option
	High	Licence to print money	Casino finance

Figure 12.8 – Financial risk assessment of strategic plan options

Figure 12.8 shows how the level of financial risk could be assessed. Products requiring little investment, but offering low returns, if they are to be proceeded with at all, are most likely to be funded from retained profits – hence the label of 'piggy-bank finance' for that quarter of the matrix. Those options which require extensive capital investment, but which are still judged to offer low returns in the short-term are only likely to be proceeded where long-term gains are considered to be more important, or where an organisation can write off the investment against possible tax liability. Such options fall within the top right-hand quarter.

Those options which are costly but potentially very profitable will normally require an organisation to pay a high price in return for investment cash, hence the term 'casino finance'. The most popular option will always be that which offers good return for very little additional outlay – the 'license to print money'.

Strategic implementation phase

When the strategic options have been evaluated and selected, it is now necessary for the plan to answer the third question – 'How are we going to get there?' This phase will plan in detail the implementation of the chosen strategic objectives beginning with the identification of the resources required to achieve the plan objective, and their likely sources.

As this is a marketing plan, rather than a full business plan, it will only be necessary to cover those resources required to achieve marketing objectives. Plans for new premises, equipment, personnel or systems will only be included in so far as they are necessary to the marketing function. Production planning, and plans for the actual raising of additional capital, lie outside its scope, and will be covered by separate plans produced within those functional departments.

Cash flow, breakeven and profit projections will need to be included in the planning process, and in the plan document, because they remind marketing personnel of the importance of profitability as an objective for their organisation, and set the targets that the organisation will be expected to achieve during the currency of the plan. In order that these are accurate, all the plan elements will need to be carefully costed, and pricing geared to both organisation profit-targets and careful research of market attitudes to price. The process of determining prices for products and services, and of measuring financial performance, was dealt with in detail in Chapter 7.

Finally, timetabled action plans need to be produced showing how each stage of the plan will be achieved, by which parts of the organisation, and within what timescale. These will form the basis for work scheduling and task allocation during the period of the plan, and they need to be based on realistic assumptions of what is achievable, or the plan risks being de-railed by operational constraints.

Monitoring and evaluation

Much of the benefit of undertaking planning will be dissipated if there is no review process to match performance with the objectives set in the plan. Performance can be assessed quantifiably without difficulty. Cash flow forecasts, for example, can be measured against actual outcomes. Deadline dates can easily be checked against attainment. To ensure that it happens, the marketing plan needs to make explicit the systems and events which will be used. For example, formal reporting chains and cycles may need to be established, and meetings scheduled at which these reports are discussed. Any deviation from targets can then be considered, and possible explanations sought. Where targets have proved too demanding, or too lax, lessons should be learned for future objective-setting.

Contents of the marketing plan – a check-list

The marketing plan document, when presented for approval should consist of the following elements:
* **position statement**, showing:
  - corporate mission statement,
  - corporate objectives (to which this plan must conform),
  - organisation or brand performance for past three years,
  - market share,
  - turnover,
  - profitability,
  - market trends for past three years,
  - likely future trends;
* **selected marketing strategies**, showing:
  - aims (long- and short-term),
  - objectives (specific outcomes), for example, expected product portfolio, market share, desired turnover/volume of business, profitability, consumer satisfaction levels;
* **rationalisation for the selected strategies**, showing:
  - results of the SWOT analysis,
  - product life cycles,
  - competitor analysis (Porter matrix);

* **costed tactical proposals**, showing, for example:
  - modernisation of production process, re-positioning of brand, promotional campaigns;
* **financial projections**, showing:
  - additional capital required (if any) and sources,
  - cash flow forecast,
  - breakeven predictions,
  - profit projections;
* **action plan and timetable**, showing:
  - itemised operational activities, responsibilities and scheduling;
* **monitoring and evaluation process**;
* **appendices**, for example:
  - abstract from market research report (relevant to forecasts within the plan), draft proposals for brand repositioning.

From drawing-board to filing cabinet

Given an ideal situation, the production of a marketing plan ought to be followed by its implementation across the organisation as naturally as night follows day.

In practice, this does not always happen. There are a number of reasons for this:

* the plan was drawn up to secure additional funding (e.g. loan, government grant) rather than to guide operational activity;
* the plan is actually unworkable (perhaps because it was produced at an organisation's headquarters, without full knowledge of operating constraints, or with insufficient time allocated);
* the plan's objectives are not communicated to operational staff who are thus uninterested in its implementation;
* the plan's objectives are communicated badly to staff, who regard them as irrelevant, and may even attempt to frustrate them.

Clearly, therefore, it is not enough to produce a plan; it has to be given life by involving staff at all levels, both in its preparation, and in its implementation. It is, after all, the planning process, not the resulting document, which has greatest value for organisations.

Case study

Read the 'Colourful Growth' article from *Single Market News* (Figure 12.9).
What part has planning played in developing this business from a seasonal to a year-round one? How has the company demonstrated flexibility in its planning?

Conclusion

This book began by defining marketing as the identification, stimulation and satisfaction of customer or consumer needs at a profit. Now, in the final chapter, you have seen that it is only by undertaking a proper planning process that organisations can fulfil the whole of that definition, and hope – in the long-term – to succeed. Those organisations that do not plan, are surviving in their markets more by luck than judgement. One day, their luck will run out.

Colourful growth

How does a small family flower-growing firm, whose highly variable daffodil export season lasts between four months at best and as little as three weeks at worst, manage to remain in business throughout the year? The answer, according to Sun King Flowers of Spalding, Lincolnshire, is the ability to grow and sell cut flowers, including dried flower bouquets, to the UK trade market for most of the rest of the year.

Despite the recession and worldwide over-production of flowers, Sun King claims to be the only flower grower of its kind to stay open all year. Two and a half years ago when Sun King featured in *Single Market News* it was only in its second year of selling to Denmark and Germany. Now in less than three years, it has increased its annual sales to the Netherlands, Denmark, Germany and North Africa from an average of 1.3 million bunches to 2 million bunches.

Daffodils to Holland

Selling daffodils to Holland, centre of the international flower bulb industry was Sun King's first venture into Europe over five years ago. It is not as odd as it seems, the UK produces more daffodils than Holland where tulips form the biggest crop. ' Because the Netherlands is part of a large land mass, its spring is later than ours. So under normal conditions we can start cropping much earlier,' explains Maurice Louis who, with his wife Margaret, originally founded their business 20 years ago.

'However', Mr Louis explains 'field daffodils are affected by the uncertainties of the weather and price. We just have to plan on guesswork.' He claims that anybody can grow flowers. 'The trick is in finding buyers at the right time and price. We have a sales team, led by our marketing director son, which is expert at that. This is vastly different to selling a manufactured product. Deals are struck and orders placed by phone or fax on a day-to-day basis. Prices fluctuate in a matter of hours.'

Filling the cash-flow gap

The company started in traditional fashion by growing daffodils and tulips under glass in winter and cucumbers, tomatoes and peppers in summer. After experimenting with outdoor crops, the Louis family took the bold step of dropping the forced flower and vegetable programme completely and concentrating on outdoor flowers. Daffodils fill what would be a serious cash-flow gap in late winter and spring before the start of summer cropping.

They have 80 acres devoted to varieties of summer flowers and the production of blooms for drying. Only a small proportion of these are exported –Sweet Williams to Denmark. The rest are sold to the UK trade.

The removal of border barriers is of help to Sun King and other companies selling perishables to the European mainland by allowing them to reach customers more quickly. Maurice Louis says: 'We are constantly seeking opportunities to expand our markets and will do so as further opportunities occur Europe and worldwide'.

(Source: *Single Market News*)

Figure 12.9

Assignment 12

Harlebrook Leisure Centre

Scenario

The leisure centre at Harlebrook is owned by the Harlesmere District Council as a multi-purpose indoor facility to provide for some of the recreational and sporting needs of the people of the district (population about 80,000). The centre is operated on behalf of the council by its own in-house leisure services contractor. It makes a substantial loss, and requires a subsidy of over £1 million per annum from the council. When the contract to operate the leisure centre was placed in-house, there was a hostile letter-writing campaign in the local press. There were criticisms of standards of cleanliness and customer care at the centre.

The centre consists of a main swimming pool with gallery, suitable for staging competitive events, a smaller splash pool for children, small multi-gym, and a large multi-functional sports hall, suitable for basketball, badminton, volleyball, table tennis, etc., and also for concerts, exhibitions and shows. There is a bar and gallery overlooking the sports hall, and a sitting area with vending machines, opening onto an enclosed patio, suitable for barbecues. Changing rooms, one lecture room and several offices complete the facilities. The building was erected in 1985.

Use of the swimming pool by local schools and clubs is good, but otherwise pool attendances are declining. The figures for admissions (not revenue) for the two pools are:

	Swim tickets issued	Spectator tickets issued
1985	101,295	5,745
1986	98,598	5,106
1987	100,448	5,638
1988	101,004	5,570
1989	96,823	4,975
1990	95,456	4,397
1991	88,853	4,075
1992	89,141	4,800
1993	88,612	4,183

Usage of the sports hall has never matched expectations. A few highly successful shows and concerts have been staged. However, these are very disruptive as they require the sports hall to be closed for 12 hours before and after the event to allow tiered seating to be assembled and then removed. Commercial exhibitions and visits by touring sports teams have been few. Revenues have risen and fallen in line with the health of the local economy.

The population of the district is generally stable. It is ageing, reflecting the district's popularity with retired people. Levels of unemployment are lower than average for the UK, but there are sizeable numbers of people working in low-paid, casual and part-time jobs. These people have a lot of free time, but little cash to spare for leisure. On the other hand, there is a significant group of sunrise industries in the area. Employees of these companies are well-paid, but have much less time for leisure.

There are a wide variety of leisure facilities provided by the private sector in the district. There are several golf courses, two golf driving ranges, an artificial ski slope, two country clubs with squash courts, several health clubs attached to local hotels, and a bowling alley/laser centre.

Market research carried out recently on behalf of Harlesmere District Council has shown that the 'top ten' sports activities that people in the district participate in are as follows:

	%		%
Walking	45	Snooker	10
Swimming	22	Golf	9
Dancing	18	Cycling	9
Keep fit, Yoga	15	Badminton	8
Ten pin bowls	14	Tennis	7

(Percentage scores are based on claimed participation within previous four weeks.)

National market research obtained by Harlesmere suggests that lifestyles are changing as follows:

* leisure is less socially-focused, and more individualistic;
* facilities are moving up-market (e.g. working men's clubs are closing, wine-bars opening);
* the home is now the major location for leisure activity (e.g. computer games, satellite television);
* there is increased interest in healthy leisure pursuits (e.g. walking);
* many people regard sport as a means to an end (e.g. to get slim, to relax) rather than an end in itself.

YOUR TASKS

Assume that you have been asked to help in the carrying out of a marketing audit for the leisure centre, during which you must undertake the tasks specified below:

1   List the methods that you would use to categorise the customers of the centre (see *Market segmentation* earlier).
2   Present the information given above about pool attendances in recent years in graphic form.
3   List those factors which you would consider to influence the level of pool attendances, and which might be included in an econometric model (see earlier).
4   Recommend a forecasting technique that you consider appropriate for estimating attendances over the next three years (see earlier).
5   Draw up a list of possible sources of commercial market research data that would be useful to Harlesmere District Council, and say how you think the data obtained would be of use.
6   Make a list of the strategic options which you would expect the council's contractor to consider in drafting a marketing plan for the leisure centre.

Index